About the author

Dr Jenny O'Dea is a dietitian and nutritionist with twenty-five years experience. She is currently a senior lecturer in nutrition and health education at the University of Sydney.

Jenny is also the author of two other books about nutrition and health, and has carried out many large research studies into body image, self-concept, self-esteem and eating issues among children, adolescents and college students. Her groundbreaking PhD in Medicine from Sydney University focused on the prevention of body image problems and eating disorders among children and adolescents using a school-based, self-esteem approach, and the results of her study influenced health researchers world-wide, paving the way for a more positive approach to preventing body image problems and eating disorders in young people. She has also authored more than fifty research publications in well-known international journals.

Jenny is well known for her contributions to the media and public debate about food, nutrition, body image and health, and is a long-time advocate of commonsense and a balanced view-point when it comes to food, nutrition and eating. She believes that food should be enjoyed as both nutritious and delicious. Jenny is also mother of Isabella and Katherine, and married to Nigel, who is an excellent cook and a great ally in feeding their children healthy food.

Also by Dr Jenny O'Dea

Healthy Food Your Kids Will Love
Family Nutrition

Positive Food
for Kids

Dr Jenny O'Dea

DOUBLEDAY
SYDNEY • AUCKLAND • TORONTO • NEW YORK • LONDON

Positive Foods For Kids
A DOUBLEDAY BOOK

First published in Australia and New Zealand in 2005
by Doubleday

National Library of Australia
Cataloguing-in-Publication Entry

    O'Dea, Jenny.
    Positive food for kids.

    Includes index.
    ISBN 1 86471 091 8.

    1. Children – Nutrition. 2. Children – Health and hygiene.
    3. Food preferences in children. I. Title.

    649.3

Transworld Publishers,
a division of Random House Australia Pty Ltd
20 Alfred Street, Milsons Point, NSW 2061
http://www.randomhouse.com.au

Random House New Zealand Limited
18 Poland Road, Glenfield, Auckland

Transworld Publishers,
a division of The Random House Group Ltd
61-63 Uxbridge Road, Ealing, London W5 5SA

Random House Inc
1745 Broadway, New York, New York 10036

Cover design by Darian Causby
Cover photograph by photolibrary.com
Typeset in Sabon 11/15 pt by Midland Typesetters, Maryborough, Victoria
Printed and bound by Griffin Press, Netley, South Australia

10 9 8 7 6 5 4 3 2 1

Information in this book referring to the nutrients in popular take-away
and packaged foods were acquired from the various manufacturers in June,
July, August and October, 2004. Please note, though, that products and their
ingredients change, and that the information was correct at the time of
publication.

Contents

Introduction

I wrote this book after working for twenty-five years as a nutritionist and watching the eating habits of Australian and New Zealand children become worse and worse. In my latest research study of 5,000 school-children aged between six and eighteen years old, I was horrified to find that many weren't getting even the most basic of nutritious foods. I was alarmed to find that one in six children had eaten no fruit or vegetables in the three days prior to the study; one in five had had no fruit juice; one in four had had no cereal, pasta or rice and one in ten had had no milk or dairy food. In addition, one in three children hadn't had anything at all for breakfast or made do with drinks like water, cordial, soft drink, tea or coffee.

Many children are missing out on important nutrients that are essential for health and growth, and equally crucial nutrients required for brain development, intelligence, concentration and academic performance. Children also need good food to protect them from colds, flu and adult diseases like heart disease and cancer. Children who eat healthy food will have plenty of energy, fewer infections, strong teeth and healthy gums, and better behaviour, and will also go on to have good eating habits for life. Children who learn to eat well during their formative years will not only eat well in their own life-time, but they will also pass their good eating habits and healthy lifestyle on to their own children, ensuring the health of future generations.

Healthy eating habits can be fostered in any child and it is a common myth that some children simply won't eat healthy food. In this book I outline the many ideas, suggestions and tricks that will help you to encourage your child to eat and drink healthily. As well as my own strategies, based on years of research with thousands of children and teenagers, I also include the suggestions of more than fifty parents interviewed for this book. They are all tried and true ways of getting our children to eat and enjoy healthy food.

Seeing your children eat well is certainly a satisfying feeling, but nothing is better than knowing that you have given your child the best start in life. I hope this book will help you to discover healthy food for healthy children, for healthy lives.

Dr Jenny O'Dea

1

A Positive Approach to Feeding Your Child

Feeding your child good, nutritious food has many benefits which continue into adolescence and adulthood. Good growth, brain development, energy regulation, health protection and immunity, protection against adult diseases, protection of teeth and gums, improved behaviour, and the development of good eating habits for life, are all gained from a well balanced, nutritious diet.

Eating should also be an enjoyable and sociable part of life for people of all ages. Preparing and sharing meals with family and friends is an important part of our social development from birth, and food continues to play an important role for all of us throughout life.

Our selection of food depends on several factors, including personal likes and dislikes, beliefs and attitudes towards certain foods, childhood experiences with food and meal times, nutrition knowledge, economic factors and food advertising. Our various attitudes towards food are influenced in the home, at school, on television, in magazines and newspapers and are also affected by what our families and friends are eating.

Children are particularly susceptible to television food advertisements, which are deliberately aired between the hours of four and six o'clock each afternoon to catch the attention of young viewers. Likewise, many parents in supermarkets are nagged and eventually surrender to their child's 'pester power', buying unnecessary sweets and chocolates that are strategically displayed near the cash register.

Physical factors other than hunger also affect what children choose to eat. The taste, colour, texture and aroma of different foods affect children and coax them to eat when they may not necessarily be hungry. For these reasons children and adults sometimes eat just for comfort, pleasure or curiosity.

With all this in mind, helping children to choose wisely from a healthy selection of food can be a difficult task for many parents. Try to be aware of the factors which affect your personal food habits and those of your children by asking the following questions:

- What is your child eating?
- Why is your child eating?
- Does your child eat because they are hungry, or perhaps because they are bored, lonely or unhappy?
- Is your child easily tempted to eat unnecessary foods and drinks?
- Does your child eat sweets or snack foods between meals?
- Does your child sometimes 'graze' on food and drink all day long?
- Are meal times relaxed, or is there constant conflict around meal times and eating?
- Does your child skip proper meals or constantly snack and 'eat on the run'?
- Does your child constantly drink or sip on a bottle?
- Is food an enjoyable part of your child's life?

Try to improve your child's eating habits and take time to relax and enjoy meals with family and friends as part of a new, healthy lifestyle.

'You are what you eat'

'You are what you eat' is a well-known saying that is all too true in families who may be overweight or affected by diet and lifestyle-related diseases such as coronary heart disease, high blood pressure (hypertension), stroke, diabetes, gall bladder disease and certain cancers. We all know of people who are overweight, have suffered a heart attack or stroke, or have diabetes, but what can we do to prevent it happening to *us*?

A lifestyle based on healthy eating and moderate daily exercise is the best way to help prevent these diseases in our children – an ounce of prevention is better than a pound of cure. Unfortunately we often act late, waiting until we have become very overweight, or have developed high blood pressure, or had a heart attack. Then we decide to 'go on a diet' or 'take up some sport'. The obvious answer is to start early – to act *now*.

Encourage your children to develop healthy eating habits and to value their health. Remember, it is never too late to begin to improve your diet and your health.

Why *do* children choose healthy foods?

In my recent research study of 5,000 school children, I asked children and teenagers a rather basic question: 'Why *do* you choose to eat healthy foods?' In other words I asked them, 'What's in it for you?' The answers from children of all ages from 6 to 18 years were quite astounding. Younger children aged 6 to 11 years answered that they deliberately chose healthy foods and drinks because they:

- Give them energy and fitness
- Help them to grow and be strong
- Make them 'feel good on the inside', whereas junk and snack foods made them feel 'heavy, yucky, lazy and a bit sick on the stomach'
- Help them to concentrate at school and stay awake
- Keep their bodies healthy and reduce colds and other illnesses.

These young children could articulate quite clearly the benefits of healthy eating. You could try asking your children the same question: why do you choose healthy food and drinks? What does healthy food do for you?

In the same research study, older children and teenagers aged 12 to 18 years gave similar, but more complex answers. They also identified having energy and feeling energetic and fit as one of the main benefits of healthy eating. They gave the following answers about healthy eating, saying it:

- Helps them to grow and stay healthy, strong and avoid illnesses
- Helps them to feel 'refreshed, clean on the inside', whereas junk food and snack foods make them feel 'heavy, sick on the stomach, clogged up, slow'
- Clears the mind and helps them to concentrate better
- Makes them feel good about themselves; that they have done something good for themselves
- Improves complexion, hair, nails and general appearance
- Helps them to regulate their energy levels throughout the whole day, with no 'highs' or 'lows' in energy levels and therefore helps them to sleep better at night
- Prevents long-term health problems like being overweight and heart disease.

The positive foods approach

As parents, you can use the positive benefits of healthy eating from your child's point of view to motivate them to eat healthily. This positive foods approach has been developed from my many years of research into the eating habits of children. I've developed three basic steps:

1. Keep reminding them of the many benefits that they will receive from healthy eating.
2. Believe it yourself and convey the importance of healthy eating to your child.
3. Provide positive reinforcement and rewards such as praise and congratulation when your child eats healthy food.

The Ten Golden Rules

I've also developed ten golden rules to use when feeding your child using the positive food approach:

1. **Remember that you are the adult, you are the boss!** Do not allow your child to dictate what is going to be eaten. You decide what is going to be eaten and your child decides how much is eaten. Explain that you are the mummy or daddy and that it is your job to look after your child. Explain that you wouldn't be doing a proper job if you allowed your child to eat food that isn't good for them; that it is your job to provide the best food for your child. Let your child know that you want them to eat well because you love them and not because it's a punishment!

2. **Don't give up the first time your child says 'I don't like it'.** What they really mean is 'I'm a bit scared to try new things', 'I can't be bothered with this at the moment' or 'I'm not really very hungry at the moment'. Years of research shows that offering children new food on at least ten separate occasions will work eventually. Remember, 'try, try again!'

3. **Regularly introduce new flavours to your child from a young age** – in utero, via breastmilk and after six months of age when they begin eating solids. *Continue* to add variety to your child's diet.

4. **Be a good role model.** Eat a wide variety of foods yourself and allow your child to see you and other family members enjoying and excitedly trying new foods. Sit your baby up at the table and allow them to participate and observe you and other family members eating healthy food.

5. **Reinforce the child's positive food behaviours.** Never let a chance go by to notice your child doing something right. Regularly witness, and make positive comments to, your child eating healthy food and trying new food. Also, reward them – often the things that a child wants most from their parents is acceptance, approval, love and praise.

6. **Take advantage of your child's appetite.** Deliberately develop your child's appetite and notice how well they eat! It's not a sin to allow your child to become hungry, in fact it helps your child to 'tune in' to their own natural appetite. In turn this will help them to control their eating and their weight later in life.

PRAISING AND CONGRATULATING YOUR CHILD

Here are some ways of rewarding children for their good behaviour after they have eaten healthy food or drinks.

- Focus on your child's *positive* behaviours. *Notice* when they eat a healthy food. For example: 'Oh Sam, you ate some of your salad – well done!', 'Katie, you tried the pasta dish – very good.'
- Praise your child when they try a new food, even if they have only eaten two peas or one teaspoon of vegetable mash. Having your child simply try new foods is more than half the battle won.
- Congratulate your child for positive eating behaviour. Smile and say:
     'Excellent eating, well done', 'Terrific', 'Very Good'
     'Good job on the vegies'
     'Good boy, good girl'
     'Wow, you are eating so well (so much better) these days'
     'Fantastic! You are going to grow fit and strong after all that healthy food, good girl'
- Praise the child's eating in front of other people like teachers, grandparents, relatives and other children. For example:
     'Very good eating, Sally – Grandma, do you see what an excellent eater Sally is? She eats up all of her vege-tables. She eats really healthy foods'
- Reward good eating with hugs, cuddles and kisses and say:
     'I'm so glad you are a healthy eater'
     'You did very well trying those new foods'
     'I was so proud to see you trying that casserole at Grandma's house without complaining – very well done'.
- Remember to stay positive and don't get cross or frus-trated when your child doesn't eat well; just try again another time, using another strategy!
- Remember to notice the child's positive eating behaviours and don't over react to their problem eating behaviour.

7. **Keep the home eating environment 'emotion free'.** Don't ban or force-feed certain foods because this type of parental behaviour is known to be counterproductive. Don't put too much emphasis on eating. Carry out your strategies in a low-key manner and try to keep a lid on negative reactions and emotions. Allow your child to have lollies, chocolates, snack foods and soft drinks occasionally (not daily) but only after they have had all the foods they *need* to be healthy. Explain that they can have treat foods only when their major food groups have been eaten.

8. **Change your food storage environment and your kitchen.** Keep healthy food readily available and accessible and keep 'treat' food well and truly out of sight. If you allow children to get their own snacks and drinks (and I don't recommend this for under twelves) make sure that they are surrounded by healthy choices. Don't allow children to keep food in their rooms or in the car. Keep fruit and vegetables peeled, chopped and readily accessible and watch it disappear! One mother told me how she and her husband deliberately bought an 'upside down' fridge that had the freezer at the bottom and the fridge on top – the parents had better control over what their children ate and drank because they could not open the fridge. Subsequently their food habits got better.

9. **Stay calm, cool, collected and consistent.** If you allow meal times to become a battle of wills you won't achieve anything, so stay cool, firmly in control and don't give in to your child's demands or tantrums. Adults and older children need to agree to promote healthy eating within the family.

   Similarly, parents need to agree and support each other and not undermine attempts to encourage children to eat well. Grandparents also need to cooperate and to be aware of what parents are trying to achieve and how the children should be fed. Many grandparents delight in 'spoiling' their grandchildren, but sometimes this can damage the parents' role as the main food provider.

10. **Congratulate yourself when your child eats well** – you really are providing them with the best start in life. They may even thank you for it when they get older!

'I provide lots of healthy food for my children, but they won't eat it!'

This is a very common complaint from parents. In general, the answer is for parents not to give up too easily, or too quickly, and for them to try presenting food again and again in a different way. Here are some helpful tips which are based on years of research among babies, toddlers and small children:

- Breastfeed your baby. Research evidence shows that breast-milk is full of hundreds of flavours from the mother's diet. If breastfed babies are exposed to different tastes and flavours from birth, this helps to reduce food 'neophobia', or fear of new foods, when they become older. In an experiment in the USA in 1994 breastfed babies were more likely than formula fed babies to eat vegetables.
- Start introducing a variety of foods early. When your baby is six months old and eating solids, introduce different foods and keep the variety up.
- Again, keep offering foods, even when they are repeatedly refused. As I've mentioned, research shows that you may need to offer a food up to ten times before your child accepts it.
- Children have a natural preference for sweet and salty foods. They also have a natural dislike of sour or bitter tastes – this is completely normal and instinctive among mammals as it is a natural way of avoiding poisonous foods, which are usually bitter or sour. However, this behaviour does not mean that parents should give up. If you persevere, more often than not your child will eventually get used to the taste of different foods.
- Don't offer too many sweet foods, such as sugary biscuits or cakes, soft drinks, juice and lollies. Similarly, avoid offering too many salty foods like crackers, snack foods and chips.

You'll find that they will always eat these foods and not other foods. Keep offering a variety of different foods every day and your child will eventually regularly eat some of them.

- Offer foods in a different way. Consider serving fruit and vegetables raw, cooked, mashed, pureed, diced, grated, frozen or juiced. One mother told me how her daughter would only eat tinned fruit and raw chopped vegetables – so that's how she has served them for the last five years! Her child eats at least five servings of fruit or vegetables daily and it doesn't really matter in which form they are consumed.

- Allow your child to determine *how much* they eat. Feeding experiments in the USA found that two- to five-year-old children could regulate how much food and how many kilojoules they ate over a twenty-four hour period when they were left to decide how much or how little food they wanted. Also, research shows that parents (mainly mothers) who try to control how much their child eats end up having children who can't regulate their food intake themselves. The research found that the best environment for children to be able to regulate their food intake is when parents or carers provide healthy food choices and allow children to decide how much they eat. You (the grown up) decide *what* will be eaten and your child decides *how much* will be eaten.

Competing with advertisements

Encouraging your children to eat healthy food means competing with television advertisements and peer group pressure. Children will be more likely to accept healthy food if you explain that looking good has a lot to do with eating good food. Children should know that a healthy weight, clear skin, shiny hair and healthy teeth all depend on good food, and that food gives us energy for play, sport, physical fitness and health. The saying 'You are what you eat' can be understood even by small children.

Here are some other ways of encouraging children to value healthy eating:

MANDY, FIVE YEARS OLD

Mandy is a very finicky eater who gets very upset when her parents suggest any new foods. She has a limited core of basic foods including toast, peanut butter, cheese sticks, crackers, mashed potato, raw peas, orange juice (with 1 teaspoon of sugar), white bread, Vegemite, banana, Asian noodles, chicken, rice and pasta. Mandy's parents Dave and Michelle become very frustrated with her poor eating and try to make her eat, which almost always ends in tears. After analysing Mandy's diet, I found that she could be eating more often, and although she was a normal weight for height, she was a little thin. Mandy would do better by eating small, frequent, healthy snacks, but not large meals. Chips, sweet biscuits and soft drinks were also filling her up and preventing her receiving the more nutritious foods. Dave and Michelle started by making sure she had peanut butter, toast and orange juice every morning. The teaspoon of sugar in the juice was fine because it helped her to drink it and she was not having too many kilojoules. Mandy was also given cheese sticks, crackers and juice for morning tea at school and Dave talked to the teacher and asked her to encourage Mandy to finish it as well as her lunch – a banana, half a Vegemite sandwich and chocolate milk. The teacher reported that Mandy never ate her crusts, but that's OK! Finally, Mandy's mother provided similar small snacks after school and at dinner time, with a small serving of rice, noodles or mashed potato with chicken, orange juice and raw peas.

This basic plan has now been expanded over three months to include limited but new and different foods. Mandy is still quite a fussy eater, but her parents realise that she probably always will be! They focus on making sure that she has six small nutritious snacks or milk drinks and let Mandy decide how much she will eat. As a reward for her better eating, Mandy has been allowed to have her first pet. Mandy is now learning all about how to feed her pet and how to keep it healthy!

- Remind children that their growth, muscle strength and energy levels are dependent on good foods. Children like to be able to 'do' things like running, playing, climbing and specific sports. Constantly reinforce that the ability to do these things comes from good nutrition.
- Measure your child's height regularly. Help them to recognise how their bodies are growing, e.g. height, hair length, finger-nails, shoe size. Encourage children to eat well in order to promote continued growth.
- Reinforce their 'healthy' status. Remind them that they haven't been sick for a long time because they eat well and this helps their body to fight germs, bacteria and viruses.
- Tell them how proud of them you are when they eat healthy foods.
- Have older children keep a food diary for one or two days and then go through it with them, praising their healthy choices and suggesting how they might make more healthy choices, e.g. choosing grapes instead of lollies, milk instead of soft drink, cheese and crackers instead of chips.

You can also improve your child's acceptance of healthy food by using the same strategies used every day by food manufacturers and television advertisements. To 'sell' your own 'products' at home, try giving them a catchy new name in the same way that food companies advertise their products. For example, 'The Magic Fairy Drink' (page 154) is much more attractive to children than 'a milk drink'. There are other recipes in this book which will give you ideas for catchy titles, or you can ask your child to invent names and recipes themselves.

The enjoyment of food can also be improved simply by eating in different spots in the house. Try a different room, a different table, on the floor, in the garden, on the balcony, in the park or on the beach. You can also invite young friends to help prepare or share meals.

Most importantly, allow children to become involved in food preparation. Let them grow vegetables, cook meals, 'invent' new

JAMES, FIVE YEARS OLD

James is the son of Cheryl and Max who also have a daughter, Kate, aged twelve. Cheryl dotes on little James and he is the apple of both parents' eye.

They both worry, though, that James doesn't eat well enough. After interviewing both parents, I found that James will always eat a dinner of fish fingers, or eggs on toast and vegetable mash which Max always cooks separately for him at five o'clock when he gets home from work. The mash consists of mashed potato with camouflaged carrot, peas and corn mixed in with it. James also eats pureed fruit such as apples, pears, peaches but won't eat wholemeal bread, grain bread or any other 'adult food'. Kate, on the other hand, eats everything her parents eat without any fuss or bother! This family situation is surprisingly common where parents tend to 'baby' their youngest child and allow them to dictate what is eaten. From the age of twelve months, most children should be sitting up at the table and eating what the rest of the family eats. Preparing separate meals for children sends the message that children's food is different and that they can have this unnecessary special treatment for the rest of their lives.

After much discussion, Cheryl and Max decided that it was time to help their baby grow up a little and join the rest of the family at the dinner table. This meant serving the family dinner a little earlier than usual. For the first few weeks, James got to eat his familiar foods at dinner and of course his vegetable mash was made up every night. After a few weeks, Cheryl and Max encouraged James to try some other food at the dinner table, and whenever he tried a new food, the whole family would clap and laugh and congratulate their 'big boy'! James is now broadening his repertoire of foods and drinks and he is relishing his new role.

healthy recipes and learn to read food labels. Teach them to look for fat, salt and sugar on food labels and decide for themselves if the food is acceptable in moderation or not at all. Children can also learn good nutrition by experiences with family pets, especially by feeding *them* healthy food. Don't throw fat off-cuts to the dog or it will end up with a heart attack! Perhaps your dog, cat, or horse is overweight and could do with less food and more exercise.

Keeping a record of your child's eating patterns

The most common worry among parents is that their child 'eats like a sparrow', or 'seems to live on thin air'. This is not always accurate, though. You may be astonished to find out how much a child can eat and drink when you keep a careful record for a few days. Use the food diary on page 57 to record your child's food and drinks for one or two days. Children are often willing to join in and record what they eat and drink as well.

The food diary can tell you:

- How much your children really eat
- What types of foods they eat most often
- The time of day when they are most hungry
- How they spend their pocket money
- Whether they are filling up on drinks or not
- If they are grazing, snacking or eating just three meals
- Whether they eat more or less on weekends
- How their mood (or your mood!) affects their eating patterns.

Don't worry if your child seems to eat the same food day in, day out. Children are often quite content to eat plain foods which would seem boring to adults. You can check your child's diet against the Five Food Groups (pages 50–51) and the Healthy Eating Pyramid (page 53) in the chapter on nutrition.

Appetite

If you are worried that young James 'never eats a thing' or 'has been losing weight ever since the day he was born' – relax!

MASON, THREE YEARS OLD

Young Mason will always happily eat his favourite, 'core' foods: wheat breakfast biscuits, milk, toast with honey, chocolate milk, banana, apple juice, peeled apples, pasta, white bread, chicken, peanut butter sandwiches, cheese sticks, meat, mashed potato, peas, raw carrots, ice cream and tinned peaches. He will sometimes eat oranges, mandarins, lettuce, grated carrot and raw green beans. Janine, his mother, worries sometimes that her son is not getting a great enough variety of foods and gets frustrated that he won't try new foods or new dishes that she cooks for the family. This is very typical and Mason is a very typical three-year-old! However, when Janine kept a diary of Mason's food intake for two days and checked it against the Five Food Groups (see pages 50–51) she found that her son *was* eating from the cereals and grains, milk and dairy foods, fruit, vegetables and meat food groups daily. Mason is quite happy to eat the same foods day in day out – even though they do seem bland and boring to Janine.

Janine is now much happier about Mason's diet, but continues to encourage Mason to try new foods and new dishes. She's also stopped letting Mason go to the fridge to get drinks which she realised he was doing eight times a day when she kept his food diary. She takes advantage of Mason's greater appetite at lunchtime and gives him the main meal of the day then and also uses this time of day to try new foods when he is hungry but not tired or distracted. Janine sits down and eats lunch with him and they eat the same foods. She has discovered that he will eat some raw vegetables like green beans, carrots, peas, bean sprouts, celery and cabbage and she puts them on his plate before she cooks them for the rest of the family. She has also discovered that he will eat raw, grated zucchini and grated apple with sultanas in it, so Janine is continuing to experiment with raw fruits and vegetables cut into different shapes and served as juices or soups. Mason will now eat Janine's pumpkin soup with a teaspoon of added light cream. This makes her very happy! They will add new foods to their list of 'likes' at a slow and steady rate, to allow Mason time to get used to all the different aspects of a particular dish. By introducing new food in this unthreatening way, Janine is helping Mason learn about the world of food in a very healthy manner and now realises that it takes years for children to add new foods to their repertoire of foods. She feels confident that, by the age of five or six, Mason will be eating a greater variety of foods with the rest of the family.

You are not alone. Children's appetites vary from day to day. They may not know instinctively which foods are good for them, but they do know when they have had enough. Encouraging children to 'clean up the plate' will only lead to weight problems when they get older. A child can lose his or her appetite by being upset at meal times, being tired, or by eating snacks close to meal times. If meal times are associated with tension, constant nagging about table manners, force-feeding or family fights then the child will not feel like eating. Try to relax and make meal times fun and enjoyable, and, again, never try to force your child to eat.

Lack of fresh air and activity can result in a temporary loss of appetite, so make sure children receive plenty of exercise every day. You may also need to check the school bag for lolly wrappers or empty chip packets. Remember, healthy between-meal snacks are acceptable but these will decrease the appetite if eaten close to meal times.

A very common cause of lack of appetite in children is frequent drinking. Children have only small stomachs that become quickly 'full' with fluids. For this reason, limit your child's fluid intake before meals. Don't allow your child to continually go to the refrigerator for foods and drinks as this 'grazing' behaviour dampens their appetite. Letting your child experience hunger is not a bad thing – it will help them to recognise when they are hungry and to eat accordingly. Many children and adults never really become hungry because of their constant grazing and are then unable to recognise their own body cues and follow their natural feeding instincts. Allow your child to develop an appetite before meals. Rest assured, they will eat what you have prepared! Three meals and two or three snacks is what most children need.

Likes and dislikes

All children are individuals and have firm likes and dislikes which develop as soon as they start eating solids. These may be related to bad experiences with a certain food in early childhood, like eating food when it was too hot, or are simply the copying of the dislikes of their parents. Some children insist that they will not eat the gravy because 'it has mushrooms in it', or they 'can't eat the peas because they are touching the carrots'. Some children separate food into lovely little piles and then proceed to eat each pile bit by bit; others will 'save the best food until last'. This type of behaviour is quite normal, as children like to explore and identify different foods as having different colours, textures, flavours and smells. Substitutes can be given for dislikes without any fear of 'spoiling' the child.

Young children usually have a 'core' of foods with which they are familiar and which they are happy to eat often. Always keep in mind that parents need to offer new foods at least ten times before the child will readily accept it. Don't expect them to accept new food the first time, but don't give up or accept their explanation that 'they don't like it'. Just keep offering the food in different ways and try, try again!

'My child never eats breakfast'

Breakfast means 'to break the fast', our overnight sleep. Sometimes this overnight fast can be as long as fourteen hours if children go to bed early, and so it is important for them to refuel in the morning. Breakfast is a very important meal for children because it:

- Refuels the child's body with energy and nutrients
- Prevents mid-morning fatigue, and irritability
- Helps morning concentration, and school work
- Helps to control weight by preventing mid-morning 'snack attacks' and bingeing
- Keeps blood glucose levels steady
- Helps prevent constipation by providing dietary fibre and a regular routine
- Generally reduces cholesterol levels
- Contributes to about ⅓ of a child's daily nutrient intakes – particularly iron, fibre and calcium.
- Also, children who skip breakfast are less likely to meet all their nutrient needs.

Some children will eat the same breakfast every day so don't worry if their breakfast seems boring or monotonous – it's fine, as long as it's healthy. If your child can't manage food in the morning, a milk drink will provide all the necessary nutrients. Don't worry if your child won't drink plain milk or low fat milk – give them flavoured milk or whole milk. It is most important that your child consumes some milk or dairy foods each day. The drinks in the recipe section of this book are complete meals on their own, and most children will accept them. Also, give the child who does not eat breakfast a healthy snack to take to school – they can 'make it up' on the school bus or at play lunch.

Don't give your child money to buy breakfast with unless you can be certain that they will be able to make a healthy choice. In my recent study of 5,000 school children, I found that 20 per cent of children had nothing more than soft drink, cordial, tea, coffee or water for breakfast. Many others were choosing chips, lollies or chocolates on their way to school. When their parents asked 'Did you have some breakfast?', the child was able to truthfully answer 'yes' but the nutritional quality was very inadequate indeed. Remember, breakfast is one meal where you can supervise what your child eats and you can point them in the right direction. Many children in my study answered that they would not prepare breakfast themselves, but they would eat it if it was put in front of them, or if their parents reminded them to eat it. The role of parents in making certain that children have had something nutritious for breakfast is very important indeed.

Making time for breakfast

Many children and teenagers skip breakfast because they don't have time to sit down to eat, or they decide to do something else with their time in the mornings. As a parent, it is your responsibility to organise enough time for your child to have something nutritious for breakfast – this may simply mean setting their alarm clock fifteen minutes earlier. Other families put breakfast food out on the kitchen table or bench the night before to save time in the mornings. Other families discourage television viewing in the mornings or make certain that children have breakfast on their laps or on the coffee table while watching their favourite morning cartoons. One mother gleefully told me that she could give her two boys anything to eat while they were in this zombie-like state! She said she often gave them raw vegetables for breakfast and they never noticed or commented on what they were eating.

Here are some other tips for making time for a healthy breakfast:

- Prepare your child's school clothes, socks and shoes, books, homework, school bags and school lunches the night before so that they don't waste breakfast time searching for lost things
- Give your child a nice alarm clock or watch, and encourage them to set it for breakfast time
- Have your child bathe or shower at night-time to save time in the mornings
- Set the breakfast table the night before with plates, cups, cutlery and breakfast cereals to save time in the mornings

- Sit your child down with their breakfast and encourage them to eat or drink it. Remind them to eat or drink it when they become distracted
- Treat morning television viewing as a privilege or a reward. For example, 'You can watch TV if you finish your breakfast'. Turn the TV off when they do not comply
- Give your child a nutritious mid-morning snack or drink to take with them, that can be eaten later on
- Eat or drink breakfast yourself! Set a good example
- If you have to leave home early, take a nutritious snack or drink to eat on the way
- Send your child's toothbrush and toothpaste to school or leave a second set in their school bag. This way, they can eat on the way to school and still clean their teeth before class. This is important for older children and teenagers who are self-conscious about personal hygiene
- Campaign for your school canteen to open early and provide quick and nutritious breakfast choices and drinks
- Keep track of your child's breakfast habits for a week. Reward their breakfast eating with praise and encourage-ment. When they eat breakfast every morning, give them a reward or special treat such as a visit to the pet shop or a special outing. Some parents include their child's healthy eating habits as part of their duties to earn pocket money or an allowance.

'My child just won't drink milk!!'

This is a very common cry from distraught parents. While milk is an important food for growing children (as well as for adolescents and pregnant and breastfeeding mothers) it can be easily substi-tuted with other foods. Milk provides protein, calcium, Vitamin D and riboflavin but out of all these nutrients, calcium is the most important for teeth and bones. Calcium is also found in:

- Skim milk, skim milk powder and low fat milks
- Cheese – all types

- Cottage or ricotta cheese
- Yoghurt
- Custard or junket
- Milk puddings and ice cream
- Nuts, especially almonds
- The bones of salmon and tuna.

You can also serve milk drinks hot or cold with added flavour-ings like Milo. If all else fails, try sneaking milk powder, cheese or yoghurt into mashed potato, rissoles and patties (add milk powder), and gravies, sauces and dressings (add milk, cheese and yoghurt instead of cream). You can also add extra milk powder to bread, damper, scones and muffins, cakes, biscuits and muesli. In soups and casseroles substitute milk or yoghurt for cream. Pancakes are a good, sneaky source of milk. Make porridge with milk instead of water, or scramble eggs with extra powdered milk and cheese. You can make frozen milk ice blocks by blending milk, yoghurt and fruit together. Also, melt grated cheese on cooked vegetables in the microwave or serve them topped with white sauce or cheese sauce. You can also serve macaroni cheese rather that plain pasta, or make spaghetti with cheese sauce.

Cream and butter are not good calcium or protein foods – they provide Vitamins A and D but are high in fat and should be used sparingly but French toast can be made with very little butter or margarine. While soy milk is a good source of protein it is low in calcium unless calcium has been added – so use brands that are fortified with calcium.

'My child hates vegetables!' 'My child won't touch any fruit!'

These are also very common remarks I hear from a lot of parents. The important thing to keep in mind is that frozen, dried, juiced, tinned – as well as fresh – vegetables and fruit will provide the necessary nutrients. It doesn't matter *how* these foods are eaten, what's important is that they *are* eaten.

Try using fruit juice or vegetable juice, which can also be frozen into cubes or other shapes. Try grating raw vegetables if they won't eat them cooked (don't try this with raw potato though, as it will cause stomach-ache).

Some children love frozen bananas on ice cream sticks, but would never touch the original fruit. Frozen grapes and oranges, and cherries on toothpicks are popular, while vegetable juices can easily be 'sneaked' into gravies, sauces, soups and casseroles. Rissoles, meatloaf and pancakes can be made with grated carrot, zucchini or potato. Pumpkin scones, pumpkin soup and pumpkin bread are a nutritious source of carotene; carrot and zucchini cake can be made with very little sugar; pumpkin pie is another alternative. Also, brush cooked vegetables with a tiny amount of warmed honey to make them more interesting.

Try cutting raw vegetables and fruit into funny shapes or balls, or let children grow their own vegetables, such as bean sprouts. Vegetables and fruit are more attractive if they are fresh, bright and crunchy, so perhaps start by serving vegetable shapes with a dip after school. For example, a dip made with ricotta cheese and crushed unsweetened pineapple can be served with celery, apple or carrot sticks. The act of 'dipping' makes vegetables much more fun. Fruit can also be blended into juices and milkshakes or concealed in cakes, breads and muffins.

2

Parents as Role Models

Children's eating habits are like their other behaviour patterns: they are usually modelled on those of their parents. If you skip breakfast, nibble or drink constantly in front of the TV, bolt down your food or grimace at the sight of green vegetables, then your child will more than likely copy you.

Children eat according to the different foods available, how much money they have, what their friends or parents are eating, what food advertisements and television tell them and what they learn at school and home about the nutritional quality of food. Trying to teach your children to eat healthy food means that you have to compete with all these other factors.

Eating habits can be improved simply by parents setting a good example for children to follow. If children grow up in an environment which clearly appreciates the importance of healthy food then their eating habits will be shaped accordingly for the rest of their lives. Try to help children understand why good food is important by teaching them about nutrition at home. Parents can encourage young children to become involved in shopping and food preparation and provide them with basic information about healthy diets.

A few basic rules will help guide the children into healthy eating habits. Set down the rules about meal times, eating habits, pocket money and school lunches; show the children your shopping list and stick to your guns in the supermarket. You will need the co-operation of the whole family, including the child's grandparents and other carers. Children like to help so let them join in the shopping, choose recipes, and get involved with the cooking. Finally, remember to reward children's behaviour with praise, fun, encouragement and attention, rather than with lollies or other foods.

Food parenting style

Have you ever thought about your food parenting style? There are basically four types of food parenting style – autocratic, laissez faire, democratic and ad hoc. In addition to these four basic styles, there are various combinations of each.

Obviously, every parent and household is different and no one food parenting style is a perfect match. Within families each parent will have a different food parenting style and this may be a useful addition to the family food environment, or it may be a constant source of conflict between parents. Mothers and fathers need to discuss how they approach feeding issues with their children and they need to agree about what approaches are to be used. Then, parents need to stick to this particular style, with only occasional diversions. If you argue about what to feed the children, or if you disagree in front of the children, it will be your Achilles heel.

Research shows that the parents who are consistent about how the children are fed and those who back each other up are the ones who have the most success in getting the children to eat what the parents want.

LIAM, ELEVEN, AND CALLUM, NINE

David is the incredibly proud father of two boys, Liam and Callum, and partner of Debbie, their mum. David's eyes light up and he talks with great enthusiasm about his sons' eating habits. 'Debbie is amazing, really,' he gushes. 'The breakfast menu is like a five star hotel! I don't know how she does it, but those boys eat so well, much better than other kids.'

David knows exactly what his boys eat every day; although he doesn't prepare any of it, and he couldn't recall many occasions of having fed them when they were babies or toddlers. David says the 'food department' is Debbie's domain and that she has done a wonderful job. He appreciates that they eat what is put in front of them and that they don't complain when they eat out. He notices and praises their adventurous eating at restaurants such as yum cha and he is pleased that they will grow up to try new foods and new cuisines. David credits Debbie with most of the hard work in getting the boys to eat well, but David enforces the table manners. David says his role is to reinforce what Debbie wants them to eat and he never interferes or undermines her.

David has vivid memories of the oldest boy's first birthday party. 'We have it on video, this tiny little toddler running around eating a very healthy low fat chicken drumstick on his birthday – being attacked by a flock of seagulls!'

Autocratic

Autocratic parents make virtually all of the decisions about what, when, where and how the children eat. They decide and plan exactly what is going to be eaten and it is often a menu that is laid out in a regular, well-planned routine. For example, many autocratic parents have regular dishes on particular days of the week. They may cook a certain meal every Wednesday night and send the same thing to school each day for lunch. Autocratic parents always shop with a list and there is no negotiating with children about which foods are being bought in the supermarket and no input from children about what is being cooked. Autocratic parents insist on children eating what is served and they never give in. This type of parent is completely in control of their child's food habits and they rule with an iron fist.

This type of clear and consistent food parenting style tends to get results because children quickly learn that the parents are in control. Unfortunately, though, when taken to extremes, this type of feeding style tends to be too controlling and doesn't allow children to make their own decisions about food. In experiments, the children of autocratic parents tended to overeat when exposed to unlimited amounts of treat foods such as lollies and chips. In addition, this style is believed to result in cravings for forbidden foods as well as secretive eating, hiding foods and binge eating. Children of autocratic parents tend to crave the foods they are not allowed to have.

Laissez faire

These parents go with the flow of life and their children's food habits simply follow. Laissez faire parents do little planning around food beyond the weekly shopping trip. They do not use a shopping list and they take advantage of market forces and price discounts – whatever is on special, they will buy. These parents do not plan set menus and they do not monitor their child's eating patterns. They tend to cook and serve whatever is in the house at the time, with little forethought or planning; although they do put regular meals on the table each night and their children never go hungry. The laissez faire parent is comfortable with food preparation at the last minute and they are always confident of putting together a decent meal with no prior planning and little preparation.

However, this type of food parenting style leaves too much to chance and leaves little room for food planning or monitoring of the child's daily intake. This style only works well if the house is stocked with a good supply of healthy foods and drinks from which the family can choose. Lack of organisation around food and laissez faire patterns around food planning are considered to be one of the main reasons for poor food intakes among children.

Democratic

Democratic parents usually ask their children what they would like to eat. This process goes on for breakfast, school lunch and dinner and involves discussion and ideas for potential meals between each parent and between parent and child. Democratic

ZALI, EIGHTEEN MONTHS OLD

Zali is an absolutely delightful little girl. Rachel and Paul, despite being quite strict parents themselves, are quite laissez faire and democratic with their little girl and allow her to choose almost all of her snacks and drinks. The incredible degree of control over food that this little one has is illustrated by the fact that she has her own cupboard full of her favourite foods! When Zali wants a snack – and this timing is completely dictated by Zali – she simply goes to the cupboard and points. Her mother or father then opens the cupboard and points to the various snack foods, asking Zali which one she wants. This is bound to result in Zali being difficult to feed as she gets older because she has become used to getting exactly what she wants. Unfortunately, there will probably be a great deal of fussing and tantrum throwing when Rachel and Paul finally decide that Zali can't continue to dictate what and when she eats.

parents allow the children to choose what is eaten and they let children eat when they want to. They allow children to fix foods and snacks for themselves and they never force children to eat what they don't want to. Democratic parents will often prepare separate meals for parents and children. Democratic parents allow children to choose from supermarket shelves and allow children to take money to school to buy their own school lunch.

This type of food parenting tends to result in children 'grazing' and constantly going to the kitchen for snacks and drinks. Allowing children some say in what is eaten may work in some families, but the golden rule tends to be that the parents decide *what* is going to be eaten as well as where and when it is eaten, and the children decide *how much* is eaten. This division of responsibility around food is now considered to be the best way to feed children. Too much democracy in food selection has been shown to result in poor food choices and over-eating in experiments among children.

Ad hoc

The food parenting style of these parents is largely random and chaotic. They allow the events of each day to determine what the children eat and where and when it is eaten. The ad hoc parent is not organised around food and does not plan meals. They fit the grocery shopping in whenever they can, never use a shopping list and never work to a menu plan. They take advantage of prepared and take-away foods whenever they can and they have little recollection of what their children eat over a twenty-four hour period. The ad hoc parent lives a very busy, stressful and chaotic lifestyle and the family's food patterns have to fit into this pattern.

This parenting style is advantageous for very busy parents who spend little time at home. Unfortunately, it only works in favour of healthy food choice if the parents have access to reasonably healthy take-away and packaged foods. Research shows that the major selling items on take-away menus are not healthy, so reading up on more healthy alternatives is essential for ad hoc parents.

Control

Who is in control of eating in your home? Are you in control or is your partner? Are the children largely in control?

As I've mentioned before, in order to establish and maintain healthy eating habits, research shows that parents need to be mostly in control of their children's eating. Parents need to decide *what* is eaten as research studies have shown that children can't make rational, healthy decisions about choosing the right food. When presented with choices between healthy and unhealthy food, children inevitably choose unhealthy food, and they tend to overeat it, as well. One thing children can achieve, though, is the decision about *how much* to eat.

MADELINE, SEVEN YEARS OLD

Madeline is the daughter of Sylvia and the younger sister of Ben, aged fourteen, and Sarah, aged ten. Madeline is an extremely fussy eater. She only eats mashed potato and apple juice from the fruit and vegetable food groups and flatly refuses to try any new fruit or vegetables. Madeline is one of the worst cases of neophobia (fear of new foods) that I have ever seen as a nutritionist and I suspect that her health is probably suffering. Madeline's mother Sylvia has a very busy life and food decisions are quite clearly ad hoc. Madeline's diet has never been particularly structured and food choices are made on the run. Madeline simply won't be made to eat new foods and Sylvia has given up arguing with her in order to keep the peace. Unfortunately, Madeline's food habits are unlikely to change. However, Sylvia's partner, Dennis, is a much more autocratic parent, so there may be some hope for Madeline's diet becoming more varied. If Dennis is able to present a wider variety of foods on a regular basis, and if Madeline can be encouraged and rewarded for eating them, her food habits are likely to improve. However, if Sylvia's ad hoc food parenting style outweighs Dennis's more controlled style, Madeline's limited diet will remain the way it is, and her long-term health will probably suffer.

Several studies show that children can monitor and regulate their own food intake and they can even out their calorie intake over a twenty-four-hour period. Children who are allowed to control their own intake can decide when to stop and don't overeat. Children of over-controlling parents, however, do not instinctively know how to regulate their intake, do not learn how to stop and they overeat. Allowing your child to decide *when* to stop eating is a very important step in helping them to be in touch with their bodily needs for food, drinks and calories. It will also, eventually, help them to control their weight.

What about grandparents?

Did you know that most adults eat the same types of food that they were fed as a child? Research shows that food preferences and food patterns are well entrenched in childhood and stay with us all our lives. It is no surprise, then, that we tend to cook similar foods and follow similar food parenting styles to those of our own parents. If you felt uncomfortable or unhappy about the way your mother or father dealt with food issues in your family, then now is the time to change! You need to be careful not to perpetuate the same food or eating style that made you hate your vegetables, or the same attitudes and behaviours that made you a closet chocolate fiend! Think about how your mother or father handled the food decisions in your family. Make a list of the way food was presented to you as a child and then check which of these attitudes and behaviours you now convey to your own children – you may find you have become your mother! Be careful to try to promote a positive foods environment in your home and help to make healthy eating relaxed, enjoyable and fun.

Rewards and punishments

The 'positive foods' approach is based on the strong psychological research finding that positive reinforcement, or reward, for a child's good eating behaviour is more effective that negative reinforcement, or punishment, for a child's bad eating behaviour. Many parents punish their children for not eating what is on their dinner plate. It's inappropriate and counter-productive to punish a child for not eating. More often than not the child will get upset and won't want to eat at all. Similarly, the punished child will associate meal times with tension, fear and stress, reducing their ability to eat; and some children will associate the punishment with the particular food for the rest of their lives.

The 'positive foods' approach recognises and rewards the child's positive food behaviours and encourages that behaviour to be repeated. Appropriate rewards are recognition, praise,

ALEXANDER, EIGHT, AND DAVID, SIX

Alexander and David are the two sons of Ted and Marilyn who have just become divorced. The boys live with Marilyn and have weekends with their dad. Marilyn is quite strict with the boys' diets, but since Ted has moved out, they spend afternoons with their neighbour from around the corner, Margaret, who is an elderly lady and a grandmother substitute for the family. Margaret loves to treat the boys and just recently, she has provided an endless supply of lollies and chocolates after school, even though their mother gives them a nutritious snack before they visit. Marilyn was quite disturbed by all of the lollies and chocolates the boys were consuming, but she knew that Margaret was simply trying to be nice to the boys and that she was enjoying being their 'grandma'. After some discussion about how to resolve the issue without hurting Margaret's feelings, Marilyn and Ted got together to make some suggestions for Margaret. They explained to Margaret, with both boys listening, that they were concerned about the boys' teeth and they would like the boys to have an appetite and eat what their mother cooks for dinner. They suggested that Margaret treats the boys with inexpensive toys, comic books and the occasional video or DVD. They all agreed that Sundays might be the best day for lolly treats.

encouragement and non-food treats like being taken to the park or some other special place, or being given some other special treat. Offering food as a special treat or reward is counter-productive because it makes some foods too 'special' and therefore too desirable. The best reward for children is often the fact that their parents noticed them doing something right! Remember, your child wants and needs your acceptance, love and support, so make it clear that you can work together as a team to keep them healthy and happy.

SHAUN, NINE YEARS OLD

'He's a shocker!' declares Shaun's mother Denise, as she describes to me how her son won't eat anything new. Shaun has a very limited core of familiar foods, and he is typically neophobic when it comes to trying new foods. Denise has virtually given up trying new recipes and she and her husband Dan have stopped heatedly discussing what Shaun should and shouldn't eat. Denise gets very upset when the family goes out to visit relatives or friends and Shaun flatly refuses to eat anything that is put in front of him. 'It's so embarrassing!' cries Denise. 'I just want to sink under the table. It's a nightmare.'

Does this situation sound all too familiar? Denise's solution to this common problem is to take a packet of two-minute noodles in her handbag every time the family eats at someone else's house. She may also take a peanut butter sandwich, just for a change.

Shaun won't eat what is served for dinner because he knows that he merely has to turn up the volume in order to be given his two favourite foods. He is unlikely to change his eating behaviours until both parents agree on some basic rules. First, Shaun must not be allowed anything to eat or drink in the 1–2 hours just before dinner and he must not be given a drink with his meal as drinks are often quite filling.

Second, Dan and Denise need to make it clear to Shaun before they arrive at the relatives' or friends' house that he must eat something at the dinner table. Shaun may choose plain bread or pasta, rice or potato separate to any mixed dish. Many children will not eat a mixed meal but will happily eat meals where food is kept separate on their plate. Shaun also needs to know that he will not be getting a special meal from Mum's handbag, and that he certainly won't get dessert, lollies or other treats unless he eats something (not necessarily everything) from his dinner plate. For this to work, his parents need to be clear, firm and calm, and the host or hostess must not offer any special alternatives for Shaun. He also needs to be encouraged, praised and rewarded for his positive eating behaviours, but no food rewards should be given. Denise and Dan have tried this strategy a couple of times with Shaun and he did manage to eat some bread and potato the first time and some pasta the second time. This, Denise reports, is true progress!

3

The Importance of Good Nutrition

Feeding your child good, nutritious food has many important benefits which continue into adolescence and adulthood:

- Growth and brain development
- Health protection and immunity
- Protection against adult diseases
- Energy regulation
- Protection of teeth and gums
- Improved behaviour
- Development of good eating habits for life.

Growth and brain development

With good, nutritious food your child is provided with all of the essential nutrients to nourish every part of their rapidly growing bodies. This ensures the best start in life and allows them to grow to their full potential – both physically and mentally.

Good nutrition is extremely important for babies, toddlers and children because their bodies are growing so rapidly. Poor nutrition can be largely tolerated by adults without dangerous consequences because their growth has finished, but babies and children most definitely can't.

In a person's life, their growth rate is the greatest from birth to one year of age when their birth weight triples and their length increases by an average of 17 centimetres. One of the most important aspects of providing good food is the nutrition for the growing brain, which is crucial for babies, toddlers and children. The growth and development of a child's brain continues from birth right through to sixteen years of age, and their intelligence, ability to concentrate and their school performance are all dependent on receiving the right foods and nutrients every day from a young age. The circumference of a baby's brain and head grows by 6 centimetres in the first three months of life and has increased by 12 centimetres from birth to their first birthday, and has increased by about 16 centimetres by the age of three years. This huge surge in the size of the brain will determine the child's intelligence and how well they perform at school. Obviously, every other part of your child's body is growing too, including the skin, blood, immune cells, lymphatic system, muscles, organs, hair, bones and teeth.

As well, cells making up all parts of the child's body are being repaired and replaced every day.

As a result, any period of poor nutrition during childhood will delay the growth, development and repair of these essential body cells, leaving the child prone to growth failure, shorter height, poor immunity and poor brain function.

In a recent study of 5,000 school children, I found a disturbing difference in height of 2.3 centimetres in the children with the poorest diets (these kids also happened to be the least well-off economically). Another concerning finding of this study was the fact that this poor bone growth (reflected in the children's lower height) may also suggest poor brain growth. If a child's diet is so inadequate as to result in lower bone growth, then it's likely that other parts of the body are not growing properly as well – namely, the child's brain. This sort of growth failure due to inadequate nutrition is common in poor, developing countries where children do not have enough food. It is also seen in cases where children are not fed the nutritious foods that promote growth. The overall result for the child is inadequate brain growth, lower intelligence and poor school performance. Below average academic achievement is seen in children who are hungry and distracted, such as those who go to school without any breakfast, but is also seen in children whose brain size and function have been hampered by inadequate nutrition. One of the best functions of good nutrition in children is the production of full brain development, intelligence and the achievement of the child's full academic ability.

The important thing to remember is that poor physical development is *irreversible*, so any deficiencies in the nutrition of a baby, toddler or child can't be made up later on. If you measure your head circumference using a tape measure and then measure your child's you'll find that your child has a lot of growing to do, and this growth is solely dependent on good nutrition.

Here is a summary of growth patterns in babies, toddlers and children:

Birth to twelve months
- This first year of life is the greatest period of growth in a human
- Growth is directly reflected by nutrient intake
- Head circumference nearly doubles in the first twelve months
- Head circumference increases by about 6 centimetres in the first three months, 9 centimetres by six months of age, and 12 centimetres by twelve months of age
- Birth weight doubles in the first five months and has tripled in the first twelve months
- Birth length increases by about 16–18 centimetres in the first six months and increases by about 25 centimetres in the first 12 months
- In this stage of life, 50 per cent of the baby's food intake is used by the brain.

Toddlers, one to three years
- Growth slows down slightly from one to three years, explaining the reduction in a child's appetite often observed by parents at this time
- Head circumference increases by 3–4 centimetres from one to three years

- 70 per cent of the adult brain size is achieved by age three
- To predict your child's adult height, double their height at age two.

Children, three to ten years
- Growth during this middle phase of childhood is slow and steady in both boys and girls
- Children average growth of about 5–6 centimetres and 2–3 kilograms per year until their ninth or tenth birthday
- Brain growth continues slowly and steadily until full brain development is achieved at around sixteen years of age
- 95 per cent of the adult brain size is achieved by age seven
- The total amount of body fat begins to decrease in toddlers and continues until six to eight years of age when it begins to rise again in both boys and girls
- Puberty may begin in girls as young as eight years of age, including development of the breast bud, nipple, underarm and pubic hair, and widening of the hipbones
- Both boys and girls naturally develop a layer of body fat at about age eight to ten, which is used as a source of energy to fuel their growth spurt in puberty
- After age eight and nine girls naturally have more body fat than boys and this gives them a rounder, more curvaceous figure
- Girls begin the puberty growth spurt from about nine to eleven years, which is, on average, about two years before boys
- Boys develop more muscle (and therefore more strength) than girls at puberty and girls develop more fat.

Health protection and immunity
The human body has many ways of protecting itself from viruses and bacteria but specific nutrients are needed each day in order to do this. Your child will be healthier and more able to fight off infections and illnesses if they receive good nutrition every day.

Good nutrition is essential for the production of protective immune cells that fight infection and disease in babies and children. Breastmilk, the child's first food, contains many anti-infection agents such as immunoglobulins, which are anti-viral agents, and lactoferrin, an anti-bacterial agent. These provide a constant supply of infection-fighting agents for babies and toddlers for as long as they are breastfed.

Breastfed babies and toddlers are known to have fewer colds, ear infections and bouts of gastroenteritis than formula-fed babies, and breast-fed babies also fight off illnesses more quickly than formula-fed babies. Full breastfeeding with no other additional food, drinks or water is recommended by the World Health Organisation (WHO) until the baby is six months old. Additional foods, apart from breastmilk, also provide the child with the ability to produce immunoglobulins and other infection fighting agents.

The size of the child's lymphatic system doubles in size by age seven and then doubles again up to the age of twelve. Good daily nutrition must be provided for the child's body to produce immune tissue and the white blood cells which engulf and destroy viruses and bacteria. The child's immune system can even fight off cancer cells and other infective agents that may enter the child's body.

Children who suffer malnutrition develop more infections than well-nourished children because they produce fewer white blood cells, immunoglobulins, anti-bodies and other immune cells. Inadequate nutrition and immunity becomes a nasty, vicious cycle in poorly nourished and undernourished children because infection and illness often affect a child's appetite and their nutritional intake.

A poorly nourished child gets sick, eats less and becomes even more poorly nourished and prone to further infection and further malnutrition. Also, the sick child can't concentrate, or misses out on important schoolwork, and their academic performance suffers.

With all this in mind, childhood is a very important time for the provision of protein, iron, zinc and Vitamin C, which are all required daily to build the child's immune system. Children who are lacking in any of these nutrients will be more prone to colds and viral infections, and the common childhood illnesses such as earache, chicken pox and gastroenteritis. Children with good nutrition are able to grow properly, stay well and develop to their full physical and mental ability.

Protection against adult diseases

The major diseases that are common in many families have their origins in childhood. Heart disease, high blood pressure, type 2 diabetes and certain cancers can all be prevented by good nutrition in childhood and throughout life.

Good nutrition in childhood helps to fight short-term infections but also fights adult diseases that may start to develop in childhood and adolescence. Children's immune systems fight a constant battle against infections and also protects them from the development of cancer cells. Many nutrients in food, particularly in fruits and vegetables, protect children against cell damage and cell changes that can cause cancer. Dietary fibre, antioxidants (beta carotene, Vitamin C, Vitamin E) and other phytochemicals (indoles, isothiocyanates, phytosterols, phosterols, isoflavones and flavenoids) found in fruits, vegetables, berries, garlic, onions, legumes and tea prevent body cells becoming abnormal or cancerous. Different foods contain thousands of different substances and chemicals and much is still unknown about which substances in foods protect us from cancer, but we do know for certain that fruit and vegetables reduce the risk. Many researchers believe that the chemicals in foods that protect us from cancer combine and act in conjunction with one another, and this is why it's better to eat the foods rather than take individual supplements. In any case, providing fruit and vegetables to babies, toddlers and children is known to reduce their risk of cancer.

A low fat diet, particularly a diet low in saturated fats, protects your child's arteries from the build up of fatty deposits and cholesterol, known as atherosclerosis. Blocked arteries in the heart can cause heart disease, and blocked or narrowed arteries in the kidneys and brain can cause kidney disease or stroke. A blockage or reduced blood supply to other parts of the body can also affect eyesight and your general circulation. Similarly, a low salt diet can help keep your child's blood pressure within a normal range.

Overweight and obesity often begin in childhood or adolescence and a healthy diet will certainly protect your child from these weight problems and help them grow normally. Overweight children can have health problems such as atherosclerosis, type 2 diabetes and high blood pressure.

Giving your child a nutritious diet will ensure daily health but will also reduce their risk of developing illnesses and disease later in life. This is important for all children, but particularly important for children from families where parents, grandparents and other relatives suffer from nutrition-related illnesses such as heart disease, high blood pressure, stroke, diabetes, certain kidney stones, gall bladder disease, osteoporosis (thin bones), diverticulitis, haemorrhoids (piles), and several cancers such as bowel, stomach, prostate and breast cancer. Children can be protected from all of these diseases by good nutrition, and will also learn to develop good life-long eating habits which they will then be able to pass on to their own children.

Energy regulation

Most children have a lot of energy, but some, especially those who don't have a nutritious breakfast, suffer a mid-morning slump in energy and concentration. Providing regular nutritious food and drink helps your child maintain a consistent supply of energy throughout the day. In turn, this helps them to settle at night-time.

Protection of teeth and gums

As a child's baby and adult teeth are fully formed in utero, good nutrition is essential for the mother during pregnancy.

ANDREW, TEN YEARS OLD

Andrew's mother, Julie, is at her wit's end worrying about her son's eating habits. She knows about the importance of healthy eating and she worries that as her son gets older and becomes a teenager, his body won't be able to cope with colds, flus and all the bumps and knocks of adolescence. She worries that he will break a bone and that it will not heal properly.

Julie's husband Mark, the main caregiver for the children at the moment, is quite used to eating an early supper at 5 or 5.30 pm. While Julie is still at work Mark cooks a 'special supper' for the children, which is a little too rich for Julie's liking – chips, devon, crumbed meats and chicken, sausages, fish fingers, pizza and potato gems – all very high fat foods. When Julie arrives home from work around 6.30 pm, Mark then cooks a separate dinner for them, which is much more healthy than the children's menu.

After discussion with Julie, it became clear that her nutrition knowledge was quite good but that Mark's was pretty non-existent! Julie started to suggest some more healthy dinner options for the children such as mashed potato instead of chips, grilled chicken drumsticks instead of fish fingers, and salad vegetables, which Andrew is happy to eat raw. Julie also suggested the children start joining them for dinner – at least a few nights a week and that their 5 o'clock dinner is preceded by a more healthful after school snack.

Andrew started trying different foods, because by dinnertime he was very hungry. Julie kept reassuring Mark that it was OK to allow Andrew to become hungry and that it actually helped to improve his eating habits. Andrew went to a family barbeque recently and both Mark and Julie spotted him eating barbequed chicken and corn on the cob without being nagged to eat it. 'Now we're really getting somewhere!' said Julie.

Good child nutrition then ensures the protection of teeth and gums for life.

Improved behaviour

Children are unable to behave properly when they are hungry or poorly nourished. A good diet, especially a good breakfast, helps children to settle at school in the mornings and regular meals, snacks and drinks help to moderate the child's behaviour over a twenty-four-hour period.

Development of good eating habits for life

Children develop their eating habits from birth and many stay with the child for life. Encouraging good eating habits helps the child when they are young, but also ensures that they will have a nutritious diet for life and pass on their good eating habits to their own children.

Children's needs

Children need food to provide the nutrients required for energy, growth, repair of old tissues, regulation of body processes and protection against disease. These are:

- **Protein** for growth and repair. Found in meat, fish, poultry, eggs, milk, cheese, yoghurt, dried beans, peas and lentils, nuts, peanut butter, tofu.
- **Carbohydrates** for energy and fibre. Found in bread, cereals, pasta, rice, oats, wheat, fruits and vegetables. Wholegrain breads and cereals, and fruits and vegetables, provide the fibre to help keep bowel movements regular.
- **Fats** for energy and to provide the fat-soluble vitamins A, E, D and K. Found in butter, margarine, oils and cream. Fats are also found in other foods such as some fruits, vegetables, meats, cereal foods and dairy foods.
- **Vitamins** are needed but contrary to popular belief, we only need vitamins in tiny amounts from food to help growth and to burn up food for energy. Important vitamins for

children are Vitamin C (found in fruits and vegetables), Vitamin A (found in yellow, green and orange fruits, and vegetables) and the B group vitamins – Thiamine (B1), Riboflavin (B2), Niacin (B3) (found in bread, cereal, meat, milk and eggs).

- **Minerals** are needed for growth and the regulation of body functions. Important minerals for children are calcium for bones and teeth (from milk, cheese and yoghurt), and iron (from meat, fish, poultry, bread, cereals, green vegetables and legumes). Iron is needed to make blood.
- **Water** is vital for all life. Our kidneys need water to make the urine in which we get rid of body wastes. Children need water to prevent dehydration, especially in hot weather.

As different foods contain different nutrients, we need to eat a variety of foods each day to combine these nutrients in the right amounts. However, no one single food is essential in a child's diet – if they have a variety of foods from the table of food groups opposite they'll get enough nutrients.

Important nutrients

Protein
Children need 2 grams of protein for each kilogram of body weight – roughly double the amount needed by fully grown adults! For example, if a child weighs 20 kg they will need around 30–40 grams of protein each day to stay healthy. This is not usually a major problem in developed countries. Most children receive more than enough protein from food. For example, 1 cup of milk, 1 egg, 1 lamb chop, 2 slices of sandwich cheese and 1 cup of baked beans all provide between 6 and 10 grams of protein each. However, poor diets, domi-nated by non-nutritious food and drinks such as biscuits, snack foods, chips, two-minute noodles, lollies, soft drinks and cordial will not supply the child with enough protein to promote growth.

Recommended Daily Nutrients for babies, toddlers, children and teens

| | BABIES | | TODDLERS | | | CHILDREN | | TEENS | | | |
	BREASTFED	BOTTLEFED	7–12 MONTHS	1–3 YEARS	4–7 YEARS	8–11 YEARS BOYS	8–11 YEARS GIRLS	12–15 YEARS BOYS	12–15 YEARS GIRLS	16–18 YEARS BOYS	16–18 YEARS GIRLS
Protein (grams)	see (a)	2.0 g per kilogram body weight	1.6 g per kilogram body weight	14–18 g per day	18–24 g per day	27–38 g per day	27–39 g per day	42–60 g per day	44–55 g per day	64–70 g per day	57 g per day
Calcium (mg)	300	500	550	700	800	800	900	1200	1000	1000	800
Iron (mg)	0.5	3.0	9.0	6–8	6–8	6–8	10–13	10–13	10–13	10–13	10–13
Vitamin C (mg)	25	25	30	30	30	30	30	30	30	40	30
Sodium (mg)	140–280	140–280	320–580	320–1150	460–1730	600–2300	600–2300	920–2300	920–2300	920–2300	920–2300
Fibre (grams) Also, see (b)	After the age of 2 years the fibre recommendation is 5 grams plus the child's age. E.g. a 7-year-old needs at least 5 + 7 grams of fibre per day = at least 12 grams of fibre per day.										
Energy (kilojoules) Also, see (c)	395–520 kj (a) per kilo body weight	395–520 kj (a) per kilo body weight	395–435 kj per kilo body weight	4,800–6,000 kj	6,500–7,900 kj	7,900–9,000 kj	8,000–10,000 kj	11,000–13,500 kj			
Water (ml) Also, see (d)	1,000–1,500 ml (4–6 cups)	1,200–1,600 ml (5–7 cups)	1,600–2,800 ml (7–11 cups)			2,000–3,000 ml (8–12 cups)					

(a) There is no specific recommendation about protein as it is assumed that breastfed babies receive enough protein from mother's milk.
(b) A minimum of 5 grams plus the child's age after the age of 2 is currently recommended, but this recommendation is likely to rise to 10 grams plus the child's age in the near future. The current recommendation is a minimum requirement.
(c) Energy requirements vary according to growth rates and how active the child is.
(d) Fluid needs are increased in hot or humid weather and when the child is vomiting or has diarrhoea.

Some vegetarian children are at risk of nutritional deficiency because vegetarian foods tend to be very filling and the child may be 'full' before nutritional needs have been met. It is easier to meet the protein, energy, vitamin and mineral needs of vegetarian children if milk based foods and eggs are included in their diet. Look at the table opposite to see where your child's protein comes from.

Calcium

This important nutrient is essential, yet all too often children receive inadequate amounts. Calcium is necessary for the growth of teeth and bones, and is found in milk, cheese, yoghurt, powdered milk and the bones of tinned fish. Growing children need nearly twice as much calcium as adults and should be drinking at least 600–750 ml of milk or the equivalent from other dairy foods each day, such as cheese, yoghurt, custard, milk powder or milk puddings. Look at the table on page 46 to see where your child's calcium comes from.

Iron

Iron is required to make red blood cells which carry oxygen throughout the body. Children who do not eat enough iron will become tired, faint, pale, uninterested in play and may complain of headaches. They will also be susceptible to colds, flus and other infections, as daily iron is required to build the immune system. Iron is an essential building block for brain tissue and iron deficiency can result in poor mental development and lower intelligence. Your doctor can supply iron supplements if your child is anaemic, but otherwise it is best to keep up a good iron intake to prevent any deficiency. Haem iron (from animal sources) is better absorbed than non-haem iron (from cereal and vegetable sources). Approximately 20 per cent of the haem iron in food is absorbed, but only 2–5 per cent of non-haem iron is absorbed. The best sources of haem iron are from meat, fish and chicken. Vitamin C helps non-haem iron to be 'taken up' by the body, so make sure your child also has a serve of fruit, vegetables or juices with the same meal to supply Vitamin C (the iron and

Good sources of dietary protein

Food	Amount	Protein (grams)
Chicken, lean, breast	100 g	28.0
Chicken, lean, leg	100 g	27.0
Meat, lean, cooked	100 g	27.0
Fish, average, cooked	100 g	22.0
Tuna/salmon, tinned, in brine or oil	100 g	22.1
Lobster, prawn, cooked	100 g	22.0
Mussels	12 cooked	20.0
Crab, cooked	100 g	12.6
Scallops, cooked	6	13.0
Yoghurt, natural	1 tub (200 g)	11.6
Tofu (soybean curd)	½ cup	10.0
Peanuts	¼ cup	9.8
Milk	1 cup	9.0
Soy drink	1 cup	8.9
Yoghurt, fruit flavoured	1 tub (200 g)	8.6
Soya beans, canned, drained	½ cup	8.6
Mixed nuts	¼ cup	8.1
Pasta, white, cooked	1 cup	7.2
Peanut butter	1 tablespoon	6.8
Baked beans	½ cup	6.4
Red kidney beans, lentils, mixed beans (canned)	½ cup, drained	6.4
Egg, boiled	1 medium	6.3
Avocado	½ pear	6.0
Oysters, raw	6	6.0
Rice, brown, boiled	1 cup	5.7
Rolled oats, raw, e.g. muesli	½ cup	5.0
Cheese, processed, cheddar	1 slice (21 g)	4.5
Rice, white, boiled	1 cup	4.4
Tahini (sesame seed paste)	1 tablespoon	4.3
Cheese, cheddar	1 cube (2.5 cm)	4.1
Rolled oats, cooked	1 cup	4.1
Sunflower seeds	1 tablespoon	3.4
Breakfast biscuits, wholewheat	2 biscuits	3.4
Bread, wholemeal	1 slice	3.0
Hummus	¼ cup	3.0
Peas, green, boiled	⅓ cup	2.6
Bread, white	1 slice	2.4
Carrots, zucchini, broccoli	½ cup	1.6
Fruit – banana, apple, orange	1 piece	1.0

Good sources of calcium

FOOD	SERVING SIZE	CALCIUM (MG)
Milk (skim)	1 cup (250 ml)	375
Yoghurt (low fat, natural)	1 container (200 g)	360
Yoghurt (low fat, fruit)	1 container (200 g)	320
Milk (low fat)	1 cup	310
Soy drink (fortified with calcium)	1 cup	290
Yoghurt (whole, plain, natural)	1 container (200 g)	290
Salmon (canned, solids and liquids – bones included)	½ cup	280
Milk (whole)	1 cup	275
Cheddar cheese	2.5 cm cube (30 g)	240
Sardines (canned and drained – bones included)	¼ cup	175
Fruche (low fat)	200 g	160
Tofu – firm (with calcium coagulant)	½ cup (100 g)	160
Custard, whole milk	½ cup	150
Prawns	100 g	150
Figs, dried	5 figs	150
Ice cream	2 scoops	130
Hummus	1 cup (246 g)	124
Milk chocolate	50 g	125
Milo	2 tablespoons	110
Ricotta cheese	3 tablespoons	100
Baked beans	1 cup	90
Tahini paste	1 tablespoon	90
Chocolate bar (Mars Bar, Milky Way, Snickers)	1 bar	80
Tofu – soft (with calcium coagulant)	½ cup (100 g)	80
Almonds (dry roasted)	¼ cup	73
Potato (mashed with milk)	1 cup (210 g)	55
Cottage cheese	3 tablespoons	30
Broccoli (cooked)	1 cup	30
Dark chocolate	50 g	25
Peanut butter	2 tablespoons	20
Mineral water	1 cup	4–18

Vitamin C will combine in the stomach to produce the better-absorbed haem iron). Good combinations are fruit juice with breakfast cereal, or bread, pasta or rice with tomato sauce, baked beans with juice or salad, and peanut butter with juice. This is another reason why eating a variety of different foods is important for your child. If your child does not like meat or is a vegetarian, try serving other foods which contain iron, such as wheatgerm, wholegrain bread and cereals, peas, lentils or kidney beans, baked beans or leafy green vegetables. You can also make meat or fish paste spread in a blender, and make salmon and tuna patties or dips.

Good sources of haem and non-haem iron

Foods containing HAEM IRON	IRON (MG)	Foods containing NON-HAEM IRON	IRON (MG)
Liver (100 g)	11.1	Bran breakfast cereal (30 g)	5.4
Kidney (50 g)	5.7	Pasta, wholemeal (1 cup boiled)	3.1
Bran breakfast cereal (30 g)	5.4	Cornflakes (30 g)	2.8
		Milo, Ovaltine (2 tablespoons)	2.8
Beef (120 g)	3.6	Breakfast wheat biscuits	2.6
Lamb (120 g)	3.0	(2 biscuits)	
		Baked beans, lentils (½ cup cooked)	2.2
Cornflakes (30 g)	2.8	Spinach (½ cup, boiled)	2.2
Salmon, tuna (150 g)	2.6	Dried apricots (10 apricot halves)	2.2
Pork (1 chop)	1.8	Bread, wholemeal (2 slices)	1.4
Chicken (120 g)	0.8	Broccoli (⅔ cup, boiled)	1.0
Fish (120 g)	0.5	Peanut butter (2 tablespoons)	1.0
		Egg (1 whole)	0.9
		Rice, brown, boiled (1 cup)	0.8
		Pasta, white (1 cup boiled)	0.7
		Rice, white, boiled (1 cup)	0.6
		Nuts (15 g)	0.6
		Bread, white (2 slices)	0.6

Fibre

Fibre is required to keep bowel movements regular and soft. After the age of two years of age, your child needs the minimum of 5 grams plus their age. For example, a seven-year-old needs at least 5 grams + 7 grams = at least 12 grams of fibre per day. A high fibre diet is unsuitable for children under two years because it is too 'filling' and the child will become full quickly and will not be able to eat enough food to provide sufficient energy for growth and development. See the table opposite.

Food groups

Cereals and bread

Required for energy, vitamins, minerals and fibre. All products made from flour, grain, rice, oats and rye including bread, cereals, spaghetti, crisp-bread, scones and pasta constitute this group. Wholegrain varieties should be included to provide fibre. Children need at least four serves daily. An example of one serving from this group would be 1 slice of bread, 1 scone or ½–1 cup of cereal, rice or pasta.

Vegetables

These provide energy, vitamins, minerals and fibre. Vegetables also provide protective substances such as antioxidants and phytochemicals; the most brightly coloured vegetables contain the most protective substances. One piece of tomato or potato will supply your child with enough Vitamin C for the day and, likewise, one serve of green, yellow or orange fruit or vegetable will supply Vitamin A; and two serves of other fruits or vegetables will supply the B group vitamins, fibre and other protective agents (fresh, raw, tinned, frozen or dried fruit and vegetables are all suitable for this).

Fish, meat, eggs and legumes

Will provide protein, vitamins and minerals and are particularly good sources of iron. This group includes all meats, poultry, fish, egg dishes, dried beans, peas, lentils and nuts. One or two

Good sources of dietary fibre

Food	Serving Size	Fibre (g)
Muesli, natural, uncooked	½ cup	7.0
Beans (baked beans, kidney, mixed beans, cooked lentils)	½ cup	6.0
Passionfruit	2	5.6
Peas, green	½ cup	4.6
Pasta, wholemeal, cooked	½ cup	4.6
Wheat biscuits	2 biscuits	4.1
Sweet corn	1 medium cob	4.0
Bran cereals	½ cup	3.8
Prunes	6	3.5
Porridge, cooked	1 cup	3.4
Apple (with skin), banana, pear, orange	1 medium piece	3.0
Kiwi fruit	2, medium	3.0
Strawberries	½ cup, sliced	2.8
Broccoli, cooked	½ cup	2.5
Carrot, cooked	1 medium or ½ cup	2.5
Bread, mixed grain	1 slice	2.3
Apricots	2 fresh	2.1
Bread, wholemeal	1 slice	2.0
Beans, green, sliced, cooked or raw	½ cup	2.0
Cabbage, cauliflower, cooked or raw	½ cup	2.0
Melon (rockmelon, watermelon, honeydew)	1 cup chopped	2.0
Avocado	½ medium	1.9
Apricots	4 dried	1.8
Potato, peeled, baked	1 medium	1.8
Bread, white (high fibre)	1 slice	1.8
Lettuce	2 medium leaves	1.7
Sultanas	1 tablespoon	1.7
Rice, brown, cooked	½ cup	1.6
Bean sprouts, raw	½ cup	1.5
Bread, white	1 slice	1.4
Crumpets, wholemeal	1	1.4
Pasta, white, cooked	½ cup	1.3
Corn Flakes, Rice Bubbles	1 cup	1.0
Mushrooms, raw, sliced	½ cup	1.0
Cherries	7 large	1.0
Zucchini, cooked	½ cup	0.9
Crumpets, white	1	0.9
Pumpkin, cooked	½ cup	0.8
Rice, white, cooked	½ cup	0.8
Tomato	½ medium	0.7
Tofu	½ cup	0.7
Celery	1 full stalk	0.5
Cucumber (unpeeled)	5 slices	0.4
Fruit juice	1 cup	0

servings daily will provide sufficient protein for children. Some people have an aversion to red meat, but lean red meat is a very nutritious food and can supply a rich source of protein, thiamin (Vitamin B), iron, zinc and Vitamin B12. Small amounts of red meat can certainly be part of a nutritious, healthy diet for children as young as eight months old.

Milk and dairy products

These supply protein, vitamins and calcium. Includes skim milk, milk powder, evaporated milk, fat-reduced milks, cheese, yoghurt and buttermilk. Children need 600 millilitres (ml) daily. This may sound like a lot of milk at first, but children need a lot of calcium to build strong bones and teeth. One cup of yoghurt or 30 grams of cheese supplies approximately the same amount of calcium and protein as one cup of milk (250 ml) so you can provide variety as well as calcium.

Look at the Five Food Groups chart below to see how many servings of each food group your child needs, and also to see appropriate serving sizes.

Five Food Groups daily servings for children aged 1–12 years

| FOOD | SERVING SIZE | AGE GROUP | |
		1–7 YEARS	6–9 YEARS
Bread and cereal	2 slices of bread 1 bread roll 1 cup cooked rice, noodles, pasta 1 cup breakfast cereal 1 cup cooked porridge ½ cup raw muesli 4 crispbread or 6 water crackers	4–7 servings per day	6–9 servings per day
Milk and dairy foods	1 cup (250 ml) milk or custard 1 tub (200 g) yoghurt 1 square (40 g)	2–3 servings per day	3 servings per day

FOOD	SERVING SIZE	AGE GROUP	
		1–7 YEARS	6–9 YEARS
Vegetables	cheese (2 slices/ ½ cup grated) 2 scoops ice cream (try low fat) 1 cup soy drink (calcium fortified) All vegetables, ½ cup cooked, 1 medium potato (raw, frozen, canned, dried), ½ cup grated carrot/ lettuce/salad Legumes and beans (e.g. baked beans), ¼ cup Tofu, ¼ cup	2–3 servings per day	3–4 servings per day
Fruit	1 piece fruit (e.g. apple, orange, banana) 2 pieces small fruit (e.g. plums, kiwi fruit, apricot) ½ cup 100% fruit juice 8 strawberries, 20 grapes ¼–½ cup cooked fruit ¼ cup grapes, berries, tomato 4 pieces dried fruit (e.g. apricots) 1½ tablespoons dried fruit (e.g. sultanas)	1–2 servings per day	3–4 servings per day
Meat and meat substitutes	100 g cooked (2 slices) lean meat, fish, chicken ½ cup mince, 2 small chops ½ cup tuna or salmon 2 eggs Peanut butter (1 tablespoon) ⅓ cup nuts ½ cup baked beans	1 serving per day	1–2 servings per day

Dietary guidelines

Poor nutrition will affect a child's health and lead to such health problems as obesity, heart disease, high blood pressure, certain types of cancer, diabetes, gall bladder disease, gout and constipation in later life. But even in childhood one or many symptoms may suggest that your child is not eating the right foods: being over- or under-weight, poor growth and development, persistent constipation, raised blood fats, dental caries and unhealthy gums, constant tiredness, irritability, lack of energy and an inability to concentrate at school. A high incidence of infection and illness can also be the result of a poor diet and can set a pattern which is often not broken later in life.

As a parent you need to set the example and encourage your children from a young age to treat good nutrition, growth and development seriously and take on the following guidelines as 'rules for life':

- Encourage and support breastfeeding
- Children and adolescents need enough nutritious foods to grow and develop normally.
  - * Growth should be checked regularly for young children
  - * Physical activity is important for all children and adolescents
- Enjoy a wide variety of nutritious foods:
  - * Eat plenty of vegetables, legumes and fruit
  - * Eat plenty of cereals (including breads, rice, pasta and noodles), preferably wholegrain
  - * Include lean meat, fish, poultry and/or alternatives in your diet
  - * Include milks, yoghurts, cheeses and/or alternatives, noting that reduced fat milks are not suitable for young children under two years because of their high energy needs, but reduced fat varieties should be encouraged for older children and adolescents
  - * Choose water as a drink.
- And care should be taken to:
  - * Limit saturated fat, and moderate your total fat intake, noting that low-fat diets are not suitable for infants and toddlers

* Choose foods low in salt
* Consume only moderate amounts of sugars and foods containing added sugar.

The Healthy Eating Pyramid

The Healthy Eating Pyramid is a concept that even small children can understand, and can be followed by the whole family. Use it as a guide to planning meals and shopping. The pyramid shows how much of each food type your child should choose. The main part of a healthy diet should come from bread and cereals such as pasta, rice, breakfast cereals and other grain and flour products, together with plenty of vegetables and fruits. One or two daily servings of lean meat, poultry, fish, dried beans, peas, lentils, nuts or eggs should be included as well as milk, cheese or yoghurt. Children require only small amounts of butter, margarine, oils, cream and other fats.

Adapted version of the Healthy Eating Pyramid reproduced with the permission of the Australian Nutrition Foundation Inc.

A Healthy Day's Meals

When planning and shopping for family meals and menus put your knowledge of good nutrition into practice. Here is just one menu suggestion which shows you how to apply the Five Food Groups plan and the Healthy Eating Pyramid to plan meals for your children.

Remember, you can combine a variety of fresh, frozen, packaged, canned and take-away foods to make up a diet which is both nutritious and delicious.

Breakfast
- ½ to 1 cup of cereal (avoid sugar and honey-coated varieties), include 1 tablespoon of wheatgerm or bran with refined cereals
- 1 cup of milk (try low fat or non-fat)
- Toast (1 slice) with butter or polyunsaturated margarine, and topping e.g. peanut butter, cheese, baked beans, tomato
- ½ cup of 100% juice

Mid-morning snack
- 1 piece of fruit or milk drink, yoghurt, cheese sticks, custard, wheat crackers

Lunch
- Sandwich (2 slices of bread or a roll)
- Filling (e.g. cheese, meat) with salad

or

- Cheese sticks, wholewheat cracker biscuits
- 5 cherry tomatoes
- 1 piece of fruit or ½ cup 100% juice

Afternoon snack
- Fruit, crunchy vegetables, sandwich, pikelet or 1 slice of cake (try some wholemeal varieties)
- 1 cup milk drink or ½ cup 100% juice

Evening meal
- Lean meat, chicken, fish (including suitable take-aways, frozen foods or ethnic dishes)
- Potato, rice or pasta

- 2 cooked vegetables or salad
- Bread (optional)
- 1 cup milk or ½ cup 100% juice

or

- Vegetarian dish, such as pasta sauce with tomato and vegetables
- Bread (optional)
- 1 cup milk or ½ cup 100% juice

Dessert
- Fruit (fresh, stewed or canned)
- Milk dessert, e.g. yoghurt, ice cream, custard

Your child's food diary

Many parents complain that their child hardly eats at all when they are actually growing perfectly well and thriving, and many parents are confident their child is eating well when in fact they are missing out on some essential nutrients. Keeping track of your child's daily intake using a simple food diary like the one on pages 56 and 57 will help you observe their eating patterns and check their nutrient intake and number of food servings consumed each day.

Monitor your child's food intake for two or more consecutive days, then refer to the table of food servings on page 50 to see if your child is getting enough of each food group. Then, if you're feeling motivated enough, check your child's protein, iron, calcium and fibre intakes using the specific nutrient tables on pages 45, 46, 47 and 49. Don't worry if your child doesn't meet the nutritional requirements perfectly as it tends to even out over several days. What is most important is whether or not your child is within the recommended ranges for the Five Food Groups. If the variety of the food groups is met, then your child should be receiving all of the required nutrients in the appropriate amounts.

Nutrition problems in children
Constipation
'Normal' bowel patterns can cover a wide range of frequency in children as well as adults. Some children who have 'lazy bowels'

Children's Food Diary

Child's Name: Maddison   Age: 3   Day: Monday   Date: _____

TIME	PLACE	WHAT HE/SHE ATE OR DRANK	HOW MUCH HE/SHE ATE OR DRANK	WHAT HE/SHE WAS DOING	HOW HE/SHE WAS FEELING	HOW YOU WERE FEELING
Example: 7.30am	Home at kitchen table	Toast	1 slice	Sitting at table	Tired etc	Rushed to get to school on time
10.30 am	Shopping mall	Chocolate Milk	200 ml	Sitting on bench at the mall	Happy. Distracted by all of the activity at the mall	Glad to sit down for a break!
1.15 pm	In car on the way home from mall	Banana	1 medium	Sitting in car seat	Drowsy – just woke up	O.K. Nearly home!
1.30 pm	Home, kitchen table	Bread, mixed grain Peanut butter Milk	1 slice 2 tablespoons 1 cup	Sitting at kitchen table	Happy	Relaxed – sitting with Maddison eating same lunch

Children's Food Diary

Child's Name: _____   Age: _____   Day: _____
Date: _____

Time	Place	What he/she ate or drank	How much he/she ate or drank	What he/she was doing	How he/she was feeling	How you were feeling

can go for two or three days without a bowel movement, while their brother or sister may have two or three bowel movements per day. Don't worry if your child seems to have too few or too many bowel movements within sensible limits; every child is different. More regular bowel movements can be produced by giving children food such as wholemeal bread, wholegrain cereals, bran, brown rice, wholegrain spaghetti and noodles, which are high in dietary fibre. Wholegrain crisp breads, cakes and biscuits, nuts, fruits, vegetables and juices are also good sources of fibre as are dried beans and lentils such as soya beans, red kidney beans and baked beans. Children must also be given plenty of water or fluids with fibrous foods, as the fibre acts by absorbing water and stimulates bowel movements. Constipation in babies and toddlers is most often related to dehydration, especially when the child is too young to ask for a drink. Keep in mind that constipation isn't necessarily defined by 'how often' a child goes, but more by what the bowel movement consists of, e.g. a child is constipated if their stools are hard, dense and pellet-like that they need to strain, or have difficulty, getting out.

Bowel movements can also be regulated by encouraging children to settle into a routine in the morning. The simple act of eating breakfast can often improve bowel movements – constipated children are often those who don't eat breakfast. The presence of food or liquid in the stomach in the morning can 'signal' a bowel movement, so it's good to eat breakfast at around the same time each morning and allow at least fifteen minutes to an hour afterwards to wait for your child to go to the toilet. Rushing children from the table to the car or school bus can interfere with bowel movements and actually worsen constipation. Bowel movements should not be forced as this causes haemorrhoids or piles. So teach your children not to 'push' with difficult bowel movements. Ideally, a child shouldn't take any longer than two or three minutes; sitting on the toilet for a long time (such as reading) shouldn't be encouraged as this puts strain on the muscles surrounding the bowel, rectum and anus and can contribute to haemorrhoids.

Children also need physical exercise to keep them fit, slim and healthy. A lack of exercise can lead to constipation, so parents should encourage daily exercise such as walking to school.

You can probably remember your grandmother telling you about certain foods that cause constipation. In particular she probably warned you about cheese and milk as being 'binding foods' which prevent bowel movements – this is an old wives' tale and completely untrue. The only reason these foods could be at all 'constipating' is because they contain no dietary fibre and therefore do not stimulate bowel movements. But children will not become constipated simply by eating milk, cheese or any other food and they should not be restricted from a child's diet.

So, how much dietary fibre should your child eat each day? The current nutritional recommendations suggest the '5 plus age' estimate for daily grams of dietary fibre in children older than two years (see page 49). It is likely that this recommendation will be revised soon to a '10 plus age' recommendation, so the current '5 plus age' recommendation is considered as a minimum. Children who meet this dietary fibre recommendation tend to have one or more soft bowel movements each day. Children who have less tend to become constipated or have bowel movements every second or third day. Regular, soft bowel movements prevent haemorrhoids (piles) in childhood and prevent diverticulitis (painful inflammation of the bowel) and bowel cancer later in life. Make sure your child has at least five servings of fruit or vegetables each day (including legumes like baked beans) and 4–5 servings of breads and cereals like wholemeal bread, breakfast cereal, porridge, or wholemeal pasta or rice.

Diet and dental health

A pleasant smile showing strong white teeth is an important part of a child's self image, and healthy teeth and gums are also important for the proper development of speech and the chewing of food.

It's only within recent years that dental caries (tooth decay) has proven to be preventable in both children and adults; it is a

CALEB, TEN YEARS OLD

Caleb is a happy, healthy and very energetic boy, but his mother Ros would like to see him eat better. Of her three children, Caleb is definitely the worst eater. His core foods include Rice Bubbles, whole milk, Milo, toast, honey, sweet biscuits, water, muesli bars, crumpets, grated cheese, meat, potato, peas and carrots. Caleb will only eat Rice Bubbles for breakfast but he will also have them for afternoon tea then again at five o'clock just before dinner and then again for supper. Ros knows that Caleb is very active and has a good appetite but he is prone to constipation and has bowel movements every two days.

After analysing Caleb's daily food intake we found his dietary fibre content to be much less than the minimum of 15 grams recommended for his age. Ros increased his fibre intake by sprinkling one teaspoon of bran on his beloved Rice Bubbles at breakfast, choosing a higher fibre bread, giving him a packet of sultanas instead of sweet biscuits at play lunch, providing wholemeal crumpets and cutting up carrot sticks and melon. He is still allowed to have his Rice Bubbles (which helps him consume milk and provides a low fat and relatively low sugar meal with some iron, protein and zinc) but he is offered chopped fruit first and he devours it all with gusto. Caleb's dietary fibre intake increased and his bowel movements have improved.

misleading belief that some children are born with 'bad teeth' and nothing can be done to make very much difference. As I mentioned earlier in the chapter, teeth are completely formed in the womb and become visible when they start to 'cut' through the gums, usually between four and eight months of age. The mother's diet can affect development of her child's teeth making it important for pregnant women to receive enough calcium, protein, fluoride from drinking water, and other nutrients necessary for tooth formation.

It is clear that the food we eat contributes to the development of tooth decay and this begins at a very young age. Tooth decay occurs when micro-organisms in the mouth convert sugars from food into acids. These acids can dissolve the outer coating of tooth enamel, resulting in a hole. The filling of holes, tooth extractions and expensive dental bills are an unnecessary burden on children and parents, and can be minimised by teaching good oral hygiene and healthy eating habits from a very young age. Start cleaning your child's teeth as soon as they arrive. Choose children's toothpaste as adult toothpaste can be swallowed and result in the child getting too much fluoride.

HARRY, THREE YEARS OLD

Helen and Tony are the parents of delightful little Harry. He is a 'pretty good eater', but is in the habit of going to bed with a bottle of chocolate milk. The two young parents can't seem to get him to sleep without the bottle and they were both unaware of how damaging the milk is to little Harry's teeth, as it supplies a constant coating of sugar during his ten hour overnight sleep. After discussing it with them, we came up with a few strategies. First, Harry was taken to the super-market to choose his own toothbrush and toothpaste, with the repeated promise that he could only have his treat if he brushed his teeth last thing before bed. Harry chose a cute little Tigger toothbrush and was delighted to use it.

Second, Helen and Tony had to find a new way to settle Harry at night – one that didn't involve chocolate milk! They started by bathing him after his dinner, brushing his teeth (for which he received lots of praise) and then giving him 'special storytime with Daddy'.

Finally, Tony put him to bed and gave him gentle rubs on the back until he was nearly asleep. Then Tony said goodnight and left the room. The first week was horrendous with Harry crying for his bottle but the parents stayed firm and calm and soon Harry learned to settle into his new routine.

Rinsing the mouth with water can also reduce the amount of sugars, micro-organisms and acids from teeth. Regular check-ups at the dentist and the use of fluoridated water and fluoridated toothpaste have been proven to reduce tooth decay enormously since the 1950s. Children these days have virtually no tooth decay compared to those of forty years ago and this is mainly due to proper cleaning and the use of fluoridated water and fluoridated toothpaste.

Important foods for the development of healthy teeth are fruits, vegetables, wholegrain breads and cereals, milk, cheese and nuts; these foods have also been shown to be 'anticariogenic' or protective against tooth decay. 'Cariogenic' foods, or those that cause tooth decay, include sweet and sticky foods such as sugar, honey, jams, lollies, 'health' bars, sultanas, biscuits, cakes, sweetened drinks, ice blocks, ice creams and any other sweet or sticky food. Naturally occurring sugars, like those found in fruit, vegetables and milk, can be cariogenic under certain conditions – like the continual sipping of fruit juices or milk. This is a particular problem with young children who are allowed to breastfeed or bottlefeed continuously through the night because their teeth are constantly in contact with lactose, the natural sugar in milk. This gives oral bacteria all night to produce acid from the sugar, which then attacks the teeth.

Fruit, vegetables and milk are excellent foods for children but the mouth should be properly cleansed or rinsed when children clean their teeth after meals and snacks at home, and parents should encourage children to rinse with water at school or when they are out. Send a bottle of water to school with your child – sipping on water will clean their teeth. Sugar-free gum also makes the mouth produce extra saliva, which naturally cleans the teeth but is only recommended for older children, as it can be a choking hazard for children under five. Remember to always set an example by following these healthy habits yourself; clean your teeth together. Once these good habits are established in early childhood, they'll ensure healthy teeth and an attractive smile throughout your child's life.

CHRISTIE, SIX YEARS OLD

Christie is described by her mother, Gloria, as a fussy eater. Her grandmother cooks traditional dinners and Christie is happy to eat most fruit and salad vegetables, especially cucumber, but she picks the cooked vegetables out of her dinner every night.

Christie's father, Roy, loves to spoil her with soft drinks and chocolates after school. Her grandpa also lives with the family and he spoils Christie too! At age four, Gloria took Christie for her first dental check-up and her teeth were fine, but by age five, Christie had cavities in all four of her back teeth. Each filling to Christie's teeth cost $80 and Gloria was very upset. Gloria decided that she had to intervene to prevent Christie getting further tooth decay. She laid down the law at home and stopped Roy and Grandpa giving her lollies, chocolates and soft drinks after school. Gloria made sure that Christie drank only water after school and that she had a fruit snack. Night time brushing became very important and now Gloria will even wake Christie up if she goes to sleep without brushing her teeth. 'I know it's cruel', says Gloria, 'but it's so important, and the dentist is worse!'

Gloria now tells Christie that there will be no more toys (especially Barbie) unless she brushes her teeth properly every morning and night. So far, Gloria's plan has worked and Christie's teeth are in much better shape.

Avoid accidents with food

All infants and children put things in their mouths which can cause choking if it is swallowed or inhaled, and one of the most common causes of choking in small children is food.

Children under five years of age are at particular risk of choking and should never be given nuts, particularly peanuts, unless they are finely chopped. Meat should be cut into small pieces and all small or fine bones and skin removed from fish, meat and chicken. Apples, carrots, celery and cheese can be grated for toddlers. Remove the skins of sausages and frankfurts and the seeds and pips from fruit. Toddlers can also choke on whole peas by 'inhaling' them, so it's a good idea to mash peas for very small children. Always have your child seated when they are eating or drinking and never allow them to 'graze' or eat or drink while running or playing as this contributes to irregular breathing patterns and increases the risk of inhaling food pieces. Remember to always supervise your children when they are eating or drinking. Your child will soon learn that meals, snacks and drinks are eaten quietly at the table or in the high chair and this will become a 'normal' pattern.

If your child is choking, follow these steps:

- If the child is making noises, breathing or crying, they are not choking seriously. Try to settle the child and see if they can clear the food themselves
- If the food is stringy, pull the food out yourself but do not push it further down the child's throat
- If the child is not breathing, bend the child over to allow the food to come out of the child's throat
- Give four sharp blows to the child's upper back between the shoulder blades to dislodge the food
- If the child is still not breathing call an ambulance on 000 (111 in New Zealand). The operator will tell you what to do next
- Do not squeeze the child's stomach or apply the Heimlich manoeuvre as this method is no longer considered safe and it may contribute to further choking.

Dehydration

Your child's body is approximately 60 per cent water and any fluid losses from sweat, breath, urine and faeces needs to be replaced daily. Dehydration can occur very quickly and easily in babies, toddlers and children, and this is usually caused by vomiting, diarrhoea or excessive heat. If your child is irritable, has few wet nappies, has skin that does not spring back quickly when pinched or has dark, yellow urine, they could be dehydrated.

Slight dehydration can be managed by giving your baby breast-feeds or child drinks of water, keeping them relatively cool and waiting until they produce urine which is mostly clear and not yellow. Severe dehydration is a medical emergency and the child must be taken to hospital or a doctor's surgery as soon as possible. Treatment may require insertion of a drip to restore the child's fluid balance or the prescription of an electrolyte solution. Severe dehydration is life-threatening and symptoms are drowsiness, lethargy, sunken eyes, lack of urination and severe weight loss.

Children who have been vomiting or those who have diarrhoea should *never* be given full strength lemonade, cordial, juice or other soft drinks because these can cause sudden 'osmotic' diarrhoea which further dehydrates the child. Appropriate fluids are electrolyte solutions made up *exactly* as per the directions or juice or flat soft drinks (no bubbles) made up to 1 part juice/soft-drink to 4 parts cooled, boiled water. Children should slowly sip the fluid until they feel better and they are producing normal urine. See the table on page 43 for your child's fluid needs.

Constipation is sometimes a sign of slight dehydration in children, which may be caused by the child not drinking enough fluid to produce soft bowel movements.

Remember, if you are breastfeeding then you will need to drink around an extra litre of fluid in order to prevent yourself becoming dehydrated.

Caffeine

Caffeine is a natural stimulant found in many common foods and drinks including tea, coffee, cocoa, soft drinks, energy drinks and chocolate. Some 'natural' remedies and herbal products may also contain caffeine, especially guarana, which has seven times the concentration of caffeine as coffee. Over the counter drugs such as cold and flu tablets and cough mixtures may also contain caffeine. Common side effects include wakefulness, diuresis (production of extra urine), stomach upsets (e.g. diarrhoea), nervousness, headaches, trembling and rapid heart beats. Caffeine can also cause sleeping problems and bedwetting in children and some studies show a rise in blood pressure and blood fats in children who have had more than 140 milligrams of caffeine per day. Other studies have shown that children who consume more than 95 milligrams of caffeine can show signs of increased anxiety (worrying and uneasiness) and may suffer nightmares. Children under the age of twelve years should not consume any caffeine with the exception of some occasional chocolate. Breastfeeding mothers can safely consume around four cups of regular strength coffee per day, but more than that amount can result in high levels of caffeine in their breastmilk.

Have a look at the following chart which shows the caffeine content of some common foods and drinks.

Caffeine content		
FOODS AND DRINKS	**SIZE OF SERVING**	**AVERAGE MILLIGRAMS (MG) OF CAFFEINE**
Coffee – brewed (drip, percolated) e.g. cappuccino, expresso	1 cup	130
– brewed, plunger	1 cup	94
Energy drinks	250 ml can	80
Coffee, instant	1 cup	74
Tea – iced tea	375 ml can	60
– leaf tea or tea bags	1 cup	45
– green tea	1 cup	45
Soft drink – cola	375 ml	45
– diet cola	375 ml	30
Chocolate – bakers chocolate	30 g	25
– dark chocolate	30 g	20
– milk chocolate	30 g	10
Cocoa	1 cup	10
Chocolate sauce syrup	1 tablespoon	4
Coffee, decaf, instant or brewed	1 cup	3
Tea, herbal	1 cup	0–3
Soft drink, caffeine free	375 ml	0

4

True or False?

I am often asked nutrition and food-related questions from parents and grandparents. Here is my advice on some very common ideas and questions about nutrition. Try testing your own knowledge, or, better still, quiz your children!

'Adding bran to the diet is the best way to relieve constipation.'

False: • Adding bran alone may not necessarily relieve constipation and may actually make it worse.
  • Increasing various types of dietary fibre from foods such as fruit, vegetables, wholemeal bread and grains, breakfast cereal, beans, peas, lentils and nuts is the most enjoyable and effective method to prevent constipation.
  • Fluid intake must also be increased, because fibre absorbs water as it passes through the bowel.

'Unpasteurised milk is more nutritious than pasteurised milk.'

False: • Most milk for sale in Australia is pasteurised using the 'High Temperature, Short Time' (HTST) process which involves heating the milk to 72°C for 15 seconds.
  • This process destroys almost all bacteria present and makes the milk safe for human consumption.
  • Pasteurisation causes some damage to the Vitamin C and thiamine content of milk, but milk is not an important source of these two nutrients.

- As pasteurisation destroys dangerous bacteria in milk it extends storage life.
- Unpasteurised milk can contain micro-organisms which cause illness if consumed by humans.

'Brown eggs or free range eggs are more nutritious than white eggs.'

False: There is no nutritional difference between these different types of eggs. Eggs are a good source of protein, vitamins (Vitamin A, thiamine (B1), riboflavin (B2), niacin (B3) and minerals (iron and zinc)). Eggs can be part of a varied and balanced diet.

'Skipping breakfast helps people lose weight.'

False: Research has shown quite the opposite, that people who skip breakfast are more likely to binge later in the day. Skipping breakfast leads to mid-morning fatigue, hunger pangs, lack of concentration and irritability, particularly among people who are used to eating breakfast.

'Combining fruit juice with bread and cereals increases iron absorption.'

True: Foods such as grain products, legumes, bread, wheatgerm and breakfast cereal contain significant amounts of iron. The Vitamin C in fruit juice enhances iron absorption. Other sources of Vitamin C include fruit, juices, vegetables and vegetable juice.

'Two cups of pasta has less fat than one sausage roll.'

True: Cereals and bread are virtually fat free but pastry contains a lot of fat.

'Guava is the fruit that contains the most Vitamin C.'

True: One whole guava (113 g) contains 270 mg Vitamin C.

'A piece of rump steak provides about 1 milligram of iron.'

False: 100 g of rump steak contains about 4 mg of iron.

'Swiss cheese contains less calcium than other cheeses.'
False: Swiss cheese contains more calcium than other cheeses.

'Carrots are a better source of dietary fibre than celery.'
True: A medium sized carrot provides 2.3 grams of dietary fibre.
The same amount of celery provides 1.2 grams.

'Breakfast cereals are low in iron and B group vitamins.'
False: Breakfast cereals are high in iron and the B group vitamins
(thiamin, niacin, riboflavin).

**'One slice of mixed grain bread contains more dietary fibre
than one slice of wholemeal bread.'**
False: 1 slice of mixed grain bread provides 1.4 g dietary fibre.
1 slice of wholemeal bread provides 2.0 g dietary fibre.
1 slice of white bread provides 0.8 g dietary fibre.

**'Sour cream contains about the same number of kilojoules as
other types of cream.'**
True: Sour cream has a different flavour to other types of cream,
but the same fat content.

**'Which is the best source of dietary fibre? Yoghurt, beef,
Vegemite, chicken or eggs?'**
None! Dietary fibre is only found in plant foods such as fruit,
vegetables, breads and cereals.

'Fruit and vegetables may prevent cancer.'
True: Certain antioxidants in fruit and vegetables (beta-carotene,
Vitamin C, Vitamin E) may play a role in preventing cancer.
Dietary fibre in foods helps prevent bowel cancer.

'Frozen vegetables are just as nutritious as fresh vegetables.'
True: Frozen vegetables are usually picked and snap frozen
straight away, so there is little time for vitamin content to
diminish. Frozen vegetables do not have salt or sugar added, and
are a nutritious food.

'Humans do not require added salt in their diets.'
True: Salted food became a necessity for humans when there was no other method of food preservation, but the invention of the refrigerator changed the need for salted food. Humans require a tiny amount of sodium which can easily be obtained from food without adding it.

'Sugar causes hyperactivity in children.'
False: Sugar is one of the factors that contributes to dental decay, but it is not linked to hyperactivity. Some children may react adversely to the chemicals in food (both added and naturally occurring chemicals) but this must be properly tested by a doctor or dietitian.

'In a healthy diet, "junk food" should be completely avoided.'
False: A healthy diet can contain any food or drink – it's the frequency and the amount that counts. There is no such thing as a 'junk food', only 'junk diets'. Balance and moderation are the key elements to a healthy diet.

'Sugar should be eliminated from a healthy diet.'
False: Sweetened foods are acceptable in moderation in a balanced diet. Nutritious foods containing natural or added sugars such as milk, fruit, flavoured yoghurt, ice cream, sweetened breakfast cereal and juices can be included in a healthy diet. Foods primarily containing sugar such as lollies and soft drinks can be eaten occasionally, but not daily.

'Legumes are a good source of dietary fibre.'
True: Legumes are vegetables such as baked beans, split peas, lentils, soya beans, chick peas (garbanzo), kidney beans, broad beans, lima beans, navy beans and borlotti beans. Legumes are a major source of dietary fibre, protein and minerals such as iron.

'Some food components can hinder iron absorption.'
True: Large amounts of some foods like unprocessed bran, tea (more than 6 cups per day) and drugs like antacids can hinder the amount of iron absorbed from foods. Combining different foods such as those containing Vitamin C (e.g. fruit and vegetables) and meat can improve the absorption of iron in the small intestine.

'Sweating increases the need for vitamins and minerals.'
False: Sweat contains some minerals such as sodium, iron and zinc, but these are usually present in very small amounts and are easily replenished by eating food. People who sweat heavily should replace the water lost, not the salt.

'"Low cholesterol" usually means "low fat"'
False: Cholesterol is only found in animal products. Fruits such as olives and avocadoes are 'cholesterol free' yet still contain quite a lot of fat. The use of 'low cholesterol' on food products is often a marketing trend. It is most important to choose foods that are low in fat.

'Exercise makes you hungry.'
False: Studies have shown that exercise actually helps regulate appetite and vigorous exercise suppresses the appetite. People who exercise for long periods of time will need extra energy from food, but their bodies will also be more 'in tune' with their appetite. People who do little physical activity are likely to eat more due to boredom.

'Children can participate in weight training.'
True: Small children (six to twelve years old) should not lift heavy weights, but aerobic activities for older children using small hand weights can be safe if properly supervised. Adolescents can benefit from moderate weight training in supervised situations where injury is minimised. Lifting heavy weights can cause back injury, hernia and muscle tearing.

'Mental activity (e.g. studying for an exam) burns up extra energy.'

False: Only physical activity (moving the body) burns up extra energy. Activities such as thinking, studying, playing chess, being nervous or being stressed require no energy.

'Children can't tolerate exercise in the heat or cold as well as adults.'

True: Children can't maintain normal body temperature as efficiently as adults due to a higher skin surface area to body mass ratio, and a less effective sweating system. Children should not exercise vigorously for more than 30 minutes in hot, humid or cold conditions (e.g. swimming in cold water) and should be well-clothed in cold conditions. Drinking water should be encouraged during and after all activities.

'Steroids have dangerous effects on the body.'

True: The human body manufactures its own steroids e.g. oestrogen, testosterone, cholesterol and growth hormone. Many of these steroids are involved in normal growth and development. However, the artificial use of steroids (usually obtained from animal sources) may cause the bones to stop growing, height stunting, raised blood cholesterol, breast development in males, body and facial hair growth in females, aggression, testicular atrophy (shrinking), liver damage and reduced sex drive.

'Milk causes mucus.'

False: There is no scientific evidence for this old wives' tale. Milk and dairy products may increase the feeling of a mucusy mouth, but there is no actual increase in the amount of mucus or phlegm. Some children may be allergic to milk, but they must be properly tested by a doctor or dietitian before this important food group is eliminated from their diet.

'Combining certain foods at meal times can cause gastrointestinal upsets.'

False: This new age concept of food combining is completely without foundation and makes little sense. Fans of this regime insist that certain foods should not be eaten before a certain time and that combining food groups (e.g. fruit and meat) will cause adverse reactions. The human gastrointestinal tract is perfectly capable of digesting and absorbing any combination of food at any time of day. The resulting nutrients can be readily absorbed by this extremely efficient system.

'Carbohydrates are less fattening than protein, fats and alcohol.'

True: Carbohydrates provide 16 kilojoules per gram when metabolised within the body's cells. Protein provides 17 kilojoules per gram, alcohol provides 29 kilojoules per gram and fats provide 37 kilojoules per gram. High fat foods are the most 'fattening' as they provide the most energy.

'Cod liver oil should be given to children to prevent rickets.'

False: Rickets is a bone disease of children caused by a Vitamin D deficiency. Rickets was a common problem during the Industrial Revolution, when children's diets were poor and when they received little sunlight. Vitamin D is manufactured by the body when 7-dehydrocholesterol present in the skin reacts with the UV light. A few minutes of sunlight each day ensures that people make enough Vitamin D. This vitamin is also present in milk, butter and margarine.

'Weight control diets can safely cut out milk and meat.'

False: Weight control diets must include all the food groups to ensure that all the nutrients (and thus a healthy diet) are being consumed.

'The best way to maintain a healthy weight is to eat foods low in fat.'

True: Foods such as bread, rice, pasta, breakfast cereal, oats, fruits and vegetables contain almost no fat. Avocadoes and olives are the exception (avocadoes are 20% fat and olives are 10%).

'Breads and cereals are fattening.'

False: Breads and cereals such as rice, oats, barley, pasta and breakfast cereal are very low in fat. Eating these foods with added fat e.g. butter, margarine, mayonnaise, or peanut butter is what makes them more 'fattening'.

'Physical activity can help control weight.'

True: Moving the body burns up energy. Excess energy eaten as food or drink will be stored as fat by the body if not used up. The body will use these fat stores as a source of energy when food intake is restricted.

'Playing computer games uses up a lot of energy.'

False: Moving the body burns up energy – but the most energy is used when the whole body moves, not just one finger!

'Certain foods can help burn fat e.g. grapefruit, Chinese tea.'

False: Nothing helps burn fat except physical activity and eating less.

'Teenagers can safely diet to lose weight.'

False: Teenage boys and girls (especially those aged 11–16 years) should be gradually gaining weight and height because they are growing. Gaining height means you also have to gain weight – this is normal. Dieting is dangerous for teenagers because it can stop growth, stunt height, prevent girls having their periods, upset hormones, thin the bones (osteoporosis) and cause nutrient deficiencies. Teenagers can eat healthy low fat foods and ensure daily physical activity to maintain a healthy weight.

'Girls generally begin the growth spurt before boys the same age.'
True: Girls begin the growth spurt on average two years before boys.

'Skinny girls get their periods earlier than large girls.'
False: Girls must reach a certain weight and body fat percentage before they get their first period. Very underweight girls and women lose their periods until normal weight is regained.

'All boys' voices have a sudden break, then they become deep.'
False: The voice 'breaks' in response to the larynx (voice box) and vocal chords growing larger and therefore being able to make different sounds. This happens over 12–18 months in the middle of the boys' growth spurt.

'Physical maturity happens at the same rate as emotional maturity.'
False: Some children grow and develop before their peers, but their emotional maturity takes longer. A twelve-year-old may be more developed than his or her peers, but is still at the same social and emotional developmental stage as other twelve-year-olds.

'Different parts of the body develop at different rates.'
True: The hands and feet grow first, then the limbs, then the trunk and torso.

'You have reached your maximum height at age sixteen for girls and eighteen years for boys.'
True: Maximum height in most people is generally achieved by these ages. Late maturers will continue growing past these ages.

'Saturated fats cause blood cholesterol to rise.'
True: Foods containing saturated fats can cause blood cholesterol levels to rise if eaten often and in large amounts. Cholesterol can build up in arteries, blocking the blood supply. Polyunsaturated

and monounsaturated fats help lower blood cholesterol. Eating less of all types of fat is recommended for health, particularly saturated fats.

'Fish oils can thin the blood.'

True: The type of fatty acids found in fish (Omega 3 fatty acids) have been found to reduce thrombosis (blood clotting) and lower blood cholesterol. Aspirin also acts as an anti-thrombogenic agent.

'Vegetarian foods are low in fat.'

False: Some vegetarian foods can be high in fat, for example deep fried foods, vegetarian pasties, foods containing large amounts of cream, sour cream, cheese, or coconut cream. Fat-reduced and low fat varieties of these foods can usually be obtained.

'Vitamin B12 is manufactured in the gastrointestinal tract.'

True: Vitamin B12 is produced by micro-organisms in the gastrointestinal tracts of animals and humans, as well as in microorganisms in dirt or manure on unwashed plant foods. Bacteria produce Vitamin B12 in the human gut, but it appears to be produced beyond the ileum, which is the site for absorption in the intestine. Hence, any Vitamin B12 produced in the human gut is not absorbed.

'Protein foods need to be very carefully matched and combined to provide a "complete" protein.'

False: Plant sources of protein alone can provide adequate amounts of the essential and non-essential amino acids required by the body for growth. The dietary sources of amino acids must be varied to ensure adequate amounts of the amino acids and must be part of a diet which is adequate in energy, otherwise the protein will be used as a source of energy.

'Mushrooms are a good source of Vitamin B12.'

False: Washed mushrooms contain no active Vitamin B12, but the bacteria in soil or manure on unwashed mushrooms may produce some Vitamin B12.

'All soy drinks are fortified with calcium.'
False: Not all soy drinks contain added calcium. Check the label on soy drinks. A well-fortified soy drink should contain approximately 120 milligrams of calcium per 100 millilitres of drink.

'Honey is a good source of vitamin and minerals such as calcium.'
False: The main components of honey are sugar and water. One tablespoon of honey contains one milligram of calcium and less than a milligram of vitamins and other minerals. Considering that the Recommended Dietary Intake for calcium is approximately 1000 mg for adolescents, honey is a very poor source of calcium. Honey is a source of potassium – a mineral which is easily obtained in the diet because it is distributed in many different foods.

'Bone meal, oyster shells and dolomite are good calcium supplements.'
False: The purity and safety of these products varies greatly and these products are not recommended for adults or children. Bone acts as a sink for heavy metals (e.g. in the bones of old horses) and some preparations of dolomite and bonemeal have been found to contain dangerous levels of lead, arsenic, cadmium and mercury.

'A diet low in calcium can be remedied by taking a calcium supplement.'
False: A diet low in calcium is likely to be a poor diet for many other nutrients. Diets which exclude one or more of the Five Food Groups (fruits, vegetables, milk and dairy products, meat and meat substitutes (e.g. eggs, nuts), and breads, cereals and grains) are likely to be deficient in several macro- and micro-nutrients. Calcium supplements are expensive and they may

interfere with the absorption of magnesium and iron. Calcium is best obtained from food because other food factors such as Vitamin D, lactose and stomach acid increase its absorption, and also contain other nutrients as well as calcium.

'Children should never eat take-away foods.'

False: Take-away foods have become part of our lives and it is estimated that Australians already spend approximately one-third of their food budget on meals prepared outside the home. The majority of these meals are take-away meals. These foods can be served to children as part of a nutritionally balanced diet but parents need to make certain that the food chosen is suitable.

'I should give my child a vitamin supplement "just in case" he is not getting enough.'

False: If your child is eating a variety of foods from the Five Food Groups they will be obtaining enough vitamins and minerals. Children need only tiny amounts of vitamins; for example, a child will receive the daily allowance of Vitamin C by simply eating half an orange, or six strawberries, or a few slices of capsicum, or ½ cup of cooked cabbage, or broccoli, or brussel sprouts or cauli-flower. Recently it has been discovered that vitamins and minerals may be toxic in large amounts and this is of particular concern for children because they may be affected at much lower doses than adults. The vitamins which are most toxic in large amounts are Vitamin A, Vitamin D and Vitamin K, although other vitamins such as Vitamin B6 have also shown to be toxic.

Some children may need a vitamin and mineral supplement if their diet is severely restricted (such as those with multiple food sensitivity) or following long illnesses, and these children can be given a low dose multivitamin supplement. Vitamin and mineral supplements designed for adult use are unsuitable for children as the dosage is too high.

5

Special Children, Special Diets

Growth in children

Children do not always grow as quickly or as big as their parents would like. Children are individuals, and their height and weight depend not only on nutrition but also on family trends, cultural background and race and their weight at birth. The child of two very tall parents will also tend to be tall, and likewise a seemingly small child may come from a family of smaller relatives.

The charts of Body Mass Index on page 83 give an overview of average weight for height in boys and girls and this will give you some idea of your child's desirable weight in relation to height and age. These figures are designed for use as a broad guideline and should not be used to compare one child with another, because every child will be different, even within the same family. The chart may be used to detect early health problems such as being over-weight and a failure to thrive, which can be treated much more easily if they are detected in the early stages. Children who show problems such as their weight being out of proportion with their height or low weight or height for age may need this problem discussed with a doctor or paediatrician. Any sudden weight loss or weight gain should also be referred to a doctor or dietitian as there may be some other cause unrelated to nutrition.

The overweight child

If your child is overweight in relation to height and age, it is most likely to be caused by underactivity rather than overeating.

Most doctors and dietitians agree that kilojoule restriction diets for overweight children are undesirable because they can compromise growth. Most overweight children and teenagers become more slender as they grow in height and parents can help by encouraging healthy food choices, fewer sugary and fatty foods, more daily exercise and emotional support and encouragement. Parents and teachers can help to bolster the child's self confidence by fostering regular daily exercise, in which the child's size is not much of a disadvantage, for example, walking the dog, walking to school, walking to do the shopping or playing in the backyard. By joining in play and exercise with children, parents will be setting a good example as well as making it more fun.

What influences my child's weight?

Many factors influence your child's weight as they are growing up. Body weight is not just affected by what we eat. Here are the other main things that affect weight:

Height

Tall children tend to be heavier than shorter children. As your child grows in height they will also increase their weight. Girls in particular need to understand that as their height increases, then so too will their weight.

Eating habits

There is no doubt that a child's eating habits influence their height and their weight. Children who do not consume enough protein and calcium (largely from milk, cheese, yoghurt and other dairy foods) will not reach their full height potential and their bones will not be as strong as they could be. Research shows that children who don't reach their full height potential may become overweight more easily. Similarly, children who constantly graze on foods and drinks will consume too many kilojoules and this will be stored by the body as fat.

Physical activity

Being physically active is natural for most children. Children are naturally active, fidgety and full of energy and they love to move and play. The problem with physical activity these days is that children become distracted by other activities such as television, computer games, homework and mobile phones and lose the opportunity to play and be active. These children are at risk of becoming overweight and unfit.

Metabolic rate

Everyone burns up energy at a different rate and this is known as the metabolic rate. Children inherit their metabolic rate from their parents, so some children will have a fast metabolic rate and will burn their food up as energy very quickly whilst others will have a slower rate. Everybody's metabolic rate can be increased by physical activity and muscle mass, so encouraging your child to play and be active will help to increase their metabolism and reduce the risk of being or becoming overweight.

Stage of growth

Children at different growth stages put on varying amounts of weight. The weight of your baby will double in the first five months of life and it will triple by the child's first birthday. This rapid weight gain is matched with a rapid increase in length.

In toddlers and school-aged children weight gain tends to be slow and steady and then rapid again during puberty and adolescence. Girls will lay down a storage layer of body fat at about age nine or ten years and this energy store will be used to fuel the rapid growth and height spurt that most girls experience between eleven and fourteen years of age. The 'puppy fat' stage is normal and should not be confused with being overweight. Boys experience the same stage of pre-pubertal puppy fat storage at a later age, around twelve to fourteen years. During their teenage growth spurt girls put on about 4–5 kilograms a year between the ages of eleven and fourteen years and grow about 6–10 centimetres per year. Boys can gain up to 12 centimetres and

5–8 kilograms per year between the ages of thirteen to sixteen years. Remember, every child begins puberty at a different age, so every child's weight and height spurt will be different.

Family patterns

Children's body shape, size, weight and height are largely determined by genetics. Some children take after their mother or father and some take after their grandparents. For example, height is largely determined by the height of parents. You can estimate your child's adult height by following these guidelines:

- Measure the mother's height and the father's height in centimetres (for example, Mum is 155 cm and Dad is 173 cm)
- Average the two heights (155 + 173 = 328/2 = 164 cm)
- Add 6.5 cm to the average for boys (e.g. 164 + 6.5 = 170.5 cm)
- Take away 6.5 cm from the average for girls (e.g. 164 – 6.5 = 157.5 cm)

This method does not always work accurately for every child, but it is a reliable estimate.

Is my child overweight or underweight?

If your child is growing and is healthy and happy then their weight for height is probably right. You can check your child's height and weight by calculating your child's body mass index (BMI):

- Measure your child's weight without shoes or heavy clothing in kilograms
- Measure your child's height without shoes in metres (e.g. 1.10 m)
- Calculate your child's BMI which equals their weight divided by their height (in metres) squared: $\frac{weight}{height \times height}$
- Your child's BMI will be a number anywhere between 13 and 34
- Plot your child's BMI on either the girl or the boy chart opposite by finding their age along the bottom line and their BMI up the side
- See whether your child's BMI falls within the Underweight Range or Overweight Range

• See your child health nurse, doctor or dietitian if you are concerned about your child's growth or health.

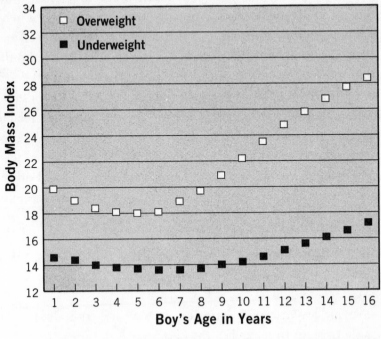

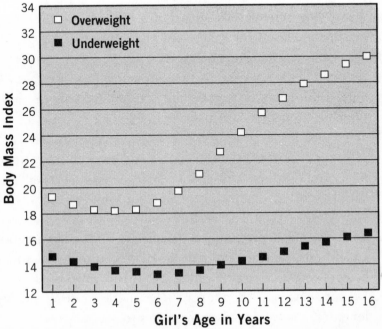

Is your child an emotional eater?

Some children (and many adults!) eat for comfort. Children learn from a very young age that food, comfort and love often come hand in hand, and this is especially true among babies who quickly learn how pleasant it is to receive a warm milk feed and a cuddle from Mum! Unfortunately, some children grow into the habit of seeking comfort and emotional satisfaction from food. Do you think your child is eating for comfort? Does your child eat because they are bored, lonely, sad, depressed or feeling neglected and unloved? If you think this is happening, take care to talk to your child about their feelings of sadness, anger, fear, happiness, loneliness or boredom and make sure you and others provide your child with enough attention, fun and interaction in their daily lives.

Top 10 tips for fostering a healthy weight for your child

1. Provide healthy food options every day for your child to be able to learn to make healthy choices.
2. Allow your child to self-regulate how much they eat. Encourage them to know for themselves when to stop eating.
3. Don't expect your child to always eat everything on their plate. As one old saying goes, 'Wastage is better than waistage'. If your child doesn't eat everything you have served, you have probably given them too much food.
4. Serve three meals and two or three snacks per day. This will satisfy the appetite of most children and prevent overeating.
5. Be a good role model for your child. You need to eat well and eat appropriate amounts because your child will inevitably copy your eating and drinking habits.
6. Eat as a family – preferably at the table so that children do not get distracted. This way they learn that eating is a social activity and learn to stop eating when they leave the table.
7. Do not allow your child to 'graze' on snacks or drinks all day long. It's unnecessary and contributes to overweight.

8. Don't allow children to store food or drinks other that water in their school bags, desks, lockers, bedrooms or in the car. Children don't need to be constantly eating and drinking all day long, and shouldn't feel as though they'll miss out on food and drinks.

9. Encourage your child to eat breakfast as this helps to regulate their food intake over the whole day and prevents snack attacks and food binges.

10. Encourage as much daily play time and physical activity as possible for your child. Turn the TV off or keep a daily 1–2 hour limit on TV or computer games. Children need to play not only for their physical health but also for their social and mental health – they need to develop into sociable, healthy and interesting individuals, not boring couch potatoes or obsessive computer addicts, so encourage your child to play and interact with other children as much as possible every day.

Building your child's self-esteem

Children who have low self-esteem may become overweight because they tend to isolate themselves from other children and may eat because of boredom, loneliness and as a way to help themselves feel better. Overweight children may also have low self-esteem because they feel less worthy than other children, or because they get teased about their weight. Self-esteem is so important for all children and parents can do a lot to foster good self-esteem or a sense of self worth and self respect in their children. Here are a few tips for fostering self-esteem in your child.

Provide unconditional love

Love and accept your child the way they are. Every child is different and your child will not necessarily be like you. Accept that your child is a separate individual.

Identify your child's uniqueness

Help your child to explore the different facets of their self-image by identifying the many varied things that make them unique.

Start on different physical features like eye colour, hair, skin and other unique features, then explore other features such as likes and dislikes, hobbies, special talents and abilities. Delve into their personal features, like their generosity, friendliness, honesty, compassion, sense of humour, positive outlook, patience and determination.

Reinforce the idea that everybody is different
Teach your children to accept the fact that every person on the planet is different and unique, and help them to respect others and be tolerant of other people's differences.

Help your child experience success
Children need opportunities to succeed at something in life. Give your child easy tasks to complete, such as clearing the plates from the dinner table, so that they can feel competent and helpful. Remember to thank your child and praise them for their help.

Praise your child's positive features and behaviours
Make certain that you notice your child's positive features and praise them for it. When your child is helpful, considerate, thoughtful, generous, determined, kind, funny or respectful, let them know that you have noticed that special aspect of themselves.

SOPHIE

Sophie was always a big child. She was a big baby and her height and weight were always on the top line of her growth charts when mother Gai took her to the baby health clinic. Despite the nurse reassuring Gai and Sophie's father Steve that their daughter was perfectly healthy and that she was just bigger than other girls of her age, the young parents continued to fret about Sophie being too big and feared she would become overweight. Gai received the same advice from a paediatrician, who checked Sophie's blood pressure, hormones and bone growth and reported that Sophie was normal, healthy, happy and that she would always be bigger than other girls the same age. Gai was advised by the hospital dietitian about what to do to avoid Sophie becoming overweight, as she obviously took after her grandfather who was a very big, solid man with a tendency to put on weight easily. (Sophie's younger brother Chris was slim like his mother.) With all these things in mind, Gai and Steve were able to promote Sophie's growth, physical health and self-esteem by:

- providing healthy meals, snacks and water as the preferred drink. This meant having to placate young Chris's whining for junkfoods and soft drinks but Gai and Steve explained firmly to the whole family that these were 'sometimes foods' and that for the most part, the family was going to focus on healthy foods and drinks.
- providing a constant 'taxi' for Sophie's physical activities which included swimming, physical culture and soccer. Gai encouraged Sophie to continue with these activities and made sure that Sophie spent after school time and weekends doing some sort of physical activity. Sophie always remained healthy and very physically fit despite being heavy.
- explaining to Sophie that she was bigger than other girls and that this was not going to change; that her body build was large and solid and that was just the way she was made.
- encouraging the whole family, including grandparents, aunts, uncles, cousins and family friends (all of whom are slim!) to help Sophie accept herself the way she was so that she would avoid developing body image problems or low self-esteem as a result of being self-conscious about her weight.

Sophie grew and developed over the years from being a tall and solid little toddler to a tubby primary school student to a tall, solid teenager who was certainly much bigger than her teenage girlfriends. Sophie grew up healthy and happy with much love and support from her family and she has the sweetest and most helpful and generous nature. She is now a bigger than average, size 16 university student with a strong sense of self-worth and a balanced life, which can largely be put down to the love and acceptance that was provided by her parents, family and friends. Sophie is lucky to have escaped the dieting merry-go-round that most big children and teenagers get trapped in, to try to change their naturally determined body shape and size. Thank goodness Sophie's parents had the good sense to realise that their daughter's physical fitness, physical health and her mental and emotional state were more important than simply focussing on her weight.

Vegetarian eating

Vegetarian eating is not new or unusual, in fact, many of the world's most ancient cultures have survived and flourished on a traditionally vegetarian diet. Vegetarian eating has become more popular in Australia since the 1950s, with many people regularly choosing vegetarian or semi-vegetarian meals. The reasons for choosing a vegetarian diet are many and varied, for example religious (Hindus, Buddhists, Seventh Day Adventists), cultural (Asian or Mexican), environmental (land use, animal rights), ethical (world hunger issues, animal welfare, killing of animals), economic (vegetarian foods are inexpensive), and health. Studies of vegetarian populations, such as the well-known Seventh Day Adventist studies, have reported lower rates of coronary heart disease, blood cholesterol, lower blood pressure, less obesity and fewer cases of cancer, particularly colon cancer, and type 2 diabetes.

Health benefits

Studies show that vegetarian eating provides a low fat, low cholesterol diet because of its high fruit, vegetable, dietary fibre and antioxidant content. In addition, recent research shows that the phytoestrogens found in soy products such as soya drinks and tofu may have special benefits for women like reducing hot flushes.

Many vegetarians are also likely to be health conscious people who do not smoke, drink alcohol, consume excessive caffeine and who generally have a healthy lifestyle, and these combined factors may contribute to the better overall health of vegetarians.

Types of vegetarian diets

There are many, varied styles of vegetarian eating, and the most common type is a 'lacto-ovo' diet, which usually contains mixed and balanced amounts of breads, cereals, rice, pasta, legumes (beans, baked beans, dried peas, seeds, lentils), nuts, vegetables, fruit, peanut butter, milk, cheese, margarine, sugar, and oils. Following is an outline of some other styles of vegetarianism, as well as a sample of a nutritious lacto-ovo vegetarian diet, illustrated as a Healthy Eating Pyramid.

Growth of vegetarian children and adolescents

A varied vegetarian diet providing good amounts of energy, protein, vitamins and minerals will meet all of the requirements of a growing child.

Growth in vegan or strict vegetarian children can be compromised however – several cases of severe protein-energy malnutrition and deficiencies of iron and Vitamins B12 and D have been reported in infants and children who were fed inappropriate, strict vegetarian diets – but several studies have shown that growth in Seventh-Day Adventist children (lacto-ovo-vegetarians) has been shown to be similar to omnivorous children with good, varied diets. Catch-up growth by age ten has been found to be possible in vegan children but overall vegetarian children still tend to be lighter than those on a mixed diet. Older vegan children and adolescents can get the same amounts of energy and protein as those on an omnivorous mixed diet, provided there is enough energy to prevent protein being used as an energy source, and that

TYPE OF VEGETARIAN DIET	NUTRITIONAL RISK TO CHILDREN
Lacto-ovo vegetarians The most common type of vegetarian diet. These people avoid flesh foods, but include eggs, milk, dairy foods, fruit, vegetables, breads and cereals.	Very low nutritional risk. Need attention to good sources of absorbable dietary iron.
Lacto vegetarians Do not eat flesh foods or eggs, but include milk, yoghurt, other dairy foods and most other foods. find	Low nutritional risk. For children it is important to monitor total kilojoules, and good sources of protein and absorbable dietary iron.
Semi vegetarians Don't eat red meat but may occasionally include fish or other 'white' meats. Include most other foods.	Low nutritional risk. Nutritionally adequate if the child's diet is mixed with good sources of protein (milk, cheese, yoghurt, eggs, fish, chicken, nuts, peanut butter).
'New-Age' vegetarians May eat a traditional diet and simply remove the meat from meals e.g., eat a plateful of vegetables or rice.	May have high nutritional risk. Nutritional adequacy depends on quality of protein. Diet will be adequate if it includes milk, dairy foods, eggs, vegetables, fruit, bread and cereals. This type of 'vegetarian' diet is often associated with eating disorders in adolescents.
Vegans Don't eat any animal products and may avoid food which contains animal products such as butter, milk and honey. Also avoid cosmetics which contain animal products, and avoid wearing animal fibres such as leather and wool.	High nutritional risk, particularly in babies, children, adolescents, pregnant and lactating women. Likely to be low in kilojoules, iron, calcium, zinc, Vitamin B12, and protein.
Fruitarians Don't eat anything other than raw fruit, berries and some nuts.	Very high nutritional risk. Unlike some primates, humans

Fruitarians believe this is a 'natural' diet, from which humans evolved.	can't survive on this diet! Extremely low in calories, protein, fat, iron, zinc, calcium, Vitamin B12.
Zen Macrobiotic vegetarians Very restricted dietary regime based on the teachings of George Ohsawa. Large amounts of brown rice, small amounts of fruit, vegetables, legumes.	Very high nutritional risk. Inadequate calories, protein, zinc, iron, calcium and Vitamin B12. Several deaths have been recorded from this extreme diet.

Healthy Eating Pyramid
for Lacto-ovo Vegetarians

Eat in small amounts
Oil, Margarine, Reduced-fat
spreads, Butter, Sugar

Eat moderately
Milk, Yoghurt, Eggs,
Tofu, Cheese

Eat most
Vegetables,
Dried peas,
Beans and
Lentils,
Cereals,
Unsalted
nuts,
Seeds,
Fruit,
Bread

© Copyright The Australian Nutrition Foundation Inc. 2000

Nutrition **Australia**
www.nutritionaustralia.org

Optimal health through food variety and physical activity

Adapted version of the Healthy Eating Pyramid reproduced with the permission of the Australian Nutrition Foundation Inc.

the protein sources are of good quality. Reports have also shown that the onset of menstruation, or menarche, is later among leaner Seventh-Day Adventist vegetarian girls. This has also been found in some studies of vegetarian British and Chinese girls.

Nutritional risk in adolescent vegetarians

As I've mentioned, a vegetarian diet containing a variety of different foods will usually provide children and adolescents with enough energy, protein, vitamins and minerals, to promote normal growth and development. Problems tend to arise when the diet becomes too limited in the amount of food and kilojoules, the variety of different food groups or when the diet is restricted to only a few different foods. Children and adolescents have high energy and nutrient needs to meet the demands of their growth spurt as well as physical activity. In fact, the nutrient needs of adolescents are usually far greater than those of fully grown adults, a point which is largely missed by parents who may be concerned about the large appetites and volumes of food eaten by their teenagers.

Energy and protein

The high energy needs of children means that they need to eat large amounts of food, and the type of food needs to be of high nutrient density to provide enough calories, protein and other important nutrients. Diets high in fibre, like the vegan diet, are unsuitable for children because they tend to 'fill up' before they have consumed enough energy, protein and other nutrients. This is one reason why vegetarian diets are advantageous for overweight adults, because the food is filling and quickly satisfying. Unfortunately, though, eating a diet of predominantly bread, cereals, rice, pasta, fruit and vegetables provides poor sources of protein and is unlikely to meet the energy, protein and nutrient needs of children. Also, a vegetarian diet contains a higher percentage of dietary fibre and the phytic acid in dietary fibre has the potential to interfere with micronutrient absorption, by binding minerals such as iron and zinc.

Good sources of protein include milk, eggs, cheese, yoghurt, soy drink, tofu, peanut butter, nuts, dried peas, beans, baked beans and lentils. Children can have low-fat milk and dairy foods, but only after five years of age because younger children need the extra energy and fat soluble vitamins provided by whole milk and dairy foods.

Fats

Humans can manufacture all but two of the essential fatty acids – linoleic acid (Omega-6 fatty acid) and linolenic acid (Omega-3 fatty acid). These fatty acids are known as essential fatty acids because they *must* be supplied in the diet and are needed to build cell membranes, and to maintain normal growth and development. A varied and nutritious vegetarian diet containing grains, seeds, nuts, leafy green vegetables, beans and lentils (especially soya beans), vegetable oils and margarine will provide enough of the essential fatty acids to maintain health and growth.

Iron

The non-haem iron in plant foods is not as well absorbed as the haem iron from animal meats. Vegetarian children need large amounts of iron (see table of nutrient needs, page 47) to ensure growth, and adolescent girls need iron to offset the losses from menstruation. The Vitamin C in vegetables, juices and fruit improves the absorption of non-haem iron so eating a variety of foods at the same meal will enhance the absorption of dietary iron in vegetarian diets. Foods such as breakfast cereals, baked beans, dried peas and beans, legumes, nuts, seeds, leafy green vegetables, dried fruits and peanut butter and tahini (sesame seed paste) are good vegetarian sources of iron.

Calcium

Calcium is often deficient in the diets of strict vegetarians such as vegans and fruitarians and 'New Age' vegetarians. Calcium can be well supplied by milk, hard cheeses (not soft cheeses like cottage or ricotta), yoghurt, ice cream, calcium fortified soy drinks, almonds, tahini, bok choy and broccoli.

Zinc

Zinc is important for the functioning of many enzymes and for growth and development. The clinical signs of zinc deficiency include poor wound healing and an impaired immune response.

Zinc is supplied by milk, dairy foods and other foods previously mentioned as good sources of protein (see page 45).

Vitamin B12 (cyanocobalamin)

Vitamin B12 deficiency has been found among strict vegetarians, vegans and their children and the young breastfed babies of vegans. Even though the recommended dietary intake for Vitamin B12 is minute and deficiency takes years to develop, Vitamin B12 deficiency may still result from diets which do not contain any animal products. Vitamin B12 deficiency is characterised by large cell anaemia (megaloblastic anaemia) and a smooth, sore tongue. These symptoms are accompanied by fatigue, skin hypersensitivity and nerve disorders such as tremors. Vegetarians who eat milk, dairy foods or eggs will receive enough Vitamin B12, but vegans and other strict vegetarians should pay close attention to this vitamin. Vegans should take Vitamin B12 supplements and should not rely on spirulina, seaweed, tempeh (fermented soya beans) or other fermented foods as a source of B12 because these sources all have variable B12 content, and a staggering 80–94 per cent of the Vitamin B12 content of these foods is inactive.

Vitamin D

Children who follow a vegan diet may only be getting small amounts of dietary Vitamin D, but they will be able to produce Vitamin D from the cholesterol on their skin if they are exposed to enough sunlight. Five to ten minutes of sunlight on the cheeks will supply enough Vitamin D. Vegans who spend a lot of time indoors or are bedridden will need Vitamin D supplementation.

Food allergy

A small number of children will have some sort of allergy to certain proteins in food in the first few months of life. This

Example of a healthy eating plan for lacto-ovo vegetarian children

Food	Kilojoules	Protein (g)	Iron (mg)	Calcium (mg)
Breakfast				
Breakfast cereal (30 g)	398	3.4	2.6	10.0
Milk (½ cup) (low fat)	585	10.8	0.1	375
Toast (wholemeal, 1 slice)	282	3.0	0.7	16.0
Butter/margarine (1 teaspoon)	269	0	0	0
Fruit juice (200 ml)	300	1.0	0	11.0
Morning snack				
Banana	501	2.0	0.7	7.0
Water	0	0	0	0
Lunch				
Bread (wholemeal, 2 slices)	564	6.0	1.4	32.0
Peanut butter (2 tablespoons)	1238	13.6	1.0	24.0
Cheese slice	291	4.5	0	131
Water	0	0	0	0
Milo (2 table-spoons with 200 ml milk)	852	10.0	4.0	368
Afternoon snack				
Apple	230	0.3	0.2	5
Evening meal				
Baked potato (1 medium)	306	2.9	0.6	3
Baked beans (½ cup)	393	6.4	2.2	47
Salad, lettuce, tomato, cucumber	98	1.0	1.0	8
Fruit flavoured yoghurt, 1 tub, 200 g	737	8.6	0.4	255
TOTAL	**7044**	**73.5**	**14.9**	**1292**
Average Recommended Dietary Intake for 4–10 year-old child	**6500–7900**	**18–39**	**6–10**	**800–1000**

usually shows up with the introduction of solids or cow's milk. Egg, seafood, cow's milk, cereals and peanuts are the main culprits. By the age of five years, less than one per cent of children will still have this true food allergy, and this may persist through adulthood. Allergy symptoms tend to run in families and show up as eczema, asthma, hives, swelling of the skin on contact, vomiting, stomach pains and diarrhoea. These symptoms can be severe and often occur soon after the food is eaten. Occasionally very allergic children, particularly those with nut allergies, will react simply by smelling the food or using any utensil that has come into contact with it. It is important to have any suspected food allergy properly diagnosed by a qualified doctor or dietitian as these symptoms may be caused by many factors other than food.

The restriction of foods such as milk, wheat and fruit from a child's diet can have disastrous effects unless supervised by a doctor or dietitian, so make certain it is absolutely necessary before you start limiting any of these foods.

Food sensitivity, food intolerance and hyperactivity

Children displaying severe behavioural changes, which are also accompanied by other physical symptoms like hives, abdominal pain, headaches or diarrhoea, have usually been repeatedly consuming foods which contain chemicals to which they are sensitive. The chemicals that are most commonly the cause of these reactions in children are salicylates, amines, azo dyes and preservatives. Salicylates occur naturally in foods such as tomatoes, oranges and apples. Children drinking large quantities (over a litre a day) of fruit juice may react to the natural salicylates. Coloured foods containing azo dyes are green cordial, red iceblocks and coloured lollies and affect the sensitive child most severely if they have been eaten frequently and in large amounts.

Amines are found in chocolate, cheese and bananas and children with sensitivity symptoms are often found to have been eating a lot of these foods. It is important to note that only sensitive individuals will be affected by the natural and artificial chemicals occurring in foods. The addition of chemicals to processed food is very strictly controlled by food law and government departments of health which ensure that processed foods are safe for us to consume.

People (including children) who react badly to particular foods are said to have 'food sensitivity' and this problem is more common than true food allergy. Food sensitivity is caused by the chemicals which occur naturally in food or those that are added to food during processing. Only people with sensitivity to the certain chemicals will be affected. Symptoms most commonly experienced in sensitive children and adults include hives and swelling of the skin, migraine headaches and stomach upsets. In some people there may be marked drowsiness, irritability, depression and tiredness, although these symptoms can be caused by other factors. Some children can display hyperactivity as severe bursts of aggression, restlessness, irritability and disturbed sleep patterns, which are out of character for the child.

These changes in behaviour are usually accompanied by one of the other signs of food sensitivity such as hives, headaches, stomach pain or diarrhoea. If your doctor suspects that your child is sensitive to the chemicals in food, it will be necessary for the child to follow a very strict elimination diet, but this should *never* be undertaken without supervision of a dietitian and doctor. It is believed that perhaps 5–10% of the population is affected to some degree by food sensitivity.

Remember, though, that it is normal for children to be very active and busy! Some parents mistake very active behaviour with hyperactivity. The truly hyperactive child (otherwise known as ADHD – Attention Deficit Hyperactivity Disorder) will usually show impulsive, inappropriate behaviours, be overactive, can't concentrate, has poor short-term memory, learning weaknesses and may also have behavioural problems such as defiant behaviour and poor coordination. Recent research has found that ADHD runs in families, is caused by slight changes in the structure and function of the child's brain, and is related to the balance of chemicals in the child's brain. ADHD is not caused by poor parenting, too much sugar or food additives. Some children, less than 10 per cent, have improved behaviour by restricting some foods and food additives, but these children must be properly supervised and monitored by a doctor and dietitian. Herbal remedies, vitamin and mineral supplements and other 'natural' products have not been helpful in treating ADHD and some children may actually be made worse by some of these treatments, particularly if they are a natural stimulant such as ginseng, or contain caffeine such as guarana.

6

Food on the Run – 101 Healthy School Lunches

When children are left to their own devices for lunch at school it can often spell nutritional disaster. Buying snack foods, chips, lollies, ice blocks and soft drinks at lunchtime can undo all the good nutrition a child receives at home; a healthy lunch is vital to the nutritious diet of any child. The good news is that school canteens are steadily changing to serve more nutritious food, so it is becoming more likely that your child will be able to choose a healthy meal when buying lunch at school.

Some parents worry that cold foods, such as sandwiches, are not as nutritionally sound as a hot, home-cooked meal, but this is not so. A carefully chosen or packed lunch, whether hot or cold, can provide a child with the energy and nutrients required to last throughout the afternoon. Lunch at home can be more adventurous when you have time to prepare food and relax over the meal. Similarly, time-saving quick and easy lunches don't have to consist of a meat pie and sauce. This chapter shows you quick food for school lunches that are also healthy and enjoyable.

Sandwich suggestions
Never underestimate the nutritional quality of the humble sandwich! A healthy sandwich can easily supply a third of a child's requirements for protein, iron, Vitamin C, niacin, thiamine and, if served with cheese, yoghurt or with a milk drink, it will provide protein, calcium and riboflavin as well.

Bread is a very nutritious food whether it is white, brown or wholemeal. It is a very unfortunate myth that white bread is a non-nutritious food. Sandwiches are best made from wholemeal bread because it contains slightly more vitamins, iron and zinc and much more dietary fibre than other breads, but white bread in Australia is fortified with iron and B vitamins and is a good food for both children and adults. Some children who like to eat only white bread will get enough nutrients from it, but will also need another source of fibre such as wholegrain cereals or fruits and vegetables.

Bread does not have to be spread with butter or margarine – this is just a habit to which we have become accustomed. Try moistening sandwiches with yoghurt, chutney, cranberry sauce or a small spread of light mayonnaise. *Never* sprinkle salt on children's food.

Try some of these healthy sandwich ideas:

- Cheese with grated carrot, lettuce and sultanas
- Chicken, chopped celery and walnuts
- Sliced meat, shredded lettuce and chutney
- Cottage cheese, chopped apple and dates
- Banana, peanut butter and raisins
- Salad sandwich served with a cold chicken drumstick
- Mashed egg with grated cheese
- Peanut butter, bean sprouts and currants
- Salmon, bean sprouts and chopped celery
- Tuna, mayonnaise and tomato
- Baked beans (drained) with lettuce and grated cheese
- Peanut butter, chopped walnuts and lettuce
- Grated carrot, peanut butter and celery
- Pineapple and walnut (well-drained, crushed pineapple)
- Alfalfa sprouts, grated carrot and sultanas
- Cottage cheese and walnuts
- Peanut butter and mashed banana
- Avocado and chicken
- Asparagus, ham and cheese

- Turkey with cranberry sauce
- Lettuce, meat and fruit chutney
- Grated apple, ricotta cheese and raisins
- Cheese and sultanas
- Grated cheese with celery
- Tuna, low fat mayonnaise and shredded lettuce
- Salmon and corn kernels
- Mashed potato and ham
- Chicken and walnut with a little mayonnaise
- Curried egg and lettuce
- Soya beans mashed with bean sprouts and pepper
- Cottage cheese and alfalfa sprouts
- Salmon and cucumber
- Chicken and asparagus
- Chopped dates and peanut butter
- Ricotta cheese and pineapple (well drained)
- Prawn, lettuce and low fat mayonnaise
- Tuna and capsicum
- Cottage cheese and cucumber.

Remember, there are hundreds of different types of breads. Try serving rolls for a change, or breads such as fruit loaf or muesli bread, rye, pumpernickel, herb bread, Lebanese flat bread, crispbreads, muffins and pocket bread. Pikelets, scones, damper and pancakes can also be nutritious lunch ideas topped with healthy spreads and fillings. You can make your own bread; you can also buy salt-free and salt-reduced bread from supermarkets and bakeries.

Open-faced rye bread
To make open-faced sandwiches, top dark rye or pumpernickel bread with colourful toppings and serve for special lunches:

- Avocado slices, bean sprouts and chicken
- Chicken with peaches
- Edam cheese with ham
- Prawns, lettuce and cocktail sauce

- Roast beef with mustard
- Pork with pineapple
- Egg slices and lettuce
- Cottage cheese and walnuts
- Apple chutney and lean roast pork.

The big lunch-box mistakes

Many parents who were interviewed for this book were genuinely concerned about their child's nutrition, health and welfare, yet many were sending their children to school or pre-school with a completely inappropriate lunch. Many parents were unaware of the pitfalls of some popular lunch-box items.

Here are some hints on avoiding the big lunchbox mistakes:

- Don't pack too much food, or too many items, for your child to choose from. Children can't make healthy, rational decisions about food and drinks until they are teenagers.
- Pack only what you want them to eat and what you expect them to eat. If you don't expect any leftovers, then there probably won't be any! Remind your child you expect them to eat their lunch.
- Don't put lollies, rolled fruit, fruit bars, biscuits, muesli bars or chocolates in the lunchbox as a treat for afterwards. Your child will eat the treats first and will not eat the rest of their lunch.
- Don't send extra money to school with your child for an 'after lunch treat'. They will inevitably spend it before they eat what you have packed.
- Never include chips in the lunchbox. Chips are a non-nutritious, fun snack food suitable for treats and parties, but they do not provide enough protein, vitamins or minerals for your child's lunch. They also contain a lot of salt which may make your child unusually thirsty.
- Don't pack too much drink – your child will fill up on it and will not eat the food you supply. Avoid this by packing one

small juice or milk drink as well as a separate bottle of water. Tell your child to have the juice or milk at recess or lunch and the water at other times when they are thirsty.

- Make certain your child can easily open any packs or drink bottles that you send. Children will avoid trying to open difficult packs and may not eat what you send.

Follow these tips for easy and successful packaging:

- Buy a good, strong, spacious lunchbox for your child.
- Cut and peel fruit like oranges, apples or mandarins. If you cover cut fruit in plastic cling wrap and brush with a little orange or lemon juice, it will not turn brown.
- 'Start' to peel the top of the banana, or slice it to make peeling easier. Congratulate your child for peeling it themselves.
- Slice melon and wrap it in plastic or foil.
- Cut fruit, vegetables, cheese and meat into easy, bite-size chunks.
- Cut kiwi fruit and passionfruit into halves, wrap in plastic or foil and send a plastic spoon for easy, mess-free eating.
- Partially open the top of small yoghurt or custard packs.
- Snip the end off plastic-wrapped foods and straws for juice and milk packs.
- Freeze drinks and yoghurts in hot weather and provide a frozen icepack to keep other items cool.

The Top Ten Tips for school lunches

1. Grated cheese – pre-grated packs, light and reduced fat. Toss a handful in the lunchbox every day
2. Light cream cheese and light processed cheese spread
3. Wrap breads – pita, Lebanese, lavash
4. Fruit snack packs
5. Cherry and grape tomatoes
6. Rice cream snack packs
7. Mini yoghurts
8. Mini custards

9. Chicken drumsticks
10. Wholegrain crackers

101 Healthy School Lunches

1. Peanut butter sandwich, banana, juice pack
2. Cheese sticks (2), water cracker biscuits (6), juice pack
3. Yoghurt (200 g container), strawberries (5), water crackers (3), juice
4. Chicken drumstick, buttered bread (2 slices), juice
5. Watermelon (sliced, wrapped in foil), cheese sticks (2), rice cakes (2 buttered), water or juice
6. Rice cakes (2 large), peanut butter, juice
7. Cheese and Vegemite sandwich, mandarin, juice
8. Vitawheat biscuits (4), light cream cheese, orange wedges (4), juice
9. Weetbix or Vitabrits, spread with light cream cheese and fruit jam, juice
10. Wheatmeal biscuits (4), spread with peanut butter and sultanas, juice
11. Pita pocket bread, grated cheese, shredded lettuce and carrot, juice
12. Pikelets (4), spread with light cream cheese and sultanas or chopped dried apricots, strawberries (4) or grapes (10) and water
13. Hot canned soup (made with milk where possible), buttered bread (2 slices), water
14. Lettuce leaf cups (2), grated cheese, grated carrot, sultanas, crackers (4), and water
15. Chicken kebab on small wooden skewer (cooked the night before), buttered bread (2 slices) or pita pocket, grapes (10), water
16. Yoghurt, muesli bar or breakfast bar (not chocolate coated or chocolate chip!), banana, water
17. Mini breakfast cereal pack (with plastic spoon), banana small carton of milk
18. Fruit salad (fresh, canned or packaged), yoghurt, water

19. Banana bread (scrape of margarine), strawberries (5), flavoured milk
20. Breakfast cereal (in small plastic container), fruit yoghurt, juice
21. Baked beans (in small plastic container with plastic spoon), bread (2 slices lightly buttered), juice
22. Celery sticks, ricotta or light cream cheese, light peanut butter, juice
23. Frozen banana rolled in coconut, cheese stick, juice
24. Pita pocket, bean sprouts, light mayonnaise, slice of meat or chicken, grated cheese, juice
25. Lavash bread, spread with light mayonnaise, grated cheese, grated carrot, lettuce and sliced ham, juice
26. Tiny can of tuna (pack with plastic spoon or fork), bread roll (lightly buttered), lettuce, flavoured milk
27. Lavash bread, ricotta cheese, raisins and grated carrot, juice
28. Fried rice (pack plastic spoon), chicken drumstick, juice
29. Corn cob, bread roll (lightly buttered), chicken drumsticks, water
30. Fruit snack pack, small custard container, bread roll, juice
31. Avocado (½ with spoon), buttered bread roll, chicken kebab or drumstick, juice
32. Cherry tomatoes (6), grated cheese, crackers (6), juice
33. Hard-boiled egg, bread roll, cherry tomatoes (5), juice
34. *Corn Fritters* (2) (see recipe page 159), bread (2 slices), cherry tomatoes, water or flavoured milk
35. Lebanese bread, hummus, tomato pieces, grated cheese, juice
36. Bagel, light cream cheese, fruit jam and flavoured milk
37. Rice cream snack pack, dates or raisins, banana, juice
38. Pineapple ring, light cream cheese, rice crackers (2), Milo drink pack
39. Lebanese bread, chicken pieces, diced apple, celery and walnuts, light mayonnaise, flavoured milk
40. Lavash bread, light guacamole dip, three-bean mix, diced tomatoes, grated cheese and juice

41. Lebanese or pita bread, ricotta cheese, bean sprouts, light peanut butter and juice
42. Cooked pasta, chicken pieces, sweet corn kernels, grated cheese, cooked mixed vegetables and juice
43. Kebabs of cheese cubes and fruit pieces, buttered bread, flavoured milk
44. Jaffle with ham and cheese (made the night before and refrigerated), juice
45. Fruit or raisin bread jaffle filled with canned pie apple, sultanas and ricotta cheese, juice
46. Pikelets (4) with ricotta and sliced strawberries, juice or water
47. Pumpernickel bread topped with lettuce leaves, sliced apple and light cream cheese and sultanas (brush the apple with lemon or orange juice to prevent browning), juice or water
48. *Spring rolls* (see recipe, page 159), Milo drink pack
49. *Vegetable Cakes* (see recipe, page 225), grape tomatoes (5), flavoured milk
50. Fruit scones (plain or lightly buttered), with fruit jam or berries (strawberries, blueberries, raspberries), flavoured milk
51. Filo pastry triangles made by brushing with milk, filling with grated cheese, ricotta cheese and frozen spinach, juice
52. Rice cakes (2), light cream cheese, chopped dates and dried apricots, juice
53. *Muffin Munch* (see recipe, page 151), flavoured milk
54. Cheese and ham roll from the bakery and flavoured milk
55. Meatballs, buttered bread (2 slices), grape tomatoes (5) and juice
56. Frozen banana, bread roll, flavoured milk
57. Extra lean sausage, grated cheese, grape tomatoes, bread roll (lightly buttered), juice
58. French mini toasts (6 square toasts) spread with light cheese, ricotta or cottage cheese and cucumber slices and cherry tomatoes, milk or juice drink
59. Roast beef slice filled with cream cheese, salad, light mayonnaise and held together with toothpicks, bread roll and juice
60. Fruit bun, flavoured milk, cheese stick

61. Baked potato, light mayonnaise, slice of ham, carrot sticks, water or juice
62. Sultanas, nuts and dried apricots with wheatmeal biscuits (4) and peanut butter, flavoured milk
63. Milo drink pack with rice cakes (2), margarine and Vegemite
64. Finger bun, flavoured milk and melon pieces
65. Custard and fruit mini pack and crackers (4), juice
66. Low fat dip (e.g. Weight Watchers) with water crackers or crispbread, vegetable sticks and juice
67. Pita pocket, hummus, lettuce, juice
68. Cooked, crisp asparagus spears with cheese slices, bread and juice
69. Cooked ravioli or tortellini with grated cheese, lettuce and cherry tomatoes, water
70. Muesli and yoghurt mini pack and banana, juice
71. Ham slices rolled with low salt pickles, light mayonnaise and grated cheese and carrot with pita bread and juice
72. *Cheesy Pancakes* (2) (see recipe, page 147), melon, fruit pieces and juice
73. Fruit and jelly snack pack with a carton of fruit yoghurt and a juice
74. Mini steamed pudding with custard snack pack and juice
75. *Date 'n' Walnut Spread* (see recipe, page 155), on rice cakes with grapes, melon and a flavoured milk
76. Crispbread with light cheddar cheese spread, cucumber, cherry tomatoes, juice
77. Custard snack pack with banana and juice
78. *Corn and Ham Spread* (see recipe, page 156), on crispbread with cherry tomatoes, juice
79. Hardboiled egg, shredded lettuce, bread roll, juice
80. *Tuna Rice* (see recipe, page 162) with juice
81. *Perfect Pears* (see recipe, page 164), bread roll and water
82. *Banana-in-a-Blanket* (see recipe, page 158), flavoured milk
83. Diet Rice mini pack with chopped fruit pieces, juice or water
84. *Bean Sprout Salad* (see recipe, page 165), with pita bread and juice

85. *Sweet Carrot Salad* (see recipe, page 167), with lettuce cups, bread (2 slices) and flavoured milk

86. Slice of quiche with bread, lettuce, grape tomatoes, cucumber slices and juice

87. *Hidden Treasure Roll* (see recipe, page 158) with a juice or flavoured milk

88. Pita pocket with turkey slices, cranberry sauce and lettuce, juice

89. *Baby Salmon Quiches* (2) (see recipe, page 163) with grape tomatoes, bean sprouts and juice

90. *Tuna Egg Surprise* (see recipe, page 162), shredded lettuce, bread roll and juice

91. *Cornmeal Bread* (see recipe, page 244), scrape of margarine, slice of ham and cheese stick (1), water

92. *Golden Pineapple Nuggets* (see recipe, page 241), cheese sticks (2), water crackers (4) and juice

93. *Tiny Corn Tarts* (see recipe, page 235), grated carrot, lettuce and cherry tomatoes, flavoured milk

94. *Coconut Log* (see recipe, page 240), shredded lettuce, crispbread (3), juice

95. *Red Cheese Balls* (see recipe, page 237), with celery sticks, pita bread triangles and fruit juice

96. *Pineapple Dip* (see recipe, page 236), apple sticks, celery sticks, fruit juice

97. *Banana Walnut Bread* (see recipe, page 241), spread with ricotta or light cream cheese and served with grapes, mandarin segments and flavoured milk

98. *Miss Muffet Spiders* (see recipe, page 236), cheese cubes, water crackers (6) and fruit juice

99. *Surprise Chicken Parcels* (see recipe, page 245), crunchy vegetable sticks and juice

100. *Cheese Pinwheels* (see recipe, page 248), snow pea sprouts, orange wedges and juice

101. *Miss Mouse* (see recipe, page 259), with bread and butter, bean sprouts and juice

7

Choices, Choices, Everywhere!

Choosing the best take-away and packaged food

Take-away food is very popular in busy households because it is quick and easy and there is no washing up. However, the problem with take-away foods is its high kilojoule fat and salt content and its low fibre content. Many fast foods are fried in oils which are high in saturated fats. Have a look at the chart, following, which illustrates the poor nutritional quality of some common take-away foods, compared to more healthy choices such as a chicken and lettuce sandwich, milkshake or yogurt with fruit salad.

Tips for choosing more healthy take-aways

Here are some helpful hints for making take-away choices more healthy:

- Limit buying take-away food to once or twice a fortnight.
- Try to eat at locations where you have a choice of different kinds of food, such as at the mall, shopping centre or food hall, so that you are able to make a variety of healthy choices.
- Always choose a 'small' sized healthy and filling drink, such as a bottle of water, fruit juice, flavoured milk or milkshake.
- Ask for 'no salt' or 'no mayonnaise', or for anything else that you or your child do not want in the meal. Large food chains will be happy to customise it for you.

FOOD	ENERGY (KJ)	PROTEIN (G)	FAT (G)	SODIUM (MG)
McDonald's				
McNuggets (6 pack)	1260	17.2	19.8	434
Quarter Pounder with cheese	2270	33.4	28.5	1180
Big Mac	2010	25.3	24.9	800
McChicken Burger	1750	18.7	19.8	699
Junior Burger with Regular Fries	1834	15.3	20.4	500
Hungry Jack's				
Whopper double beef with cheese	4150	53.8	65.1	1440
Whopper	2740	28.7	39.3	932
French Fries (regular)	1500	9.9	17.9	73
Grilled Chicken Burger	1390	17.8	17.2	886
Onion Rings	1370	4.6	16.0	475
Pizza (most large pizza chains), regular crust				
Supreme (2 slices of 8 slice pizza)	1466	18.4	14.2	736
Chicken combination (2 slices)	1468	20.2	14.0	714
Pepperoni and cheese (2 slices)	1690	20.0	20.6	868
Vegetarian (2 slices)	1330	16.8	10.6	516
KFC				
Original Recipe Chicken (2 pieces)	1903	35.9	28.9	840
Twister	2611	27.7	33.3	1403
Crispy Strips (3 pieces)	2064	43.9	21.8	822
Original Fillet Burger	1895	26.2	17.9	1093
Original Zinger Burger	2237	28.1	25.3	1044
Seasoned Chips (regular serve)	1347	4.8	13.0	356
Red Rooster				
Rooster Burger	2153	23.5	29.0	1445
Strip Sub Roll	3295	29.1	40.3	1584
Flayva Roll	2888	22.6	42.3	1348
Little Red Rooster Meal – Burger	2692	19.0	29.9	1168
Little Red Rooster Meal – Nuggets	1725	11.7	20.6	561

Food	Energy (kJ)	Protein (g)	Fat (g)	Sodium (mg)
Fish and chips (no added salt)				
1 piece of fish, battered (100 g)	1060	14.2	15.7	470
Chips (regular)	1110	3.0	13.6	256
Pies and Sausage rolls				
Meat pie	1894	15.4	27.6	1200
Sausage roll (large)	1200	8.0	17.7	630
Tomato sauce (1 tablespoon)	84	–	1.7	194
Healthy choice				
Chicken & lettuce sandwich	930	12.3	8.8	256
Yoghurt & fruit salad	518	5.6	0.3	72
Chocolate milkshake (1 scoop ice cream)	851	10.2	7.2	156
Healthy Subway (6 inch roll, no chips)				
Veggie Delight	990	9.0	3.5	520
Turkey Breast Deli	930	11.0	4.0	620
Roast Beef Deli	910	11.0	3.5	740
Ham Deli	910	11.0	3.5	700

· Note: nutritional analyses of take-away foods obtained from the manufacturer, 2004, and from Commonwealth Government nutrient analyses of foods.
· Sodium values are listed before extra salt is added after cooking.

- Steer your family towards the sandwich shop, bakery, milk bar, fruit shop, supermarket or café so that you will have a choice of more healthy foods and drinks. Stay away from fish and chips, pies, sausage rolls and pasties.
- Sit down and eat the meal slowly. This allows time for your child to 'fill up' before they ask for other food and drink.
- Tell children to finish their meal and drink before they ask for anything else. Say, 'If you are still hungry after that you can have a flavoured milk' or 'You can have some fruit when you get home'. It is amazing how quickly a child becomes 'full' when they finish their water, juice or milk!

- Avoid the 'meal deal' as they are usually combinations for poor food choices. For example, the combination of burger, chips, soft drinks, ice cream and/or chocolate bar is an unhealthy combination *but* a combination of burger, salad, coleslaw, milkshake, water bottle or juice is much healthier. However, if you do allow the meal deal ask for the soft drink to be replaced with fruit juice.
- Serve a salad while you wait for home delivery pizza. This way children will be hungry enough to eat the salad and you will only have to order one pizza.
- Avoid the 'kids menu' in take-away shops, cafés and restaurants as this will usually be limited to chips, chicken nuggets, sausage rolls or pizza. Children need to learn to eat well from the adult menu and allowing them to choose from the kids menu reinforces the idea that children are expected to eat junk food while their parents choose 'adult' food.
- Make sure that you do the ordering for your young children – don't expect them to be able to decide for themselves.
- Try walking to and from the takeaway shop or fast food chain – the excursion will do you and the children good.
- Remember, you need to set a good example and be a healthy role model yourself!

Here are some healthy and practical take-away suggestions:

- Sandwiches or rolls. Ask for 'no butter', 'just a scrape of butter', 'no salt or pepper', or 'no mayonnaise'.
- Don't worry if the only choice is white bread. Remember, any sort of bread is nutritious.
- Allow children to choose which water, juice or milk they want.
- When ordering a milkshake or fruit smoothie ask for low fat or skim milk.
- Hamburger, with lots of salad (and 'no salt or pepper'), and a bottle of water, juice or flavoured milk.
- Steak sandwich with a bottle of water. Ask to have burgers and sandwiches cut into quarters.

- Grilled fish, a buttered roll ('just a scrape of butter'), fruit juice or flavoured milk.
- Barbequed chicken (avoid the skin), bread or bread rolls, salad, coleslaw, bean salad, fruit juice.
- Corn on the cob with bread roll and flavoured milk.
- Baked potato with cheese, baked beans or a small serving (1 teaspoon) of sour cream or butter.
- Banana in a bread roll with flavoured milk. You can ask for this at the sandwich shop or make it yourself by buying the bananas and the loaf of bread from the supermarket or fruit shop.
- Yoghurt and fruit salad.
- Baked potato or wedges instead of chips ('no salt, please').
- Thick crust pizza: choose vegetarian, extra pineapple and avoid extra cheese and the very fatty, greasy meats (pepperoni, salami, cabanossi).
- Souvlaki, burrito or kebabs with salad and juice.
- Chinese meal (choose stir fry) with vegetables, steamed rice or noodles – avoid battered or crumbed choices like fried spring rolls, sweet and sour pork or chicken, and fried rice. Ask for 'no MSG' to lower the salt content.
- Steamed dim sims, fresh spring rolls in rice paper, steamed dumplings, noodle soups.

Choosing from the major fast food chains

You will be able to choose a reasonably nutritious meal for yourself and your children from the major fast food chains if you stick to some basic rules, below. And always remember – you are the parent, you are the boss!

- Avoid meal deals which usually combine unhealthy choices with unhealthy drinks and desserts.
- Choose a nutritious drink such as a bottle of water or fruit juice instead of soft drink.
- Avoid the fries – if you can, choose baked or mashed potato, or wedges instead.

- Ask for 'no added salt' – it may take a little longer for your meal to arrive, but it will be a lot lower in salt.
- Remember the golden rule – the parent decides *what* will be eaten and the child decides *how much*. You will need to make your child's selection from the menu. If you want to be democratic, you can allow your child to choose their drink from water, fruit juice or flavoured milk.
- Decide on some 'family rules' about take-away foods, such as 'No soft drinks', 'No salt', 'No playing until after eating', 'The meal should include the Five Food Groups', 'No more than once a fortnight'.

With these things in mind, you are often able to choose a nutritious meal from major fast food chains. Here is a breakdown of the most nutritious and least nutritious food from seven of the most popular chains:

MOST NUTRITIOUS	LEAST NUTRITIOUS
McDonald's Vege Burger Lean Beef Burger Roast Chicken Salad Garden Mixed Salad Berrynice Yogurt Crunch Apples Chicken Foldover Junior Burger Cheese Burger	Fries McNuggets Quarter Pounder with Cheese McOz Big Mac
Hungry Jack's Salads Spicy Chicken Wrap	Whopper/Junior Whopper Aussie Burger Bacon Deluxe Double Cheeseburger Chicken Nuggets Onion Rings French Fries
Pizza Vegetarian Ham and pineapple with extra pineapple	Meat combination pizza Thin, crispy crust Chicken and bacon

Seafood	Pepperoni
Cheese and tomato	Extra cheese
KFC	
BBQ Chicken	Popcorn Chicken Nuggets
Coleslaw	Twister
Potato	Crispy Strips
Corn on cob	Fried Chicken Pieces
	Fries
Red Rooster	
Fresh Chicken Sub 97	Crispy Fillet Burger
(97% fat free)	Real Bacon Burger
Fresh Satay Sub	Tropical Pack
Fresh Flayva 97 (97% fat free)	Chicken Nuggets
BBQ Chicken Dinner	Chips
	Chicken Strips
Fish and Chips	
Grilled fish	Battered/crumbed fish
Bread/rolls, lightly buttered	Potato scallops
Milkshake	Chiko Roll, fried dim sims
	Chips
Subway 6 inch sandwich rolls	
Veggie Delight	Italian BMT
Turkey Breast Deli	Meatball
Ham Deli	Horseradish Steak and Cheese
Roast Beef Deli	Southwest Steak and Cheese

· Note: most choices in both 'Most Nutritious' and 'Least Nutritious' categories are still high in salt, particularly for children. Take-away foods usually have salt added in their preparation and then more salt added after cooking. Always ask for 'no added salt'.

Packaged food and fats

A very active child will need more kilojoules (or more food) than a less active child, but it is a myth that they can therefore eat more fat. Dietary fat is considered to be undesirable because it is linked to being overweight, heart disease and some cancers. Nutritionists recommend that no more than approximately 30 per cent of the total energy intake should come from fat.

However, remember that nobody, including your child, is expected to eat a fat free diet. If we use the 30 per cent recommendation, this equates roughly to 40–47 grams of fat per day for a child aged one to three years; 52–63 grams of fat per day for four- to seven-year-olds and 63–79 grams for eight- to eleven-year-olds. The amount of daily fat for adults who consume around 8,000–10,000 kilojoules is approximately 63–80 grams. Naturally, the amount of kilojoules and therefore the amount of fat varies greatly between children and depends on how physically active they are.

The section on pages 119–123 provides information about various packaged foods from supermarket chains and lists the amount (percentage) of fat and sodium per 100 grams of the food. This gives you an idea of whether the food is relatively low in fat (less than 4 grams per 100 grams or 4 per cent fat), moderate in fat (5–10 grams per 100 grams or 5–10 per cent fat) or high in fat (more than 10 grams per 100 grams).

Here are some other tips about dietary fat:

- Choose lean beef, lamb, pork and chicken. Cut the fat off yourself (and take the skin off chicken). Don't feed fat or skin cut-offs to your pets, as it's bad for them, too! Avoid processed meats and crumbed meats as they are extremely high in fat, and it is mostly saturated fat.
- Cook with more healthy fats and oils such as olive oil, canola and sunflower. Avoid cooking with shortening (e.g. lard), hard fats or butter.
- Choose low fat milk for your child after the age of two years. Remember, though, that whole milk is a relatively low fat food with only about 4 per cent fat, so if your child will only drink whole milk, that's fine. It's more important that they get three serves of milk or dairy foods every day.
- Read food labels and avoid foods with ingredients such as lard, tallow, shortening or hydrogenated vegetable oils. These contain saturated fats which clog up arteries.
- Choose 'fat free' brands such as 97 and 98 per cent fat free.

Packaged food and salt

Salt (sodium chloride) is added to food to make it more flavour-some. In fact, often the only flavour that you can taste in most pre-packaged foods is salt! A child as young as six months of age will have a natural liking for sweet or salty foods and this explains why they like lollies and chips. Salt is not good for children and they do not need any salt added to their food. Most pre-packaged foods contain a lot of salt and this puts extra pressure on children's kidneys, as they have to work hard to get rid of it. Salt can also cause dehydration in small children as it makes them very thirsty. In addition, a high salt diet in childhood can raise a child's blood pressure and add to the risk of high blood pressure (hypertension) later in life.

However, children do need a tiny amount of salt daily in order for their blood sodium to remain in balance. The recommended maximum level of sodium in a child's diet is 140–280 milligrams in babies (from breastmilk or formula); 320–580 milligrams in seven- to twelve-month-olds; 320–1150 milligrams in one- to three-year-olds; 460–1730 milligrams in four- to seven-year-olds and 600–2300 milligrams in eight- to eleven-year-olds. The minimum range is the most desirable – when it comes to sodium, the less your child consumes, the better!

It's astounding to see how much sodium is actually added to packaged foods. For example, a small packet of chips (50 g) contains 359 milligrams of sodium and 15.7 grams of fat! If your child 'grazes' on these foods throughout the day, they can easily exceed the limits on fat and salt and completely miss out on the important nutrients in more healthy choices.

See the list of some common high-sodium foods on page 118.

To help reduce the sodium in your and your child's diet, you can:

- Choose products labelled with 'No Added Salt' or 'Reduced Salt'.
- Encourage your child to eat foods naturally low in salt such as fruit, vegetables, juices, water and milk.

- Ask for 'no added salt' at take-away food shops.
- Take the salt shaker off the table.
- Do not add salt when cooking as most recipes just include salt for taste. The recipe will not fail without the salt.
- Cook two-minute noodles (99% fat free) without adding the sachet of flavouring.
- Choose vacuum packed Udon, Singapore or Hokkein noodles, which are very low in fat and salt.

FOOD	SODIUM (MG) PER SERVING
Two minute noodles (including seasoning), 1 serving	1800
Soy sauce (1 tablespoon)	1262
Pretzels (50 g bag)	990
Takeaway burger	932
Stock cubes (1 cube, 1 teaspoon)	920
Pizza (2 slices, supreme)	720
Processed meat (bacon, ham, salami) 30 g	503
Soups (packet and canned) ½ cup prepared	340
Chips, snack foods (50 g bag)	320
Hot chips, salted (1 serving)	300–500
Crackers, savoury snack biscuits (20 g)	240
Cheese, cheddar, processed (30 g)	218
Sauces (BBQ, pasta sauces, tomato, gravy), 1 tablespoon	128–200
Vegemite, Marmite, Promite (1 teaspoon, 5 g)	169

The following list of common packaged or prepared foods shows you the fat and salt content and will help you to choose more healthy food for you and your family.

Meat, Chicken and Fish	Grams of Fat per 100 g (%)	Milligrams of Sodium per 100 g
Salami	41	1370
Pepperoni/cabanossi	37	1200
Polish sausage	33	880
Mettwurst	33	1470
Mortadella	29	770
Liverwurst	27	770
Spam	23	1570
Chicken nuggets	22	370
Black pudding	21	760
Kransky	21	1370
Sausages (beef, pork, chicken)	21	860
Bacon, trimmed of fat, grilled	20	1730
Hamburger mince patty	17	710
Prepared meatballs and beef burgers	17	480
Devon/Fritz/sandwich meats	16	780
Gourmet sausages	16	860
Chicken schnitzel	15	610
Processed chicken roll	15	745
Crumbed fish	15	610
Spam Lite	13	1036
Fish fingers	11	260
Lean beef gourmet sausages	10	860
Chargrilled chicken burgers	9	93
Lean Beef Hamburger Patties	8	93
Turkey/chicken mince	8	59
Extra lean gourmet sausages	4	860
Turkey/chicken sandwich slices	3	745

Other foods	Grams of Fat per 100 g (%)	Sodium (mg)
Pasta		
Beef lasagne	6	235
Canneloni	6	285
Ravioli	5	295
Tortellini	4	275
Chicken lasagne	4	235
Egg pasta	2	13
Fresh gnocchi	1	10
Dry white pasta	Less than 1	5

OTHER FOODS	GRAMS OF FAT PER 100 G (%)	SODIUM (MG)
Pasta sauces (most brands)		
Alfredo	4	537
Bacon carbonara	3	764
'Light' Alfredo	2	537
Tomato	Less than 1	370
'Light' bacon carbonara	Less than 1	764
Other sauces		
Korma	22	500
Honey mustard chicken sauce	11	490
Rogan josh	10	700
Creamy mushroom chicken sauce	10	560
Stroganoff sauce	9	430
'Light' creamy mushroom	4	420
97% fat free chicken cacciatore	2	340
Curried chicken and vegetables	2	480
Asian noodles		
Crunchy noodles	31	800
Two-Minute noodles		360
Chow Mein noodles	25	1393
Fried noodles	24	604
Pad Thai noodles	2	522
Hokkein noodles	2	140
99% Fat Free Two-Minute noodles	Less than 1	350
Singapore noodles	Less than 1	137
Udon noodles	Less than 1	109
Cheese		
Havarti	37	800
Cheddar	35	610
Cream cheese	33	338
Blue vein	32	1198
Swiss	30	370
Gloucester, Gouda, Edam	28	1072
Feta	23	850
Mozzarella	22	530
Ricotta	11	130
Cream cheese spread	7	1231

Processed cheddar cheese	7	1677
Light cream cheese spread	5	1310
Cottage	6	293
Grated cheese	33	644
'Light' grated (25% less fat)	24	540
'Extra light' grated (50% less fat)	15	758
Peanut butter		
Regular	50	629
'Light'	38	713
Ice Cream		
Regular ice cream	10	75
'Light' ice cream	4	46
Low fat ice cream	Less than 1	71
Cream		
'Pure' premium cream	56	31
Double thick cream	48	18
Sour cream	36	25
Thickened cream	35	18
'Light' sour cream	19	49
'Light' thickened cream	18	31
'Extra Light' cream	12	16
'Diet' sour cream	3	86
Breads		
Taco shells	26	290
Croissants	24	456
Pappadams (ready to eat)	23	1900
Garlic bread	17	525
Cheese twist sticks	14	1230
Roti wraps	9	392
Pikelets	8	460
Pancakes	7	280
Breadsticks	7	560
French toast	5	630
Flour tortillas	5	610
Naan	5	940
Turkish Pide bread	4	558
Mini toasts	3	830
Corn tortillas	2	610
Pumpernickel	2	370
Lebanese bread	2	243
English muffins	2	360
Crumpets	1	560

OTHER FOODS	GRAMS OF FAT PER 100 G (%)	SODIUM (MG)
Pizza base (plain, no sauce)	1	572
Most other breads	Less than 1	500
Pastry		
Shortcrust	25	510
Puff pastry	24	140
'Reduced fat' shortcrust	16	550
'Reduced fat' puff pastry	12	170
Filo pastry	3	510
Chips and snack foods		
Pringles	39	540
Popcorn (prepared as on pack)	32	453
Potato crisps	32	719
Cheezels	31	1220
Choc chip muesli bar	31	120
Microwave popcorn	29	765
Corn chips	27	510
BBQ snack biscuits	25	1360
'Baked not fried' crackers	21	1110
Jatz/Ritz crackers	19	1070
Twisties	15	1007
Muesli bar	15	180
Vita Wheat crackers	10	570
Water crackers	9	670
Japanese rice crackers	8	650
Yoghurt and desserts		
Chocolate mousse	11	44
'Light' cheesecake mini	6	71
Creamy custard yoghurt	5	110
Panacotta	5	67
Natural yogurt	4	120
Dairy desserts e.g. Yogo	4	91
Crème caramel	4	51
'Dairy snack'	3	61
Rice Cream Mini	3	158
Custard	2	56
'Diet' rice	1	67
'Trim' custard	Less than 1	103
'Light', low fat yoghurt	Less than 1	94

Frozen waffles, chips and wedges (oven baked)		
Frozen waffles	13	736
Hash browns	9	316
Potato smiles	9	384
Potato nuggets	9	453
'Crunchy' wedges	9	381
Potato gems	6	453
Frozen chips, oven baked	5	60
Potato wedges	3	381
Cakes and biscuits		
Teddy bear biscuits	15	390
Yoghurt topped muesli bars	13	115
Milk arrowroot biscuits	11	270
Muffin bar	10	340
Lamington	6	180
Jam roll	5	460
Fruit bars	4	115
Twists	3	162
Breakfast bars	3	23

8

Kids in the Kitchen

Children love to cook and be involved in the preparation of food. Allowing your child to help with the shopping, food storage and cooking helps them to learn about food, but also provides them with self-confidence and self-esteem. Children who cook for the family are so proud of themselves! In addition, involving children in food preparation helps them to learn important food skills that will stay with them for life. Children can also learn a lot from reading food labels, so start them young and help them get used to reading food labels and understanding what goes into their food.

Part of the battle of getting children to eat a variety of foods is overcoming their neophobia, or fear of new foods. Having children involved in shopping, storage and preparation of foods helps them broaden their knowledge of new foods, helps them identify a wide array of foods and reduces the shock of being asked to eat them!

In this chapter there are lots of tips and ideas for involving children in shopping, deciphering food labels and growing your own herbs and vegetables, and also some quick, safe and easy food ideas and recipes for your children to try. There are also two simple food games you can play with your kids.

Involving children in shopping

For many parents, taking the children shopping is a nightmare. Some children throw classic supermarket tantrums, some employ a never-ending stream of pestering until they finally get what they want. Some take off and have to be found by the supermarket staff! Often, children behave badly in the supermarket because they are tired, bored or hungry. Make certain that your children are up to the shopping trip because otherwise it will be a negative experience for all concerned. It may be best for you all to have a snack or drink before you go shopping, rather than afterwards. This is also a good idea if you are prone to impulse buying when you or your kids are hungry. Here are some other tips for involving children in shopping in a positive way:

- Make it absolutely clear that your child is not going to get a special treat every time they go shopping. This is an unnecessary and expensive habit which is reinforced every time you do it.
- Remember, you are the adult and you are the one who has to be firm, calm and consistent when the pestering begins.
- Involve children in the shopping experience. Get the children to help you write the shopping list, ask them to read it out to you as you go, let them fetch the products from the shelves and put them into the trolley, read the date stamp, bag and count the fruit and vegetables. Remember to thank your child for helping you – your child wants your approval, attention and love more than anything else in the shop!
- Ask your child to tell you the price of various items and choose the best value for money.
- Allow your child to have a plain bread roll or a slice of bread as they sit in the trolley.
- Allow them to choose a small inexpensive book or non-food treat if they have behaved well.

If you think that these suggestions are impossible for you to put into action, rest assured that they have all been tried successfully by parents I have spoken to. These parents reported that their children were far better behaved, less bored and truly interested in learning about foods and family budgeting.

JASMINE, THREE YEARS OLD

Jasmine is the youngest daughter of Fiona and Brett. She spends most days at home with Brett while Fiona works, and together daughter and father do the grocery shopping. To get to the supermarket they have to walk past the cake shop and Jasmine inevitably complains that she is hungry and that she must have a doughnut with pink icing. To avoid one of Jasmine's infamous tantrums, Brett always allows her to have the doughnut, even though she usually just eats the icing. In several other ways, Jasmine demands, and gets, lollies, cakes, biscuits, iceblocks and soft drinks. This makes Fiona extremely cross because she tries hard to encouarge Jasmine to eat healthier food. When Fiona takes Jasmine shopping on the weekends, she uses the following successful tactics:

- Fiona does the shopping trip in the mornings when Jasmine is not tired.
- She distracts Jasmine when she starts to say she is hungry. 'How hungry?' asks Fiona. 'Are you as hungry as a lion?', 'Are you hungry as a giraffe?', 'Are you as hungry as an elephant?'. This game usually gets them past the cake shop!
- Fiona asks Jasmine to help her with the shopping. 'Could you find me some milk?', 'Oh, thank you!', 'Where is the bread?', 'Excellent', 'Do you remember what mandarins are?', 'Can you see any?'. Jasmine enjoys helping and taking responsibility and she basks in Fiona's praise. Fiona says that she is learning that 'behaving well is its own reward'.

Fiona and Brett are now trying to be consistent together with Jasmine's behaviour and they are focussing on being firm, keeping her occupied in the supermarket and rewarding her good behaviour with praise, hugs and encouragement. Funnily enough, Jasmine observed a toddler tantrum in the supermarket recently and exclaimed, 'That little boy is being very naughty, isn't he, Daddy?'!

Teach your child to read food labels

Children are fascinated by finding out what is in their food. Helping kids to read food labels encourages them to understand the ingredient content of packaged foods but also helps them understand value for money. Here is a brief guide to reading and understanding food labels:

A description or name of the food

Each label 'names' the specific food.

Ingredient list

All of the ingredients are listed in order by weight. Generally the first three ingredients are the major components of the food. For example, the ingredients of sweet biscuits are flour, vegetable shortening, sugar, wheatmeal, brown sugar, golden syrup, raising agents (503, 500, 450), salt, flavour. You can see from this list that the main three ingredients are flour, fat and sugar. When other sugars are listed on a product ingredient label (e.g. sucrose, glucose, maltose, fructose syrup, honey, corn syrup, molasses, invert sugar) they can all add up to make sugar the overall main ingredient.

Food additives are all checked for safety by government agencies before they are allowed to be added to foods. Additives such as preservatives, colours and flavours are added to foods to improve the taste, appearance, quality, stability and shelf-life of a food. Rather than printing the whole name of the additive, manufacturers usually print the type of additive (e.g. thickener, humectant, anti-caking agent, antioxidant) and then the specific number for example, 'thickener (440)'. Some manufacturers list the name of the additive and all of the additional information. For example, 'Pectin (thickener, 440)'. Some people are allergic to certain foods (e.g. eggs, milk, nuts) or are sensitive to certain additives so all of this information is printed on the food label to allow consumers to make informed choices about their foods and drinks.

Net weight

This is the weight of the food without the weight of the packaging. Teach your children to read the net weight and compare net weight on large packages versus small packages. Sometimes large and small packages can both be 500 grams net weight! In this case, you are often paying more for packaging, so it pays to be aware. Teach your children to compare the price of similar weight products and to understand value for money.

Nutrition panel

This lists the energy (kilojoules), protein, fat (total fat and how much of the total is saturated fat), carbohydrate (total carbohydrate and how much of that is sugar or starch), dietary fibre and sodium content in the food. Nutrients are shown per average serving and per 100 grams. If, for example, a muesli bar is listed as 35 grams of sugar per 100 grams, you know that it is 35 per cent sugar. This will also be obvious from the ingredient list.

Similarly, you can see how much fat is in the food by checking the amount of fat per serving and the per cent of fat (per 100 grams). Anything below 3 per cent fat is a low fat food, anything from 7 to 15 per cent fat tends to be a moderate fat food and above 15 per cent fat is a high fat food.

Nutrition claims

- **'Use by' or 'Best Before' date:** For foods with a shelf life of less than two years, the 'Best Before' date refers to the suggested time limit on the food before it begins to spoil or go stale. It does not necessarily mean that the food will have gone 'off'. It is illegal to sell food which has gone past its date marking.
- **'Country of Origin':** The country or countries where the food was made or the country from where the ingredients came. (This information is not required in New Zealand.)
- **'Product of Australia', 'Product of New Zealand':** This means that the vast majority of ingredients and production has occurred in Australia or New Zealand.

- **'Name and address of manufacturer or distributor'**: This information must be put on the label so that consumers can contact the manufacturer if required.
- **'Allergy warning'**: Ingredients that cause common allergies are listed. Examples are gluten (for people who suffer coeliac disease), nuts, eggs, bee pollen etc.
- **'Storage and cooking instructions'**: The manufacturer has tested the food product and provides storage and cooking instructions based on these quality tests. It's sensible to follow these instructions.
- **Bar code:** The identification number for the food which is electronically scanned at the cash register.
- **'No added sugar'**: This means that no sucrose (table sugar) or glucose, honey, dextrose or maltose has been added to the food. Natural sugars, such as the fructose naturally occurring in fruit juices, are not 'added'.
- **'Fat Free'**: The produce contains less than 0.15 per cent fat.
- **'Low Fat'**: The product contains less than 3 per cent fat in a solid food, and less than 1.5 per cent fat in a liquid food.
- **'97 per cent fat free'**: The product contains about three per cent or less fat.
- **'98 per cent fat free'**: The product contains about two per cent or less fat.
- **'Reduced fat'**: The product contains at least 25 per cent less fat than the regular product. This means that it has been made with less fat than usual, but it is not necessarily low in fat!
- **'Low salt'**: No more than 120 mg of sodium per 100 grams of food *or* less than half the amount of sodium in the normal food product.
- **'Reduced salt'**: At least 25 per cent less sodium than the regular food. This means that it is made with less salt than usual, but it is still not necessarily low in salt.
- **'Low-joule'**: Liquids and drinks are less than 80 kilojoules per 100 mls and solid foods are less than 170 kilojoules per 100 grams.

- **'Cholesterol Free', 'No Cholesterol':** The food contains no cholesterol but may still contain significant amounts of fat, e.g. avocadoes. Cholesterol only comes from animal foods.
- **'High in fibre':** The product contains at least 3 grams of fibre per serve of the food.
- **'Very high in fibre':** The product contains at least 6 grams of fibre per serve of the food.
- **'No artificial colourings or flavourings':** The product contains no added synthetic colours or flavours but naturally occurring colours and flavours are permitted and often used e.g. Beta-carotene (160).
- **'No preservatives':** The product contains no added chemical preservatives.
- **'No MSG':** The product contains no added monosodium glutamate (MSG), although MSG is found naturally in tomatoes, mushrooms and some cheeses.

Other food label claims
- **'Lite' or 'Light':** This has no strict definition. It can mean a lighter flavour of food (e.g. light olive oil) or less fat, or lower in alcohol (e.g. light beer) or a thinner (e.g. 'Lite') cream, lighter weight product (e.g. lighter potato chips).
- **'Natural':** This word has no strict definition and is used in a variety of ways on food labels.

Grow your own
Growing your own vegetables in pots or in a garden plot is an excellent education for children and introduces a wide selection of fruits and vegetables that children will be keen to try. One father was astounded at the impact that growing herbs and vegetables had on his children's willingness to eat them. He had his children eating cherry tomatoes, carrots, lettuce, radishes, silverbeet and cucumbers – they were very 'vegetable phobic' before they had a vegetable patch. They all enjoyed pottering around together on weekends and the children learned a lot about

gardening, compost, worms and environmental issues. They have since started a small vegetable patch at their local school and it has been a big hit with students, staff and parents.

Vegetables

If you have only a small space you can grow herbs and miniature vegetables on your deck or windowsill. The best vegetables for this are tiny cherry tomato vines, parsley, radishes and shallots. If you have a yard with lots of space, you can plant the seeds from pumpkin, watermelon and squash. These seeds take between 4 and 12 days to sprout and require plenty of water every day. Try recycling or bucketing water from your bathtub or washing machine onto your garden.

Try buying a packet of carrot, radish or bean seeds from the supermarket or hardware shop and follow the directions on the pack. When the vegetables are ready children can use them to make sandwiches, or serve them with the special dishes they have cooked for the rest of the family.

Windowsill herb garden

Herbs are believed to have many health protection benefits and encouraging your child to eat fresh herbs will broaden their food tastes as well. Herbs can be added to salads, soups, casseroles and other cooked meals.

Your child can grow a herb garden on any windowsill as they don't take up very much space. You will need some small pots or one long window box, some soil and coarse sand, and some herb seeds or plants. These are all available at supermarkets or hardware stores. If you can't get sand easily, pet shops sell coarse sand for aquariums. Try growing the herbs you use the most, such as chives, thyme, basil, parsley and oregano.

Fill two-thirds of the pot with soil and the other one-third of the pot with coarse sand. Plant the seeds or herb plants in each pot or space them 6 centimetres apart in the window box. Water once a week and place in a sunny spot. Use scissors to snip the herbs back when they become 'scraggy' – this will help them stay bushy. Children can grow small pots of herbs to sell at school fetes and fundraisers.

Beansprouts

Children can easily grow beansprouts from dried seeds and beans such as dried mung beans, soy beans and alfalfa. You can buy these at the supermarket.

Place 1–2 tablespoons of beans in a large glass jar. Cover the top with a piece of clean stocking and place a rubber band over the top to hold it in place. Cover the beans with water and stand in a dark cupboard overnight. Drain the water off the beans the next day and rinse them with fresh water. You'll need to rinse and drain the beans every morning and afternoon to keep them fresh and clean. Lie the jar on its side in a light spot such as on the windowsill. They will sprout after a couple of days and will be ready to eat after 4–5 days. You can eat bean sprouts as a snack, in sandwiches, as a salad or cooked in a stirfry meal.

Easy, fun, nutritious and delicious recipes for kids

Children as young as three years of age can become involved in cooking and food preparation and this helps them learn about foods and different cooking methods. In other cultures children learn to master many different food preparation skills at a young age and this is an important aspect of their development. Allowing both boys and girls to participate in food preparation helps them become familiar with different foods and this can improve their acceptance of a wide range of ingredients. It also gives them an opportunity to read recipes and food labels and this is a wonderful learning experience. Many parents I have spoken to said that they had successfully used cooking as a way of practising maths with their child, particularly fractions!

Bread

Bread is made by combining flour, sugar, water and yeast. Yeast is used to make bread 'rise'. The yeast is a living cell that makes carbon dioxide gas which stretches the flour mixture and allows it to rise. Yeast requires warmth, warm water, a little sugar for food, and air before it starts to multiply to produce the gas. The bread dough is allowed to stand for 40–50 minutes to give the yeast time to make the carbon dioxide gas. Cooked bread does not contain live yeast cells, but does contain lots of nutrients to help you grow and give you energy.

3 × 7 g sachets of dried yeast
1¾ cups lukewarm water
1 teaspoon sugar
3 cups wholemeal plain flour
3 cups white plain flour
1 teaspoon salt
2 teaspoons margarine
poppy or sesame seeds

Heat the oven to 220°C. Dissolve yeast in warm water with sugar. Put flour, salt and margarine in a large mixing bowl (rub the margarine into the flour to make small breadcrumbs). Add the yeast and water mixture to flour. Mix it through the flour with clean hands. Mix the dough with the 'heel' of your hands for five minutes by folding it over to trap the air inside; this is called kneading. Then cover the bowl with a damp, clean tea towel and leave it on the kitchen bench for 40–50 minutes. This is when the yeast will start working to produce carbon dioxide gas. The mixture should double in size as the gas stretches the dough. After the dough has risen, remove it from the bowl and place it on a table or board with a little flour (this stops it sticking to your hands). Knead the dough, folding and rolling it on the board. Cut the dough in half and shape into loaves. You might like to try dividing the mixture into three and plaiting the dough to make a large bread plait. Put the loaves into a greased loaf tin or just place on a greased tray. Leave the tray on the kitchen bench for 20 minutes to allow it to rise again before you put it in the oven. Brush the top with a little water and sprinkle with poppy or sesame seeds. Bake the dough in the oven for 30 minutes until golden brown on top. You can serve bread hot or cold and you can make bread rolls by cutting the mixture into 12 pieces instead of two loaves.

Quick Bread

Bread is a fascinating recipe for children of all ages because it is basically an interesting science experiment! This quick bread produces gas using bicarbonate of soda and the rising gas helps the bread dough to rise.

2 cups plain wholemeal flour
2 cups plain white flour
2 teaspoons sugar
1 teaspoon bicarbonate of
  soda
2½ cups milk

Sift the flours, sugar and bicarbonate of soda together into a bowl. Add the milk a bit at a time and mix through the flour. Place the mixture on a board or table sprinkled with a little flour to prevent it sticking. Dust your hands with some flour and pat the dough into a round loaf. Use a knife to cut a deep cross on top of the loaf. Place the loaf on a baking tray that has been brushed with a little butter or margarine to prevent sticking. Bake the loaf in a moderately hot oven (190°C) for 1 hour until golden brown. Serve slices hot or cold with a scraping of margarine.

Scrambled Eggs on Toast

2 eggs
¼ cup milk
1 teaspoon butter or margarine

Crack the shell of each egg with the back of a knife and break the egg into a bowl. Make sure that no egg shell is in the bowl. Beat the egg in the bowl with a fork and add the milk and mix. Heat a saucepan on the stove on a moderate heat and melt the butter in the pan. Pour the egg mixture into the saucepan and stir slowly until the eggs become thicker and soft. Cook a piece of toast and serve the eggs on the toast.

Melted Cheese Roll

1 wholemeal bread roll
½ cup grated cheese
Margarine or butter
Aluminium foil

Heat the oven to 180°C before you start. Slice the roll in half. Grate the cheese and spread the roll with a scraping of margarine or butter. Place the cheese on the roll and cover with the other half of the roll. Wrap up in a piece of foil and heat in the oven for 15 minutes.

Lettuce Cup

1 lettuce
2 carrots
2 tablespoons raisins
1 tablespoon plain yoghurt
½ teaspoon lemon juice

Wash the lettuce in cold water and remove each leaf. Take 4 lettuce leaves and shred into thin strips with a knife. Peel, wash and grate the carrots using a grater. Mix the carrot, raisins, shredded lettuce, yoghurt and lemon juice together. Pile the mixture into the middle of a lettuce leaf cup and serve with meat, cheese or eggs.

Baby Pizza

1 piece pita pocket bread
1 tablespoon tomato paste
  (no added salt)
1 tomato
½ cup grated cheese

Spread the pita bread with tomato paste. Chop the tomatoes into small pieces and place on top of bread. Sprinkle with cheese and heat under the griller until the cheese melts. Try adding canned pineapple pieces for a change.

Popcorn

½ cup popping corn
1 tablespoon vegetable oil

Place the oil in a large saucepan that has a lid and heat on the stove. Add the corn and put on the lid. Shake the saucepan to cover each corn kernel with oil. Hold the lid firmly while the corn is popping. Pour into a bowl and eat hot or cold.

Corn Pikelets

½ cup wholemeal self-raising
  flour
½ cup white self-raising flour
½ tablespoon sugar
3 tablespoons skim milk powder
1 egg
¾ cup water
310 gram can sweet corn
  kernels
½ teaspoon butter or margarine

Pour the corn into a strainer and allow all the juice to run off. Mix flour, sugar and milk powder in a bowl. Make a hole in the centre and stir in the egg and water gradually. Beat until all the lumps are gone. Add the corn and mix thoroughly. Heat a frypan and melt ½ teaspoon of butter or margarine in the pan to prevent the pikelets sticking. Drop tablespoonfuls of batter into the pan and cook until bottom side is golden brown. Turn the pikelet over and cook the other side. Eat hot or cold as a snack or as a meal served with bread and salad.

Banana Milkshake

2 bananas
2 cups milk
1 tablespoon wheatgerm
1 teaspoon sugar

Make sure the milk is cold. Chill all ingredients and bowl, fork and blender jug in the freezer for 10 minutes to make them really cold. Mash the banana in the bowl with a fork until it is smooth. Place the milk, banana, wheatgerm and sugar in a blender, replace lid and blend until smooth. Pour into two glasses and share. Serves two.

Porridge

1 cup rolled oats
2 cups water
Small amount sugar or brown
  sugar

Place oats and water in a saucepan and heat over a moderate heat until it begins to bubble. Do not boil. Cook for 5–10 minutes until the oats become thick. Serve in bowls with milk and a tiny sprinkling of sugar. Brown sugar with porridge is also yummy!

Fruit Ice Blocks

Use unsweetened fruit juice, or a combination of juices such as pineapple and orange, apple and orange, apple and pear, apricot and pear or passionfruit and orange. You can blend fruit such as rockmelon, watermelon or other soft fruits in a blender and freeze the pulp. Freeze fruit juice or pulp in ice cube trays or moulds and insert a tooth pick or ice cream stick so that you can hold your ice block. You may also freeze milk and fruit smoothies in this way. Sell your products at your next school fete!

Garlic Bread

1 french bread stick
2 tablespoons margarine
1 teaspoon garlic powder or
   chopped/minced garlic
1 teaspoon lemon juice

Place the margarine in a bowl. Add the lemon juice and garlic powder and stir with a wooden spoon until it is mixed and the margarine is soft. Use a bread knife to make small slices across the bread roll, but do not cut all the way through the bottom of the roll. Using a bread and butter knife spread each side of the bread slices with a thin scraping of margarine. Roll the bread in foil and heat in the oven for 15 minutes.

Chicken Pilaf

1 cup rice (uncooked)
1 cup cooked chicken
½ cup celery
½ cup frozen peas
1 chicken stock cube
3 shallots

Chop shallots and celery and chicken into small pieces. Cook rice in boiling water until tender. Drain. Heat 1 tablespoon of oil in a frypan and cook shallots and celery. Add rice, chicken and peas and cook over low heat for five minutes. Dissolve the stock cube in 1 cup of hot water and pour over the rice. Cook and stir until all the liquid is absorbed.

Home-made Yoghurt

1 litre milk
1 cup plain yoghurt
Empty jars

Pour the milk into a saucepan and heat it until tiny bubbles appear. Do not allow the milk to boil. Heat for 15 minutes. This kills any bacteria in the milk so that the lactobacillus in the yoghurt can do its job. Cool the milk until it is lukewarm – just a little warmer than your finger. Stir in the yoghurt and pour the mixture into empty jars that have been thoroughly cleaned. Close the lids tightly. Place the jars in a large boiler or saucepan and fill with hot water from the tap. Wrap the pot in a bath towel to keep it warm. Wait at least five hours then open the jars to make sure the mixture has thickened, then chill the yoghurt. Serve with chopped fruit or a little sugar or honey. Remember not to eat it all so that you can use it to start making yoghurt next time.

Lamb Shank Soup

2 lamb shank bones
2 carrots
2 potatoes
1 onion
1 cup frozen beans
½ cup rice (uncooked)
½ teaspoon pepper

Trim the fat off the bones. Place the bones and pepper (optional) in a large pot of water and bring to the boil. Do not cover the pot. Reduce the heat so that the water is barely boiling and use a spoon to skim off any fat that floats to the top. Cook on a very low heat for three hours. Add the rice and vegetables and cook for 30 minutes. Serve with garlic bread (see recipe page 138).

Pancakes

½ cup wholemeal flour
½ cup plain white flour
1 cup milk
2 eggs
Oil or margarine for cooking

Mix the eggs and milk together in a bowl. Put the flour in a separate bowl and add the milk and eggs. Mix with an egg beater or a whisk until it is a smooth batter. Add more milk if the batter is not runny. Pour the batter into a jug so that you can easily pour into the frypan. Heat a small frypan and melt a teaspoon of oil or margarine in it. Pour in a little of the batter and tilt the pan from one side to the other so that the batter covers the bottom of the pan. Pancakes cook very quickly, so you will need to turn them over with an egg lifter when the bottom is golden brown. If you are feeling confident, you can try flipping. To serve, top each pancake with a scraping of margarine, a sprinkle of sugar, lemon juice and ½ teaspoon of honey, sliced fruit or cheese, or any other healthy topping you like.

Cinnamon Apples

4 cooking apples
1 cup sultanas
1 teaspoon cinnamon
Aluminium foil

Slice the top off each apple and remove the core, leaving a hole in the apple (apple corers are available from most supermarkets). Mix sultanas with the cinnamon and fill the apple with this mixture. Wrap the apples in aluminium foil and bake in a hot oven for 30–40 minutes until tender.

Fireplace Bread Sticks

2 cups flour
Water
Green sticks, steel skewers or
   soaked wooden skewers

These bread sticks can be cooked over an open fire and are fun to make at barbecues and picnics. Mix the flour with water in a bowl to make a soft dough. Break the dough into pieces and roll into long sausages. Twist the dough around a green stick (so that the stick will not burn) or skewer and hold using an oven mitt or cloth over the fire or barbecue until cooked.

Food games for kids

What food is that?

Ask the kids to put the following foods into the right food group; for younger children, play it as a question and answer game.

Yoghurt	Peanuts	Cheese
Cornflakes	Almonds	Chicken
Fish	Chops	Bread
Cherries	Rockmelon	Custard
Eggplant	Baked beans	Persimmon
Kiwifruit	Boiled rice	Cashews
Apple juice	Spaghetti	Cauliflower
Potatoes		

FRUIT	NUTS
CEREALS	MILK AND DAIRY PRODUCTS
VEGETABLES	MEAT AND PROTEIN FOODS

Answers

Fruit
Cherries
Rockmelon
Persimmon
Kiwifruit
Apple juice

Cereals
Bread
Boiled rice
Spaghetti
Cornflakes

Vegetables
Potatoes
Eggplant
Baked beans
Cauliflower

Nuts
Cashews
Almonds

Milk and dairy products
Yoghurt
Cheese
Custard

Meat and protein foods
Chicken
Fish

Quick Quiz – 'How does it grow?'

Get your child to answer 'true' or 'false' to the following:

	TRUE	FALSE	ANSWER
1. Apples grow on trees.			True
2. Strawberries grow on a tall bush.			False
3. Carrots grow on a vine.			False
4. Honey comes from bees.			True
5. Grapes grow on big trees.			False
6. Potatoes grow under the ground.			True
7. Oysters grow in salt water.			True
8. Peas grow on bushes and vines.			True
9. Mandarins grow on trees.			True
10. Peanuts grow on tall trees.			False
11. Walnuts grow under the ground.			False
12. Onions grow on a vine.			False

9

Recipes and Healthy Food Ideas

The importance of breakfast

Breakfast means 'to break the fast' which happens while we are sleeping. Sometimes the overnight fast can be as long as fourteen hours if children go to bed early so it is really important for them to refuel in the morning. Some children will eat the same breakfast every day so don't worry if your child's breakfast seems boring or monotonous – as long as it's healthy it's OK. If your child can't manage food in the morning, a healthy drink will provide all the necessary nutrients. The drinks in this section are complete meals on their own, and most children will accept them.

For the child who does not eat breakfast, give them a healthy snack to take to school – they can 'make it up' on the school bus or at play lunch.

A sample healthy breakfast

Remember to select foods from the Five Food Groups for a balanced meal and follow the Healthy Eating Pyramid. Also, keep in mind that children don't need very large servings of food. Some won't finish all of the food placed in front of them, but a few bites or sips are better than none! Here are three examples of a nutritious breakfast:

- Orange juice, muesli (½ cup), milk
- Fruit pieces, wholemeal toast, Creamy Cottage Eggs (page 152)
- Rockmelon segment, yoghurt (½ cup), Magic Fairy Drink (1 cup) (page 154)

Healthy breakfast ideas

Here are some quick and healthy breakfast ideas:

- Bread, muffins, rolls, crumpets, pikelets, tortillas, wrap breads or toast with egg, cheese, peanut butter or any other protein topping
- Fruit and yoghurt (plain, skim or flavoured)
- Breakfast cereal or muesli with milk
- Cottage or ricotta cheese with dried fruit
- Yoghurt and nuts
- Milk drink or smoothie
- Pancakes or pikelets or crumpets
- Melon and yoghurt
- Eggs or omelette on wholemeal bread or toast
- Porridge
- Baked beans on toast
- Banana smoothie
- Melted cheese on muffin (quick and easy in the microwave)
- Muffins or scones
- Dried fruit, nuts, cereal and milk
- Muesli and yoghurt
- Rice pudding/custard and fruit
- Egg flip
- Breakfast bar with milk or juice
- Banana and milk
- Cheese stick and juice.

Breakfast cereals and fruit juices

These foods are not essential for a healthy breakfast, but they can be very handy for busy mornings. Most ready-to-eat cereals and juices have sugar added, so check labels to see whether they show sugar, sucrose, glucose, maltose, honey or molasses. Choose cereal and juices with no added sugar or salt or make your own from the recipes following in this section. A breakfast of fruit or fruit juice, cereal or bread and milk will provide all the nutrients a child needs until lunchtime.

Toast Toppers

Toast can be a nutritious meal provided the topping is healthy. However, salty spreads and jams provide too much salt and sugar, and few nutrients, so it's good to keep an eye on how often you use these.

White or wholemeal bread is nutritious and can be toasted and topped with any of the following:

- Scrambled, boiled or poached eggs
- Grilled cheese and tomato
- Pizza topping – grated cheese, tomato, ham and onion
- Baked beans (high in protein) – with chopped ham or cheese
- Peanut butter and sultanas
- Mashed banana, chopped nuts and coconut
- Ricotta cheese, peanut butter and sultanas
- Chicken, chopped walnuts and mayonnaise
- Creamed corn and melted cheese
- Tuna, chopped apple and mayonnaise
- Cream cheese
- Meat from the night before (e.g. sliced lamb) and tomato
- Cottage cheese, pineapple and dates.

Fibre Rich Muesli

1 cup rolled oats
1 tablespoon unprocessed bran
2 tablespoons bran breakfast cereal
1 tablespoon wheatgerm
½ tablespoon brown sugar
2 tablespoons skim milk powder
1 tablespoon coconut

Mix all ingredients. Store in airtight container. Serve 2 tablespoons with hot or cold milk. Cook over low heat with milk for a good winter breakfast.

Fruity Muesli

To basic recipe (Fibre Rich Muesli, page 145) add:

1 tablespoon sultanas,
  chopped dates, raisins or
  chopped figs
1 tablespoon dried apricots
  (chopped)
1 tablespoon dried apple
  (chopped)

Nutty Muesli

To basic recipe add:

2 tablespoons chopped nuts
  (very finely chopped, without
  husks, for small children)
1 tablespoon toasted sesame
  seeds

Make up Fruity Muesli. Dry roast chopped nuts and seeds in a non-stick pan. Mix all ingredients. Serve Muesli with:
- 2–3 tablespoons yoghurt
- Sliced banana and milk
- Grated apple, cinnamon and milk
- ½ rockmelon with milk or yoghurt
- Mixed with stewed fruit and fruit juice
- Cooked with milk in winter.

Toasted Muesli

1 cup rolled oats
2 tablespoons wheatgerm
1 tablespoon unprocessed bran
2 tablespoons bran breakfast
cereal
1 tablespoon coconut
1 tablespoon polyunsaturated
oil
2 tablespoons chopped nuts
3 tablespoons chopped dried
fruit

Combine all ingredients, except the dried fruit, in baking dish with oil and 1 tablespoon water. Bake in oven (150°C) stirring regularly for 1 hour. Add dried fruit. Store in airtight container.

Pancakes

½ cup white self-raising flour
½ cup wholemeal self-raising
flour
1 egg
1 cup milk
2 tablespoons polyunsaturated
oil

Lightly beat egg and mix with flour, oil and milk. Lightly grease pan and pour 2–3 tablespoons of mixture into pan. Turn pancakes as soon as they 'bubble'. Cook until lightly browned. Serve lightly buttered or with fruit, lemon juice or small teaspoon of honey.

Cheesy Pancakes

Make as for Pancakes and add 2 tablespoons of grated cheese to mixture before cooking. Melt grated cheese on top.

Sultana Pancakes

Make as for Pancakes and add 2 tablespoons of sultanas to mixture. Serve lightly buttered or with sliced banana and cinnamon, or grated apple, cinnamon and yoghurt.

Bubble-and-squeak Pancakes

Make Pancakes and top with bubble-and-squeak. Make bubble-and-squeak with leftover vegetables from the day before heated up with 1 teaspoon butter or margarine. Mashed potato, pumpkin, carrots, beans, cabbage and zucchini are perfect.

Melt grated cheese on top and serve with grilled tomato halves (for Vitamin C). Bubble-and-squeak was invented long before Snap, Crackle and Pop!

Strawberry Ricotta Pancakes

½ cup wholemeal flour
1 cup ricotta cheese
1 tablespoon polyunsaturated
  oil
½ cup white flour
1 tablespoon milk powder
½ cup water
Sliced strawberries

Beat egg and blend with ricotta cheese and oil. Add flour, milk powder and water. Pour 2–3 tablespoons into lightly greased pan and cook until bottom is lightly browned, turn and brown other side. Serve with layers of sliced strawberries and ricotta cheese.

This may also be served as a dessert.

Pancake serving ideas

- Make a stock of pancakes the day before and separate with greaseproof paper. Reheat in microwave, pan or oven. They can also be frozen.
- Serve with fruit and yoghurt.
- Vegetable Pancakes – make up Pancake mixture and add 1 cup of grated potato, carrot or zucchini.
- See Toast Toppers (page 145) for savoury pancake ideas.

Fresh Fruit Salad

1 small rockmelon
1 red apple
1 banana
1 kiwi fruit
Lemon juice

Slice rockmelon in half, or in quarters if large. Remove seeds. Using a melon baller, make small balls from the centre of each melon. Dice apple (do not peel) and slice banana. Coat in lemon juice to prevent browning. Peel kiwi fruit and slice thinly. Arrange apple, banana, kiwi fruit and melon balls in rockmelon segment and serve topped with yoghurt, cottage cheese or nuts.

Hot Apple Oats

3½ cups apple juice
  (unsweetened)
½ cup rolled oats
½ teaspoon cinnamon

Heat apple juice in a saucepan until gently boiling. Sprinkle in the oats and cinnamon. Simmer and stir constantly until mixture thickens. Serve with banana slices or yoghurt.

Citrus Cup

1 orange
6 strawberries
½ cup grapes

Slice orange in half and run knife around the inside edge of each orange half and remove flesh. Slice the strawberries and orange segments. Combine with the grapes. Serve in the orange cup with yoghurt or muesli. This makes an excellent dessert or snack. For adults, it can be topped with a tablespoon of Grand Marnier for special occasions.

Fruit Compote

1 cup mixed dried fruit
½ cup dried apricots
  (chopped)
1 cup apple juice
  (unsweetened)

Soak fruit in apple juice overnight. Simmer gently for 5 minutes. Serve hot or cold with yoghurt, porridge or cereal.

Breakfast Damper

2 cups wholemeal flour (plain)
2 cups plain white flour
2 teaspoons sugar
1 teaspoon bicarbonate of
  soda
1½ cups milk

Sift flour, sugar and bicarbonate into a bowl. Add bran. Add milk and mix to a soft dough. Place dough on a floured surface and shape into a loaf. Cut cross on top of loaf. Bake on a lightly greased tray in a moderate oven (190°C) for 1 hour. Serve hot with butter or margarine.

Variation: To make cheese damper add 1 cup of grated tasty cheese when adding the milk.

Cinnamon Rice

3 cups cooked rice (white, gold
  or brown)
2 cups milk
1 egg (beaten)
½ tablespoon honey
½ cup raisins, sultanas or
  dates
1 teaspoon cinnamon

Combine all ingredients in a saucepan and mix well. Cook over low heat, stirring often, until mixture thickens.

Variation: Add 2 tablespoons unprocessed bran when cooking for extra fibre, if desired.

Wheaty Crunch

1 cup burghul (cracked wheat)
2 teaspoons wheatgerrn
2 teaspoons honey
1½ cups milk
¼ teaspoon cinnamon

Place burghul in saucepan, cover with water and stand overnight. In the morning drain off excess water and add remaining ingredients except cinnamon. Simmer over low heat for six minutes. Serve with cinnamon.

Variation: Try topped with yoghurt and mashed banana, sultanas, chopped dried fruit or grated apple. To make a high protein cereal for milk haters soak the burghul in milk instead of water.

Muffin Munch

4 wholemeal muffins
3 tablespoons peanut butter
1 cup ricotta cheese
2 teaspoons honey
2 tablespoons chopped walnuts
2 tablespoons dried apricots

Slice muffins and toast each half. Spread with peanut butter. Mix ricotta cheese, chopped nuts, honey and fruit and pile on to muffins. Warm under a griller for 3 minutes.

Creamy Cottage Eggs

½ cup cottage cheese
2 eggs
¼ cup chopped tomato
¼ cup chopped ham
1 teaspoon margarine or butter
wholemeal toast
chopped parsley

Mix cottage cheese and eggs in blender *or* push cheese through a sieve and then mix with eggs. Add tomato and ham. Melt 1 teaspoon of margarine or butter in a saucepan and add mixture. Stir egg mixture gently with wooden spoon until it thickens. Serve on wholemeal toast with chopped parsley (serves two).

Wholemeal Toast Fingers

1 egg
4 slices wholemeal bread
½ cup milk

Mix egg and milk in bowl with a fork. Dip each slice of bread into egg mixture. Dry fry in non-stick or lightly oiled pan until golden brown. Slice into fingers.

Variations: These high protein toast fingers are a meal on their own or can be served with eggs, baked beans, spaghetti, or other healthy toppings (see Toast Toppers, page 145).

Salt-free Peanut Butter

2 cups peanuts (unsalted)
1½ tablespoons
   polyunsaturated oil

Mix peanuts and oil in blender. Blend until the paste is smooth. Add a few more drops of oil if too thick. Store in jar with a screw lid. Serve on wholemeal toast with cheese for a high protein breakfast. (Peanut butter with no added salt is also available in most supermarkets.)

Home-made Yoghurt

1 litre milk
1 cup powdered milk
4 tablespoons plain yoghurt

Mix milk and milk powder in saucepan. Simmer milk – do not boil. Pour into glass dish or large glass jar. Cool to lukewarm and mix in yoghurt. Cover bowl with plastic or place lid on jar. Wrap in blanket and let stand in warm spot overnight.

Spiced Apple Yoghurt

1 crisp Granny Smith apple
1 teaspoon lemon juice
1 carton (200 g) natural yoghurt
¼ teaspoon cinnamon

Place apple in freezer for 30 minutes. Slice apple into chunks and grate. Toss in lemon juice. Combine all ingredients and serve.

Strawberry Frozen Yoghurt

1 tablespoon gelatine
¼ cup cold water
2 cups natural yoghurt
2 cups mashed strawberries

Mix gelatine in water and wait five minutes. Heat over low heat to dissolve. Cool. Stir in yoghurt and refrigerate in shallow dish until thickened. Add strawberries and whip up until light and airy – use a blender or egg beater. Freeze in the tray or in patty papers.

Banana Smoothie

300 mls milk
100 g yoghurt
1 banana
1 cup ice cubes

Place all ingredients in a blender and whip until frothy, or beat by hand without ice. Save the leftover drink in a jug for after school or freeze for the lunch box.

Variations: Try ½ cup apricots. pears, passionfruit pulp or strawberries.

Magic Fairy Drink

300 mls milk
1 egg
1 teaspoon sugar
½ teaspoon vanilla essence
nutmeg

This was invented by my dear mother in 1959! Beat ingredients with a blender or hand egg beater. Sprinkle with nutmeg. This drink is magic because it can be served as a whole meal for children and is especially suitable for children recovering from an illness.

Pineapple Punch

1 cup crushed pineapple
  (unsweetened)
200 g yoghurt
4 ice cubes
1 teaspoon coconut

Blend all ingredients in blender until frothy. Add juice or milk if the mixture is too thick. Sprinkle with coconut and serve with a straw. To make without a blender use pineapple juice and yoghurt without ice and use a hand egg beater.

Variation: Try pineapple juice or apple juice instead of crushed pineapple.

Luscious Lunches, Picnics and Barbecues

The key to a nutritious and delicious lunch can be summed up in two words: light and fresh. The ingredients for these lunch-time recipes are all based on light and fresh foods, combined to make appetising meals which won't be too heavy in the middle of the day. For more ideas for quick, healthy lunches, see chapter 6 'Food on the run – 101 healthy school lunches' (page 99).

Picnics and barbecues are a nice way for families to enjoy time together and you can also ensure these occasions are healthy ones for children by serving nutritious food and drinks. Choose lean meat and chicken, wholemeal buns and sandwiches with plenty of salad, or a special picnic dish from some of the recipes in this section. Serve hot or cold meat kebabs, quiche or fruit on skewers with an unsweetened drink or milk (these can be frozen beforehand) and provide a large bowl of salad or vegetable sticks that can be eaten as finger foods.

You can cook meat, fish, poultry and kebabs on the barbecue, and even damper can be wrapped in foil and cooked under hot coals. Alternatively, dough can be wrapped around green sticks and toasted over the barbecue. Potatoes, bananas, fish and corn cobs can be wrapped in aluminium foil and cooked in the hot coals of the barbecue, too.

Spreads

Date 'n' Walnut Spread

100 g dates, pitted
¼ cup water
1 tablespoon lemon juice
½ cup chopped walnuts

Combine dates, water and lemon juice in a saucepan. Cover and cook over low heat until dates are tender. Mash to make smooth. Mix in walnuts and spread on sandwiches. Store in refrigerator.

Corn and Ham Spread

½ cup creamed corn
1 cup ricotta cheese
1 slice ham (chopped)

Mix corn, ricotta cheese and chopped ham and spread on sandwiches or serve in lettuce cups with bread.

Variation: Substitute sultanas for ham.

Hummus

6 cups cooked chick peas
½ cup tahini (sesame seed paste)
1 cup lemon juice
4 cups water
1 clove garlic, chopped
3 teaspoons ground cumin
2 teaspoons ground coriander
pinch cayenne pepper

Blend chick peas and tahini, lemon juice, water and garlic until very smooth. Mix in spices. Chill overnight before serving to allow flavours to blend and develop. Use as a sandwich filling, or spread on Lebanese flat bread or crusty bread and serve with salad, chicken or meat on sandwiches. Hummus is also very handy as a dip.

Rolls, picnic and lunchbox ideas

Falafel Roll

½ cup finely chopped onions
2 teaspoons chopped garlic
¼ teaspoon ground coriander
¼ teaspoon ground cumin
olive oil
1 cup soaked burghul (cracked wheat)
1½ cups cooked and mashed chick peas
1 egg
½ cup milk

Lightly fry onion, garlic, coriander and cumin in ½ tablespoon olive oil. Add cracked wheat and mashed chick peas and mix well. Leave 1–2 hours in a covered bowl. Beat egg lightly and mix with milk. Roll chick pea mixture into balls, flatten and dip in egg and milk, and then wholemeal flour. Lightly fry in

1 cup wholemeal flour
hummus (see recipe page 156),
tabbouli (see recipe page 166)
Lebanese bread

pan with 2 tablespoons of
olive oil until golden. Serve
with hummus and tabbouli on
Lebanese bread, rolled up.

Lebanese Rolls

6 Lebanese pita breads
1 cup hummus (see recipe
  page 156)
1 cup tabbouli (see recipe
  page 166)
2 tomatoes, chopped
1 cup shredded lettuce
3 cups cooked meat or chicken
Tomato or chilli sauce

Spread whole pita bread with
hummus, then add tabbouli,
tomato, lettuce and meat. Add
a dash of tomato or chilli
sauce, if desired. Roll up
tightly into a roll and wrap
with a serviette for holding.
Roll in plastic wrap if you are
packing for a picnic or
barbecue. Serves 6.

Variation: Can also be served as open sandwiches.

Space Shuttle

2 slices bread
2 cheese sticks
2 carrot sticks (the same
  length as cheese sticks)

Remove crusts from bread.
Place carrot stick and cheese
stick on one slice of bread.
Roll up. Secure with toothpicks
and wrap in cling wrap. Serve
two per child with one piece of
fruit or fruit juice.

Robert's Roll

2 slices bread
2 tablespoons peanut butter
¼ cup grated carrot
lemon juice

Remove crusts from bread.
Combine peanut butter, carrot
and lemon juice and spread
evenly on bread. Roll up,
wrap in plastic and chill in
freezer until firm. Cut into
1 centimetre slices.

Hidden Treasure Roll

1 long bread roll
½ cup soft cream cheese
1 boiled egg (chopped)
1 tablespoon celery (chopped)
1 tablespoon carrot (grated)

Slice the end off the bread roll and remove most of the bread with a fork, leaving a hollow for the filling. Combine all other ingredients in a bowl and mix well. Spoon mixture into the roll and pack down. Replace end slice and wrap with cling wrap. Chill until filling is firm. Cut into 3 centimetre slices and press slices back into roll shape. Roll in cling wrap if it's for a school lunch or picnic.

Banana-in-a-Blanket

1 banana (not too ripe)
1 slice ham or chicken meat
lemon juice

Slice banana lengthways and dip in lemon juice to prevent browning. Place banana slices on ham and roll up diagonally. Use one or two toothpicks to secure. Serve in a chilled lunch-box with salad, bread or fruit. These may be frozen overnight.

Variation: Try using cheese sticks or apple wedges instead of the banana.

Spring Rolls

Spring roll wrappers (1 packet –
  you can buy these frozen at
  supermarkets)
Chopped, lean ham (1 cup)
Creamed corn (1 can, 125 g)
Celery (1 stick, chopped)

Combine the ham, creamed corn and celery in a bowl. Spread thawed wrappers on benchtop and spoon 1 tablespoon of ham mixture on corner of each. Brush edges of wrapper with water to make it sticky. Fold corner of wrapper over then roll up tightly and press to seal. Brush baking tray with a little margarine or oil. Bake rolls at 200°C for 15–20 minutes until golden brown. Makes 6.

Corn Fritters

⅔ cup wholemeal self-raising
  flour
1 egg (separated)
½ cup milk
1 cup corn kernels (well
  drained)

In a bowl, beat egg yolk and milk. Add corn kernels. Add flour to corn mixture and mix thoroughly. Beat egg white until stiff and fold through corn mixture. Drop ½ tablespoon of mixture into lightly oiled non-stick pan and cook until underside is golden brown. Turn with egg lifter and cook other side. Serve with Fruit Slaw (see recipe page 168) and a grilled chicken drumstick.

Corn and Liver Kebabs

350 g lambs liver (cubed)
50 g button mushrooms
1 red capsicum (cut into 2 cm
    squares)
16 mini corn cobs
1 tablespoon oil

Heat oil in frying pan and add liver. Cook until lightly browned. Add capsicum, mushrooms and lightly cook for two minutes. Thread liver, capsicum, mushrooms and corn cobs alternately on skewers and grill for ten minutes. Serve with salads and sauces (see recipes following on page 165 etc.).

Variations: For Tropical Kebabs make Corn and Liver Kebabs as above and add cubes of fresh pineapple, banana or mango. To make Fruity Chicken Kebabs use chicken cubes instead of liver, and thread on skewers with apple and celery, corn, mushrooms and capsicum.

Sausages-on-a-Stick

600 g lean minced meat
2 tablespoons wheatgerm
1 medium onion (frozen and
    then grated)
½ cup parsley (chopped)

Place mince, wheatgerm, grated onion and choppped parsley in a bowl and mix thoroughly. Divide mixture into 12 pieces and roll into small sausage shapes. Skewer each sausage with bamboo or metal skewers and cook under grill or in vertical grill. Serve 1–2 sausages per child hot or cold with salad, and a choice of sauces (see recipes following). Children may dip sausage sticks into individual sauce bowls.

Tomato Sauce

1 medium onion (finely
  chopped)
1 tablespoon oil
1 × 425 g tin whole tomatoes
  (no added salt)
2 tablespoons tomato paste
  (no added salt)
2 drops tabasco sauce
  (optional)
2 cups water

Place onion and oil in saucepan and simmer until soft. Chop tomatoes and add to saucepan with liquid from tin, and water. Add tomato paste and tabasco sauce. Bring to boil and simmer until sauce is desired consistency. Serve in individual bowls for each child to dip sausage sticks into.

Mango Chutney

3 large, ripe mangoes
1 small onion
¼ teaspoon chilli powder
⅓ cup raisins
⅓ cup currants
1 tablespoon chopped mixed
  peel
1 teaspoon grated green ginger
1 clove garlic, crushed
1 teaspoon Allspice
1 tablespoon brown sugar
⅓ cup brown vinegar
⅓ cup lemon juice

Peel and chop mangoes (removing seeds). Chop onion and place in large saucepan with chopped mango and all other ingredients. Allow to stand overnight. Bring to boil and gently simmer for 30 minutes until thickened. Sterilise glass jars and lids in boiling water and pour hot chutney into jars. Seal and store in refrigerator. Use for packed lunches or served hot or cold with Sausages-on-a-stick.

Peanut Sauce

4 tablespoons peanut butter
(salt free)
1 large onion (finely chopped)
¼ teaspoon chilli powder
½ cup water
1 teaspoon brown sugar
1 teaspoon soy sauce
1½ tablespoons lemon juice

Mix peanut butter, onion and chilli powder thoroughly in saucepan or blender. Heat in saucepan until onion is soft, stirring constantly. Add water and sugar and cook for a further three minutes. Add soy and lemon juice and mix thoroughly. Serve hot or cold.

Tuna Egg Surprise

½ cup tuna (drained)
1 tablespoon lemon juice
1 tablespoon mayonnaise
6 hard boiled eggs
½ teaspoon black pepper
paprika
shredded lettuce

Blend tuna with the lemon juice, mayonnaise and pepper. Cut 2.5 cm from the large end of each egg and carefully remove the yolks. Combine the yolks with the tuna mixture and fill each egg. Replace the cut off section of egg. Stand the eggs upright in a bed of lettuce and sprinkle with paprika for colour. Wrap eggs in plastic for lunchboxes or picnic.

Tuna Rice

1 cup brown rice
½ cup frozen peas
½ cup corn kernels
½ cup chopped red capsicum
¼ cup chopped celery
½ cup Coleslaw Dressing
(see page 167)

Cook rice in boiling water until soft (do not add salt). Cook peas in boiling water until tender, but not soft. Drain rice and mix with peas and other ingredients. Serve at home or in lunch box with a boiled egg or chicken drumstick.

Variations: For Sultana Rice add ½ cup sultanas. For Tuna Rice add ½ cup flaked, drained tuna (preferably packed in water, no added salt). For Curried Rice mix 1 teaspoon mild curry powder and 1 teaspoon honey with coleslaw dressing and add to other ingredients. Serve Curried Rice with banana and apple slices dipped in lemon juice.

Baby Salmon Quiches

Potato Pastry
1 cup white flour
½ cup wholemeal flour
½ cup skim milk powder
1 egg
2 tablespoons water
1½ cups cold mashed potato

Salmon Filling
1 small onion (finely chopped)
1 cup salmon (drained)
½ teaspoon butter or
   margarine
2 eggs
2 cups milk
1 cup plain skim yoghurt
1 cup cheddar cheese (grated)

To make pastry, combine potato, egg and water in a bowl and mix well. Add remaining ingredients and allow to stand while filling is prepared.

Place onion and salmon in saucepan with ½ teaspoon butter or margarine and heat until onion is soft.

Roll pastry out on floured board and cut into rounds. Line lightly greased patty tins with pastry.

Place 1 tablespoon salmon mixture into each quiche case. Combine eggs, milk, yoghurt and beat until smooth. Pour over salmon filling. Sprinkle with grated cheese. Bake in moderate oven for 20 minutes or until filling is firm and cheese is golden brown. Serve 1–2 quiches hot or cold to each child with salad or vegetables.

Variations: You can vary quiche fillings according to children's likes and dislikes. Some children like plain cheddar cheese fillings while others like more tasty ham, mushroom and onion varieties.

Perfect Pears

1 firm pear
2 tablespoons cottage or
   ricotta cheese
1 tablespoon sultanas

Halve the pear and scoop out core to make a small hollow. Combine cheese and sultanas. Fill each pear half with cheese mixture. Press pear halves together and wrap in cling wrap.

Pineapple Celery Boats

celery sticks
cottage or ricotta cheese
crushed pineapple
   (unsweetened)
paprika

Cut celery into 10 cm sticks. Drain pineapple and mix through cheese. Let stand and then drain excess liquid from cheese mixture. Fill celery sticks with cheese mixture and sprinkle with paprika to add colour. Serve in lunch-box with salad, bread or fruit.

Salads for all occasions

Bean Sprout Salad

1 cup bean sprouts
1½ cups boiled rice
1 cup chopped celery
2 tablespoons capsicum
1 cup grated carrot
2 cups diced chicken
½ cup slivered almonds
lemon juice
French dressing (see recipe
   following)

Cook bean sprouts in hot water for 2–3 minutes until just crisp and tender. Dry and allow to cool. Mix bean sprouts, rice, celery, capsicum, carrots, chicken and almonds. Season with pepper, lemon juice and French dressing. Chill, drain excess liquid and serve. For lunch boxes, serve 1–2 tablespoons on a bed of crisp lettuce.

French Dressing

1 cup wine vinegar
2 tablespoons olive oil
1 tablespoon lemon juice
2 tablespoons chopped parsley
¼ teaspoon ground pepper

Combine all ingredients in a glass jar or bottle. Replace lid and shake vigorously. Store in refrigerator. Can be used for two weeks.

Waldorf Salad

1 red apple
2 sticks celery (chopped)
1 tablespoon walnuts
   (chopped)
2 tablespoons low fat yoghurt
   (plain)
lemon juice of half a lemon

Combine the diced apple, celery and walnuts in a bowl and mix with the juice of half a lemon to prevent the apple browning. Mix thoroughly with yoghurt and chill. Serve in lettuce cups with baby potatoes, boiled egg halves or cold meat slices.

Crunchy Pasta Salad

100 g wholemeal pasta
1 tablespoon polyunsaturated
   vegetable oil
½ tablespoon vinegar
3 granny smith apples (sliced)
1 tablespoon lemon juice
4 stalks chopped celery
2 tablespoons raisins
2 tablespoons chopped dates
   (pitted)
2 tablespoons chopped walnuts
1 tablespoon plain low fat
   yoghurt
1 tablespoon unsweetened
   orange juice
1 tablespoon Thousand Island
   dressing
ground black pepper

Cook pasta in boiling water until tender. Drain. Toss in oil and vinegar while still hot. Toss apples in lemon juice and mix with raisins, dates and walnuts. Add to pasta and mix well. Mix yoghurt, dressing and orange juice with ground black pepper and pour over salad. Toss and serve in lunch box on bed of crisp lettuce with cold meat, chicken, tuna or cheese wedges and wholemeal bread.

Tabbouli

½ cup cracked wheat
1 cup parsley (finely chopped)
½ cup chopped mint
½ cup chopped shallots
2 chopped tomatoes

Dressing
¼ cup olive oil
¼ cup lemon juice
1 teaspoon honey

Soak cracked wheat in water for at least 30 minutes. Drain and combine with parsley, mint and shallots. To make dressing, combine oil, lemon juice and honey in jar, shake well, and add to parsley. Mix well. Stir through tomato. Serve as a salad or sandwich filling.

Sweet Carrot Salad

1 apple
½ tablespoon lemon juice
orange juice
1 teaspoon honey
1 cup grated carrot
¼ cup chopped celery
½ cup sultanas
¼ cup chopped walnuts

Grate apple and mix with the lemon juice to prevent browning. Combine orange juice and honey and mix well. Mix carrot, apple, celery, sultanas with juice mixture. Drain excess juice and mix through walnuts. Serve with cheese or Celery Boats (page 256).

Coleslaw

2 cups finely shredded cabbage
1 cup grated carrot
½ cup celery, finely diced
½ cup onion, finely chopped
½ cup French Dressing (see
    page 165) or Coleslaw
    Dressing (following)

Combine all ingredients and toss with dressing. Drain well and serve coleslaw as a salad in lunch box, or on sandwiches, rolls and hamburgers.

Coleslaw Dressing

1 cup plain low fat yoghurt
2 tablespoons mayonnaise
½ cup French Dressing
    (page 165)
½ cup dry mustard
¼ teaspoon cayenne pepper
¼ teaspoon ground pepper

Place all ingredients in clean glass jar or bottle, replace lid and shake vigorously. Store in refrigerator and discard at the use by date on the container of the yoghurt used in the recipe.

Fruit Slaw

1 red apple, chopped
1 tablespoon lemon juice
2 cups finely shredded cabbage
1 cup grated carrot
1 cup sultanas
¼ cup finely chopped celery
¼ cup finely chopped onion
½ cup crushed pineapple, well
  drained

Dressing

1 cup plain low fat yoghurt
1 tablespoon mayonnaise (low
  fat)
2 tablespoons polyunsaturated
  oil
2 tablespoons white vinegar
2 tablespoons lemon juice
½ teaspoon dry mustard
1 teaspoon brown sugar
¼ teaspoon ground pepper

Combine ingredients for dressing in a glass jar and shake vigorously. Chill in refrigerator for 1–2 hours, or overnight. To make Fruit Slaw, toss apple in lemon juice and mix with all the other ingredients and chilled dressing. Chill and toss again before serving.

Pineapple Rice Salad

½ cup brown rice
2 tablespoons pineapple
  pieces (unsweetened)
1 tablespoon low fat mayonnaise
2 tablespoons sultanas
½ cup chopped celery
1 tablespoon grated carrot

Cook rice in boiling water until soft. Drain and cool. Chop pineapple into small pieces and drain, then mix with other ingredients. Chill thoroughly.

Soups

A hearty soup with croutons, toast, bread or hot grilled sand-wiches can be served as a complete meal for children. Soups are often served before meals as an entree or as an after school snack, but can be very filling in this way and may dampen the child's appetite if more than one small serve (about 1 cup) is eaten. Soups can be a good way of providing milk for a child who does not like it, so cream soups should always be made with milk or yoghurt rather than cream. Send hot soup to school in a thermos flask or serve at home in a mug or bowl with crunchy croutons (see page 171), hot jaffles or toasted sandwiches.

Quick Tomato Soup

1 medium onion
1 teaspoon butter or margarine
1½ cups milk
1½ cups water
½ cup tomato puree (no added salt)
1 teaspoon sugar
¼ teaspoon dried mixed herbs
1 tablespoon plain flour
¼ teaspoon pepper, ground

Place peeled onion in freezer for 15 minutes to allow chopping without tears. Finely chop onion. Melt butter or margarine in large saucepan and gently cook until soft but not brown. Remove from heat and gradually stir in the milk and water, beating until smooth. Stir in the tomato puree, sugar and herbs.

Season with pepper. Simmer for 10 minutes. Garnish with chopped parsley and Crunchy Croutons (page 171).

Pumpkin Soup

½ cup split peas
2 onions (sliced)
1 tablespoon butter or margarine
1½ cups chopped pumpkin
¼ teaspoon black pepper
2 cabbage leaves (finely chopped)
¼ teaspoon dried thyme

Soak dried peas in water overnight. Lightly cook onions in butter or margarine, add pumpkin and all other ingredients. Cover with water, replace lid and simmer for an hour. Mash vegetables in soup and serve with hot bread and a dollop of yoghurt.

Chunky Chicken and Corn Soup

2 cups chicken stock (see
    page 173)
2 medium potatoes (diced)
½ cup diced carrot
1 small onion (chopped)
½ teaspoon ground black
    pepper
150 g cooked chicken (chopped)
220 g creamed corn

Place cold stock, diced potato, carrot, onion and pepper in a saucepan, bring to boil and simmer for 20 minutes. Add chicken and creamed corn and simmer for ten minutes. Serve with wholemeal toast triangles or crusty bread rolls.

Minestrone

100 g haricot beans
1 small onion
1 medium potato
1 large tomato
2 sticks celery
3 shallots
1 teaspoon olive oil
½ clove garlic
3 cups Chicken Stock
    or Vegetable Stock
    (see opposite)
1 tablespoon tomato paste
    (salt-free)
¼ teaspoon dried basil
1 teaspoon chopped parsley
1 cup small macaroni (try to
    use alphabet shapes)

Soak haricot beans in cold water overnight. Drain and gently boil in water for one hour or until tender. Drain. Peel and chop tomatoes and chop other vegetables. Heat oil in large saucepan and saute onion, shallots, parsley and basil. Add tomato paste, other vegetables and stock. Bring to the boil and simmer for 30 minutes or until vegetables are soft. Add beans and macaroni and simmer until macaroni is tender. Season with pepper and serve with chopped parsley to garnish. Serve with Crunchy Croutons (see page 171) or Cheesy Dippers (see page 172).

Chicken Stock

2 litres water
Chicken bones or carcass, or
   whole uncooked chicken
½ cup chopped celery
2 bay leaves
½ cup chopped carrot

Place all ingredients in large saucepan. Bring to boil and simmer for one hour. Remove carcass or bones and discard, or remove cooked chicken for use in other recipes. Strain stock. Allow to cool in refrigerator and skim fat from top. Freeze in litre containers for future use.

Vegetable Stock

2 onions (sliced)
2 carrots (sliced)
6 stalks celery (sliced)
1 turnip (sliced)
1 bay leaf
1 teaspoon mixed herbs
3 black peppercorns
2 litres water

Boil vegetables and water in large saucepan, skimming off vegetable froth as it rises. Continue for about 20 minutes. Add herbs and peppercorns and bay leaf and cover and simmer for two hours until the liquid has reduced by about half. Strain thoroughly and discard vegetables. Allow to cool and use for soups, sauces and other recipes. Freeze for future use in 1 litre containers.

Crunchy Croutons

6 slices bread
1 tablespoon polyunsaturated
   oil

Remove crusts from bread. Dice bread into one centimetre cubes. Heat large non-stick pan and lightly grease with oil. Toss bread cubes until crisp and golden. Let children dip croutons into soup or serve on top of hot soup.

Cheesy Dippers

1 French bread stick ½ cup grated cheese ½ teaspoon paprika	Slice bread stick in half lengthways then in half lengthways again and section into 10 cm sticks. Sprinkle each individual stick with cheese and then paprika. Grill until cheese is golden. Serve hot with soup.

Pizzas and Hamburgers

Children particularly like these foods because they are colourful, novel and fun; and by making them in your own home you can be assured that there has not been too much salt or fat added during cooking. Nutritionally these foods make a complete meal by themselves because they combine foods from each of the Five Food Groups and provide children with a variety of essential nutrients. Serving these foods with salad, vegetables, fruit juice or a milk drink will make it an even more nutritious meal which is both easy and inexpensive for parents to prepare.

If you buy these foods from take-away outlets be certain to ask for lots of salad, no butter on the buns, and no added salt.

Pizza Toppings

Prepare pizza base (see opposite) or use a whole slice of Lebanese pita bread. Spread with tomato paste or tomato sauce (try salt reduced) and sprinkle with grated cheese. Try ricotta or cheese with no added salt topped with any of the following and cook in hot oven for 15–20 minutes. If you are using pita bread, heat pizza under griller.

- Tomato Topping (see opposite).
- Tomato (sliced), onion rings and cheese.
- Capsicum (chopped), sliced mushrooms, chopped celery and cheese.
- Ham (chopped), tomato (chopped) and onion rings.

- Ham and crushed pineapple (unsweetened and well drained).
- Tuna and crushed pineapple (unsweetened and well drained).
- Ricotta cheese, chopped tomato, capsicum and onion rings.

Salty toppings such as olives, anchovies, parmesan cheese, bacon, gherkin, salami, cabanossi, and salted tomato paste are very high in sodium and should be used only occasionally, and then only in very small amounts. Using reduced-salt cheese and salt-free tomato paste is an excellent way to reduce the amount of sodium in pizza.

Pizza Dough

½ cup white self-raising flour
½ cup wholemeal self-raising
  flour
½ cup milk

Sift flour into bowl and add any bran remaining in sieve. Mix to a stiff dough with the milk. Roll out onto a lightly floured surface and shape into 20 cm (8 inch) round. Place on lightly oiled baking tray. Heat oven to 300°C.

Tomato Topping

½ cup onion rings
1 cup tomatoes (chopped)
2 tablespoons tomato paste
  (salt-free) or tomato sauce
½ teaspoon ground pepper
1 cup grated mozzarella cheese

Dry fry onion rings in saucepan until tender but not soft. Add tomatoes, tomato paste and pepper and simmer until thick. Spread on pizza dough and top with mozzarella cheese. Bake for 15–20 minutes until golden brown. Divide into four and serve each segment to child with salad and fruit juice or milk drink.

Mini Pizzas

1 slice pocket pita bread
tomato paste (no added-salt)
pizza topping

Halve pocket bread and spread each slice with tomato paste. Sprinkle with cheese. Top with selected pizza topping and place under griller. Serve one mini pizza per child with salad, fruit or juice. You can also wrap mini pizzas and freeze for a quick meal.

Home-Made Hamburgers

500 g lean minced beef
1 egg (lightly beaten)
1 onion (finely chopped)
1 carrot (grated)
1 tablespoon ground pepper
Hamburger buns
Lettuce, shredded
Tomato, sliced

Combine all ingredients and mix well. Scoop each patty with an ice cream scoop or a tablespoon and roll into balls on a floured board. Flatten into patties. Dry grill or fry in a non-stick or lightly oiled pan, or cook on the barbecue. Slice each hamburger bun in half and toast the inside of each bun under the griller. Top bun with hamburger patty, then shredded lettuce and sliced tomato. (Do not salt or butter the bun.) You can make a stack of patties for your freezer.

Variations:
- Tomato sauce topping (see page 173).
- Onion burger – top hamburger with dry-fried onion rings.
- Tropical burger – top hamburger with grilled pineapple, banana or coleslaw (see page 167). Slice one ring of unsweetened pineapple through middle to reduce thickness and grill.
- Cheese burger – place 1 slice sandwich cheese on hamburger and melt under griller.
- Egg burger – fry an egg in a lightly oiled pan before cooking the patties; keep warm under griller and top hamburger with egg.

Tacos

The taco originated in Mexico and consists of a taco shell filled with meat, beans, sauce and a topping such as lettuce, cheese, tomatoes and avocado. Taco shells can be found in supermarkets, but are often high in fat and salt so it is best to limit these to only one or two per child served with lots of salad. You may substitute pita bread for taco shells. Heat bread in the oven until crisp and fill with the taco mix. Also, choose soft flour or corn tortilla wraps from the bread section of the supermarket.

Mexican Tacos (using tortillas)

500 g lean minced beef
1 onion (finely chopped)
1 clove garlic (crushed and chopped)
¼ teaspoon chilli powder (optional)
1 teaspoon ground cumin
2 tablespoons tomato paste (no added-salt)
½ cup water
½ teaspoon ground black pepper
Soft flour or corn tortillas

Brown mince in heavy based frypan and break up lumps with a fork. Add onion and garlic and stir constantly until soft. Drain off any fat. Add all other ingredients and bring to the boil. Reduce heat and simmer for 20 minutes. Heat soft corn or flour tortillas in the microwave or frypan and half fill with meat mixture. Top and roll up the tortilla with any combination of the following:

- grated cheese
- shredded lettuce
- chopped tomato
- chopped onion
- chopped capsicum
- sliced radish
- diced avocado
- taco sauce (page 176)

Vegetarian Tacos

1 teaspoon vegetable oil
1 large onion, chopped
1 clove garlic, crushed and
   chopped
½ teaspoon chilli powder
1 large tomato, chopped
4 × 310 g cans red kidney
   beans, drained and rinsed
Cheese, grated
Lettuce, shredded
Tomato, chopped
Taco sauce (see following)

Heat oil in large, heavy based pan and cook onion, garlic and chilli powder until soft. Add tomato and cook for 1 minute. Mash beans and liquid and add to pan and cook until mixture is almost dry. Heat soft flour or corn tortillas and half fill with bean mixture. Top with cheese, lettuce, tomato and taco sauce. Serve 1–2 tacos per child with extra salad and toppings.

Variations:

- Tuna Tacos – mix 1¾ cups drained flaked tuna with 2 cups grated cheese and ¾ cup of taco sauce in a saucepan and heat until cheese melts.
- Raisin Tacos – add 1 cup raisins to any of the taco filling recipes.

Taco Sauce

½ cup tomato puree
   (no added-salt)
1 onion (frozen and then
   grated)
¼ teaspoon dried oregano
2 teaspoons vinegar
½ teaspoon sugar
¼ teaspoon chilli powder

Combine all ingredients in a saucepan and simmer for 3–5 minutes. This can be frozen for future use.

Quick, easy and healthy family meals

The evening meal has traditionally been the main meal of the day for most families in Australia and New Zealand, but this is not necessarily the pattern children prefer. Some children like to eat a large breakfast or lunch and only feel like eating a light dinner, so it is up to parents to recognise these preferences and serve the main meal according to when the family is 'most hungry'. Some families prefer to eat the main meal at lunch time. It can be upsetting for children to be force fed at the evening meal, when they are tired or not hungry and do not want a large meal.

You can improve a child's appetite at the evening meal by keeping a check on afternoon snacks and drinks which should not be eaten too close to meal times. Children will fill up quickly on drinks at meal times, too, so make sure that drinking with meals is kept to a minimum. The same is true of entrees such as soup, which tend to be quite satisfying for children and leave them uninterested in the main course!

It is also a good idea to serve any dessert well after the main course, so that children do not feel pressured to eat it all at the meal. Desserts can easily be delayed until supper time.

The main meal menu should combine foods from the Five Food Groups, including protein foods (e.g. meat, fish, poultry, eggs, milk, cheese, dried beans, peas, lentils or nuts), fruit, vegetables, bread or cereals and milk products. For example, a serving of Chinese Beef (see page 178) and a fruit dessert with yoghurt would be a well balanced meal. Remember that children's servings do not need to be as large as adults', and small portions will usually satisfy the child's appetite. For example, when serving meat, or other protein foods, an adequate child serve would be 1–2 small chops, 2 rissoles, 3–4 tablespoons of casserole or cooked dishes, 1–2 chicken drumsticks, 1–2 eggs or ½–1 cup of cooked legumes. A serving of vegetables is between two and four tablespoons, and fruit is ½ cup stewed or one whole piece of fresh fruit. Desserts are not always necessary and a piece of fresh fruit is an easy and nutritious dessert.

The following recipe ideas for main meals serve four people

and you can easily halve or double the recipe for fewer or extra people.

Remember, try to relax and enjoy the main meal of the day as it is often the only time for all the family to come together.

Beef

Chinese Beef

500 g lean fillet steak
1 carrot
2 sticks celery
6 shallots
1 cup green beans (frozen)
1 cup water
2 teaspoons soy sauce
½ teaspoon sugar
1 tablespoon cornflour
1 tablespoon vegetable oil

Trim all visible fat from the steak and slice across the grain into thin strips (2.5 cm in length). Slice carrots and celery diagonally and chop shallots. Heat the oil in a large frypan or wok and cook the carrots, celery and beans for three minutes. Add the meat, sugar, soy sauce and toss until meat is browned. Do not allow the vegetables to become soft. Blend the cornflour with the water and pour over pan. Bring to boil and allow to thicken, stirring constantly. Serve with boiled brown rice and eat with chopsticks.

Crunchy Beef Pancakes

250 g lean minced steak
2 egg yolks
4 egg whites
1 small onion, chopped
1 tablespoon parsley, chopped
¼ teaspoon dried basil
¼ teaspoon ground pepper
1 tablespoon vegetable oil
½ teaspoon baking powder

Beat egg yolks in a bowl until pale and thick. Fold in steak, pepper, baking powder, onion, parsley and basil and mix thoroughly. Beat the egg whites until they form stiff peaks and gently fold them into meat mixture using a metal spoon. Brush large non-stick frying pan with oil, drop spoonfuls of meat mixture into pan and cook until pancakes are puffed up and browned. Turn and cook other side. Serve with jacket potatoes, green vegetables or side salad.

Chilli Con Carne

500 g lean minced steak
1 green capsicum, chopped
470 g can tomatoes (no added salt)
1 onion, chopped
315 g can red kidney beans (rinsed and drained)
¼ teaspoon pepper
⅓ teaspoon mild chilli powder
2 cups water
1 tablespoon vegetable oil

Heat oil in a large saucepan and brown onion. Add minced steak and capsicum and cook until well browned. Add tomatoes with liquid from the can, kidney beans, water, chilli powder and pepper and bring to the boil. Simmer until mixture thickens (approximately 1–1½ hours) and serve with hot rice and salad.

Beef Shaslik with Pilaf

1 kg rump steak
2 onions
1 green capsicum
1 red capsicum
8 button mushrooms

Marinade

3 tablespoons red wine
1 tablespoon lemon juice
½ tablespoon soy sauce
1 clove garlic, crushed
1 tablespoon oil

Remove all visible fat from meat and cut into small cubes (2 cm). Combine ingredients for marinade, add beef cubes and allow to stand overnight in refrigerator. Cut onions and capsicum into bite size chunks and thread alternately on skewers with beef and mushrooms. Cook under griller; turn occasionally and brush with marinade. Serve with pilaf (page 208).

Ginger Beef

500 g topside steak, trimmed
   of all fat
2 tablespoons soy sauce (salt
   reduced)
2 teaspoons freshly grated
   ginger
2 cloves garlic, crushed
1 tablespoon polyunsaturated
   or olive oil
1 large onion, cut into quarters
   and separated
500 g frozen Chinese vegetables

Slice beef into thin strips and mix with the soy sauce, ginger and garlic. Marinate in refrigerator for 2 hours or overnight. Heat the oil in a large frying pan. Add onion and sauté until tender. Add beef slices and marinade and cook until beef is tender. Add vegetables and cook until tender, but not soft. Serve with steamed white or brown rice.

Beef Stroganoff

300 g steak (fillet, rump,
   topside)
1 tablespoon polyunsaturated
   oil
1 onion, chopped
1 clove garlic, crushed
½ teaspoon beef extract
freshly ground black pepper
½ cup red wine
2 cups sliced mushrooms
½ cup natural yoghurt
   (low fat)

Remove all visible fat from steak and cut into thin strips. Heat oil in a non-stick saucepan and cook meat, onion and garlic until tender. Add beef extract, pepper and red wine and simmer until meat is tender, about 30 minutes. Add mushrooms just before serving and cook until tender but not too soft. Remove from heat and gradually add yoghurt. Serve with noodles and green salad.

Lamb, veal and pork

Lamb Curry

1 kg boneless lean lamb
2 large carrots
4 sticks celery
1 onion
2 teaspoons mild curry powder
1 tablespoon honey
2 teaspoons lemon juice
2 tablespoons plain flour
1 cooking apple
1 cup tomato soup (salt reduced)
1 cup water

Some children love spicy foods while other children won't touch them. It is best to keep curries and chilli dishes very mild to allow children to discover these new flavours. Trim visible fat from lamb and cut into 2.5 cm cubes. Chop vegetables and apple and place in large saucepan with lamb, tomato soup and water. Blend flour, curry powder, honey and lemon juice and add to meat. Mix well, replace lid and simmer for two hours until meat is tender. Serve with boiled rice and a variety of side dishes known as sambals (recipes following).

Cucumber and Yoghurt Sambal

1 green cucumber, sliced
1 cup low fat plain yoghurt
1 teaspoon lemon juice
¼ teaspoon garam masala

Toss all ingredients together.

Banana and Coconut Sambal

2 bananas
1 teaspoon desiccated coconut
1 teaspoon lemon juice

Slice bananas and toss with lemon juice. Sprinkle with coconut.

Apple and Sultana Sambal

1 large granny smith apple
1 tablespoon sultanas
1 teaspoon lemon juice

Slice the apple and toss in lemon juice. Add sultanas and mix.

Minted Tomato Sambal

2 tomatoes (sliced and chopped)
½ tablespoon white vinegar
½ teaspoon sugar
½ tablespoon chopped mint

Toss all ingredients together.

Lamb and Pineapple Hot Pot

500 g lamb, diced
1 cup pineapple pieces (canned, unsweetened)
1 small onion, chopped
½ red capsicum, sliced
2 cups water
¼ teaspoon garlic flakes
¼ teaspoon pepper
¼ teaspoon paprika
2 tablespoons white wine
1 teaspoon cornflour

Remove visible fat from lamb and dice into small cubes. Brown the meat in a large saucepan and drain off any fat. Add chopped onions, capsicum, wine, spices and ½ cup of pineapple juice from the can. Simmer for five minutes. Add water, cover and simmer until the meat is tender. Blend cornflour with a little water, bring hot pot to boil and add cornflour to meat mixture. Reduce heat and stir until slightly thickened. Add pineapple pieces and heat through.

Lamb Kebabs with Rosemary

500 g boneless shoulder lamb
1 punnet cherry tomatoes
1 small capsicum, sliced
rosemary sprigs

Remove all visible fat from lamb and cut into cubes. Combine all ingredients for marinade in bowl. Add lamb,

Marinade

1 cup dry white wine

3 tablespoons chopped fresh
   rosemary

2 tablespoons lemon juice

1 tablespoon olive oil

3 shallots, chopped

2 cloves garlic, crushed

1 bay leaf

1 teaspoon brown sugar

½ teaspoon black pepper

mix well and marinate in refrigerator for several hours, preferably overnight. Thread lamb onto skewers with tomatoes, capsicum and rosemary sprigs. Grill or barbecue until meat is tender, basting with marinade. Serve with brown rice and crisp green salad.

Greek Lamb with Green Beans

600 g lean boned lamb

½ cup wholemeal plain flour

2 tablespoons olive oil

3 cloves garlic, chopped

1 large onion, sliced

425 g can tomatoes (no added
   salt)

2 tablespoons tomato paste
   (no added salt)

½ teaspoon ground cinnamon

½ teaspoon pepper

1 cup water

1 cup dry white wine

½ teaspoon thyme

500 g green beans, trimmed

½ teaspoon chopped fresh
   parsley

Trim all visible fat from meat and chop into 2.5 cm cubes. Toss meat in flour. Heat oil in a large, heavy-based casserole dish and brown meat pieces well. Add garlic and onion and simmer until onion is tender. Add tomatoes, tomato paste, cinnamon, pepper, water, wine and thyme. Simmer for 40–50 minutes. Add whole beans to meat mixture. Cook a further 20 minutes until beans are tender. Serve sprinkled with parsley and a Greek salad.

Savoury Veal and Pumpkin Ring

500 g lean minced veal
1 onion, chopped
2 tomatoes, chopped
1 tablespoon parsley, chopped

Pumpkin Topping
3 cups pumpkin (cooked and
    mashed)
2 cups potato (cooked and
    mashed)
2 tablespoons cheese, grated

Combine mince, onion, tomatoes and parsley and mix *well*. Form the mixture into a ring shape in an ovenproof dish, pressing down firmly. Bake at 150°C for 30 minutes. Drain off meat juices from dish. Combine potato, pumpkin and parsley and spread mixture on top of meat ring. Sprinkle with cheese and bake for 30 minutes. Serve hot or cold with green vegetables or salad.

Veal Birds

500 g thin slices of veal
¼ cup wholemeal plain flour
1 cup stock
½ cup celery, chopped
¼ cup walnuts, chopped
½ cup sliced mushrooms
    (optional)
¼ teaspoon pepper
1–2 tablespoons vegetable oil

Mix celery and walnuts and place 2 tablespoons on each veal slice. Roll up and secure with toothpicks. Mix flour and seasonings and coat veal with this mixture. Heat oil in large frying pan and brown meat on all sides. Add a little more oil to prevent sticking. Add stock, cover and simmer until tender (approximately 45 minutes). Add mushrooms and heat for a few minutes before serving with vegetables.

Pancit

1½ cups cooked pork or
    chicken, sliced
2 cups cabbage, shredded

This is a national dish of the Philippines. Presoak the noodles in cold water for ten

1 carrot, chopped
1 cup vermicelli noodles
1 onion, finely chopped
1 clove garlic, chopped
2 tablespoons oil
3 cups chicken stock or water
1½ tablespoons soy sauce

minutes. Sauté onion and garlic in oil and add pork, or chicken, and soy sauce. Heat stock in a saucepan and add the vegetables. Simmer until vegetables are tender. Combine meat mixture, vegetables and noodles and cook until noodles are tender.

Tropical Ham Steaks

4 small ham steaks
4 pineapple rings
  (unsweetened)
½ tablespoon vegetable oil

Brush non-stick pan with a little vegetable oil and cook ham steaks until golden brown. Cook pineapple rings until lightly browned and serve on top of ham steaks. Serve with coleslaw, salad or corn on the cob.

Thai Pork Curry

200 g pork fillets, sliced
1 teaspoon oil
½ cup zucchini strips
½ cup sliced carrot
½ cup sliced capsicum
4 shallots, chopped
2 cloves garlic, crushed
juice from ½ lime
1 teaspoon red Thai curry
  paste
1 tablespoon fish sauce
½ cup coconut milk
¼ cup evaporated skim milk

Lightly brown pork strips in oil in a non-stick pan. Add vegetables and sauté until tender but still crunchy. Add garlic, lime juice, curry paste and fish sauce. When pork is cooked (about 5 minutes) add coconut milk and heat thoroughly. Mix in evaporated milk just before serving – do not boil. Serve on a bed of rice.

Chicken
Chicken with Peanut Sauce

4 chicken drumsticks

4 chicken wings

1 cup smooth peanut butter (fat-reduced, salt free)

½ cup tomato paste (salt free)

1 onion (finely chopped)

3 drops tabasco sauce (optional)

1 red capsicum (finely chopped)

2 tablespoons water

2½ cups water

Remove skin and visible fat from chicken and place in saucepan with onion and 2 tablespoons of water. Simmer for three minutes and add 2½ cups water. Bring to boil and add capsicum, tabasco sauce and tomato paste. Blend peanut butter with a little water from the pan and add to chicken mixture. Simmer for 40 minutes and allow some of the liquid to reduce. Serve hot with rice or potatoes.

Paella

2 tablespoons vegetable oil

2 green capsicums, sliced

3 cups brown rice, cooked

2 cups tomatoes, chopped

½ teaspoon ground pepper

1 cooked chicken

500 g prawns (peeled and deveined, cooked)

1 cup onion rings

4 cups chicken stock

½ teaspoon saffron

2 red capsicums, sliced

2 cloves garlic, chopped

Heat 1 tablespoon of oil in a large, heavy based frypan. Add onions and cook until tender. Add remaining oil, capsicums, rice and garlic and cook for five minutes, stirring. Add tomatoes and ground pepper. Heat stock in a saucepan with the saffron and bring to boil. Add stock to rice mixture and cook for a further ten minutes, stirring occasionally. Remove skin and visible fat from chicken and break into serving pieces. Arrange chicken on top of paella with prawns and cook for ten minutes or until all the stock is absorbed. Serve with green salad and crusty bread.

Quick Chicken with Almonds

1 plain BBQ chicken
1 large carrot
4 sticks celery
6 shallots
1 cup mushrooms
100 g canned bamboo shoots
  (drained)
100 g blanched almonds
1½ tablespoons dry sherry
1 teaspoon grated root ginger
2 tablespoons vegetable oil

Sauce

3 teaspoons cornflour
1½ cups chicken stock
1 tablespoon soy sauce
1 tablespoon dry sherry

Slice vegetables diagonally. Remove skin and visible fat from chicken and chop into similar-sized chunky pieces. Heat ½ tablespoon of oil in a frying pan or wok and cook almonds until crisp and golden. Drain on kitchen paper. Heat remaining oil in pan and cook carrots and ginger until tender but not soft. Add celery and shallots and lastly bamboo shoots and mushrooms. Add sherry, chicken and almonds and toss over low heat. To make sauce, blend the cornflour in ½ cup of the stock in a saucepan.

Blend in other ingredients and bring to boil. Stir constantly and simmer for three minutes. Add sauce to chicken mixture and heat through. Serve with chopsticks and boiled brown rice.

Marinated Chicken Drumsticks

5 chicken drumsticks
½ cup red wine
1 tablespoon brown sugar
1 tablespoon soy sauce
2 tablespoons tomato paste
  (no added salt)
1 clove garlic, crushed
½ teaspoon ginger, ground
½ teaspoon paprika

Remove skin and visible fat from drumsticks. Combine all ingredients for marinade. Pour over chicken and marinate for at least two hours. Bake in oven at a moderate temperature for 20–30 minutes. Baste frequently with marinade.

Roast Chicken with Spicy Fruit Stuffing

1 large chicken
1 large onion, finely chopped
12 dried apricots, chopped
6 prunes, chopped
¼ cup sultanas
¼ cup currants
1 large apple, chopped
¼ teaspoon ground pepper
¼ teaspoon cinnamon
1 teaspoon dried tarragon
½ teaspoon dried thyme
2 tablespoons vegetable oil

Wash chicken and dry with kitchen paper. Sauté onion in pan with 1 tablespoon of oil until tender. Add remaining oil, dried fruit, apple, spices and herbs and cook gently for three minutes. Allow to cool slightly and stuff into chicken. Lightly brush baking dish with a little oil and bake at 180°C for 1½ hours until tender. Serve with rice and vegetables.

Hawaiian Chicken

No. 16 roasting chicken

Stuffing
2 cups cooked brown rice
1 cup unsweetened, crushed
  pineapple, drained (reserve
  juice)
1 cup chopped shallots
1 cup sultanas
2 tablespoons chopped parsley
2 tablespoons chopped lean
  bacon
1 teaspoon black pepper
½ cup pine nuts
2 tablespoons polyunsaturated
  oil

Remove visible fat from chicken. Combine all ingredients for stuffing and pack firmly into chicken. Roast chicken in a moderate oven (180°C) until golden brown and juices run clear when tested, about 1½ hours, basting occasionally with reserved pineapple juice. Serve hot or cold with coleslaw and potatoes.

Tandoori Chicken

4–6 chicken pieces
  (drumsticks, thighs, breasts)
1 cup natural yoghurt (low fat)
1 onion, finely chopped
2 teaspoons curry powder
1 teaspoon chopped garlic
1 teaspoon grated fresh ginger
1 teaspoon chopped chilli
1 teaspoon chopped, fresh
  mint leaves
freshly ground black pepper

Remove all fat and skin from chicken. Combine yoghurt with onion, curry powder, garlic, ginger, chilli, mint and pepper. Coat chicken pieces with this marinade. Marinate overnight in refrigerator. Place chicken and marinade in a baking dish and bake in a moderate oven (200°C) for 35–45 minutes or until chicken is cooked and tender. Serve with rice and sambals of cucumber in yoghurt (page 181), minted tomato (page 182), banana with coconut (page 181), and apple and sultana (page 182).

Spicy Marinated Chicken

1 cup orange juice
2 teaspoons curry powder
2 teaspoons honey
2 cloves garlic, crushed
½ teaspoon nutmeg
freshly ground black pepper
500 g chicken fillets

Mix all ingredients together, except chicken. Place chicken into a shallow dish and pour marinade over. Cover and refrigerate for 2 hours or overnight. Grill chicken, basting with marinade from time to time, until chicken is cooked. Serve with rice and salad.

Variation: Try cutting the chicken into cubes and grilling as kebabs.

Kashmiri Chicken

2 tablespoons polyunsaturated
  oil
3 onions, chopped
2 cloves garlic, crushed
2 teaspoons grated ginger root
1½ tablespoons curry powder
½ teaspoon chilli powder
  (optional)
2 whole tomatoes, peeled and
  chopped
½ cup tomato purée
  (no added salt)
2 teaspoons paprika
1 tablespoon brown sugar
3 whole cloves
1 cinnamon stick
No. 16 chicken
1 cup natural yoghurt (low fat)
½ cup evaporated skim milk
2 tablespoons chopped fresh
  mint (optional)

Gently heat oil in a large, heavy-based pan and sauté onions, garlic and ginger over low heat until onions soften. Add curry powder and chilli and gently cook for 5 minutes. Add tomatoes, tomato purée, paprika, sugar, cloves and cinnamon, cover and simmer for 15 minutes. Remove all fat and skin from chicken and chop into pieces. Add chicken to curry mixture, cover and simmer 30 minutes, or until chicken is tender. Stir occasionally to prevent sticking. Remove cloves and cinnamon stick. Add yoghurt and milk and mix thoroughly until well heated. Add water to thin mixture if desired. Serve with Basmati rice and garnish with chopped mint.

Chinese Chicken with Cashews

1 tablespoon polyunsaturated
  oil
1 cup unsalted cashews
2 large carrots, sliced diagonally
1 teaspoon grated ginger root
4 stalks celery, sliced diagonally
2 shallots, chopped
1 cup sliced mushrooms

Heat ½ tablespoon oil in a wok or large frying pan. Gently fry cashews until lightly browned. Remove from pan and drain on absorbent paper. Heat remaining oil in pan and cook carrots and ginger until tender but not

1 tablespoon dry sherry

1 cooked chicken, skin and fat removed, chopped into pieces

1 cup bean sprouts

Sauce

3 teaspoons cornflour

1½ cups chicken stock

1 tablespoon soy sauce (salt reduced)

1 tablespoon dry sherry

soft. Add celery, shallots, mushrooms, sherry, chicken pieces and cashews, and toss over low heat. To make sauce, blend cornflour with chicken stock, soy sauce and sherry. Pour sauce over chicken mixture, bring to boil and allow to thicken. Add bean sprouts and simmer for 3 minutes. Serve with boiled brown rice.

Spanish Chicken

No. 16 chicken

2 tablespoons wholemeal plain flour

2 tablespoons olive oil

4 shallots, chopped

2 cloves garlic, chopped

1 capsicum, chopped

1 cup frozen peas

3 cups cooked brown rice

425 g can tomatoes (no added salt)

2 tablespoons chopped parsley

1 bay leaf

1 teaspoon black pepper

½ teaspoon chilli powder (optional)

1 teaspoon turmeric

1 cup hot chicken stock (no added salt)

Cut chicken into pieces and remove skin and fat. Toss lightly in flour. Heat oil in a large, heavy-based pan and cook chicken until browned. Add shallots, garlic and capsicum and sauté until tender. Add peas, rice, tomatoes with liquid from can, parsley, bay leaf, pepper and chilli if desired. Dissolve turmeric in chicken stock and mix through chicken. Cover and simmer for 15 minutes. Remove bay leaf and serve.

Seafood

Baked Fish with Yoghurt

500 g white fish fillets
1 cup plain low-fat yoghurt
1 tablespoon mayonnaise
1 cup celery, chopped
1 tablespoon lemon juice
1 tablespoon parsley, chopped

Remove skin and bones from fish fillets. Line a lightly greased ovenproof dish with half the fish fillets. Combine yoghurt, mayonnaise, lemon juice and celery and spread half of this mixture over the fish.

Place remaining fish fillets on yoghurt layer and top with remaining yoghurt. Bake at 180°C for 20–30 minutes. Sprinkle with parsley and serve with colourful vegetables or salad.

Seafood Skewers

300 g green prawns
200 g scallops
1 lemon
1 orange
1 tablespoon dry sherry

Peel the prawns carefully and remove veins. Squeeze the lemon and orange juice into a bowl and add the dry sherry. Marinate the prawns and scallops in the juice overnight.

Thread prawns and scallops onto skewers and place under griller, basting occasionally with the marinade until prawns are cooked. Serve with skewered vegetable pieces or salad.

Trout with Almonds

2 fresh trout
½ cup plain flour
2 tablespoons polyunsaturated oil
½ cup blanched slivered almonds
juice of 1 lemon

Lightly dust trout in flour. Heat oil in a non-stick pan and gently cook trout for 8–10 minutes, turning once. Place trout on a serving plate and keep warm. Toss almonds in lightly oiled frying pan until golden brown. Top trout with almonds and sprinkle with lemon juice.

Fish Rolls

¼ cup onion, finely chopped
¼ cup celery, finely chopped
½ tablespoon margarine
½ cup mushrooms, sliced
4 tablespoons parsley, chopped
2 tablespoons lemon juice
500 g fish fillets

Toss onion and celery in pan with margarine until tender. Add mushrooms, parsley and lemon juice. Remove bones from fish fillets. Spread mixture on each fillet. Roll up each fillet and secure with a toothpick. Place in lightly greased baking tray and bake at 180°C for 20–25 minutes. Serve with jacket potatoes and baby carrots.

Salmon Rice Pie

Base
2 cups cooked rice
1 egg
½ onion, frozen and then
   grated

Filling
250 g salmon
2 eggs
½ cup grated cheese
¾ cup milk

To make the base, combine rice, egg and onion and press into lightly greased pie dish. Mix ingredients for filling and pour over base. Bake at 180°C for 25–30 minutes until golden. Serve hot or cold with vegetables or salad.

Capsicums with Tuna Rice

1 onion, chopped
½ cup tuna, drained
2 tomatoes, chopped
2 green capsicums
1 cup cooked rice
¼ teaspoon black pepper
1 tablespoon olive oil
½ cup ricotta cheese
paprika

Heat oil in frypan and cook onion until soft. Add tuna, tomatoes, rice and pepper and heat through. Slice the top off each capsicum and remove seeds. Fill capsicum with tuna filling. Bake in an ovenproof dish at 180°C for 30 minutes, top with ricotta cheese and sprinkle with paprika. This may be served with hot tomato sauce (page 161).

Little Fish Parcels

4 white fish fillets
2 zucchinis
1 cup mushrooms, sliced
1 teaspoon olive oil
½ tablespoon lemon juice

Slice zucchinis diagonally and spread on 4 sheets of aluminium foil. Remove bones from fish fillets and place each on top of zucchini slices. Toss mushrooms in oil and lemon juice and spread over fish. Fold ends of foil to form neat parcels and bake at 190°C for 15 minutes. Allow children to unwrap their own 'parcels', being careful not to burn themselves. Serve with foil baked potatoes (see page 161).

Variations:
• *Fish and Tomato Parcels:* combine fish fillets, slices of tomato, onion rings, chopped parsley and a squeeze of lemon juice.
• *Fish with Basil:* coat each fish fillet with lemon juice and chopped fresh basil.

Italian Seafood

1 tablespoon olive oil

1 onion, chopped

2 cloves garlic, crushed

2 × 425 g cans tomatoes (no added salt)

½ cup dry white wine

2 bay leaves

1 teaspoon chopped fresh thyme (or ½ teaspoon dried)

freshly ground black pepper

500 g white fish fillets, cubed

500 g mussels, scrubbed

250 g scallops, deveined

250 g green prawns, shelled and deveined

Heat oil in a large, heavy-based pan and sauté onion and garlic until tender. Add tomatoes with liquid from can, wine, bay leaves, thyme and pepper to taste. Cover and simmer for 10–15 minutes. Add fish and mussels. Cover and simmer gently for a further 3 minutes. Add scallops and prawns and simmer for 2–3 minutes only, to avoid toughening. Remove bay leaves and serve with a crisp green salad and crusty bread.

Mexican Chilli Prawns

1 tablespoon olive oil

1 onion, chopped

1 capsicum, cut into strips

2 large green chillies, chopped

1 cup tomato puree (no added salt)

1 teaspoon curry powder

2 tomatoes, chopped

½ cup chicken stock (no added salt)

¼ teaspoon cumin

1 bay leaf

500 g green prawns, shelled and deveined

Heat ½ tablespoon oil in a pan. Sauté onion and capsicum until tender. Add chillies, tomato puree, curry powder, tomatoes, chicken stock, cumin and bay leaf and simmer for 10–20 minutes. In a separate pan, heat remaining oil and gently cook prawns for 3 minutes only, until they turn pink (overcooked prawns will be tough). Add prawns to chilli sauce mixture, remove bay leaf and serve with steamed rice.

Curried Fish Fillets

1 tablespoon polyunsaturated
  oil
1 onion, sliced
2 cloves garlic, crushed
2 teaspoons curry powder
½ teaspoon garam masala
425 g can tomatoes, chopped
  (no added salt)
½ cup white wine
½ teaspoon black pepper
1 kg white fish fillets

Heat oil in a large, heavy-based pan or wok and sauté onion and garlic for 2 minutes. Add curry powder and garam masala and cook over low heat for 10 minutes. Add tomatoes, wine and pepper and mix thoroughly. Place fish fillets on top of curry mixture; cover and simmer until fish flakes on underside. Turn fish fillets once. Serve fish with rice and sambals.

Seafood Paella

2 tablespoons olive oil
1 onion, sliced
2 green capsicums, sliced
2 red capsicums, sliced
2 cloves garlic, crushed
3 cups brown rice, cooked
2 cups chopped tomatoes
½ teaspoon ground pepper
4 cups chicken stock (no
  added salt)
½–1 teaspoon saffron
½ cup frozen peas
1 cooked chicken
500 g cooked prawns, shelled
  and deveined
250 g scallops

Heat 1 tablespoon oil in a large, heavy-based pan and sauté onion, capsicum and garlic until just tender. Add remaining oil, rice, tomatoes and pepper and mix thoroughly. Mix stock and saffron and pour over rice mixture. Bring to boil, reduce heat and add frozen peas. Simmer 10 minutes. Remove all skin and visible fat from chicken and cut into pieces. Add to rice mixture and cook until all stock is absorbed. Add prawns and scallops and heat through for 5 minutes. Serve paella with crusty bread and salad.

Barbecued Fish

1 tablespoon polyunsaturated
  oil
2 tablespoons soy sauce (salt
  reduced)
½ cup lemon juice
½ cup brandy
2 cloves garlic, crushed
2 whole fish, cleaned and
  gutted

Combine oil, soy sauce, lemon juice, brandy and garlic in a baking dish. Make slits in both sides of fish and place into baking dish. Marinate fish for 1–2 hours, basting frequently with marinade. Place fish on barbecue plate or under grill. Cook one side of fish, then turn to cook the other side, basting frequently with marinade, until flesh flakes easily with a fork. Serve fish with salad and lemon wedges.

Pasta

Children love eating pasta because it is fun and there are many different pastas available, all of different shapes, colours and sizes and many sauces to go with them. Pasta belongs to the bread and cereals section of the Five Food Groups and is a nutritious food for both children and adults. Wholemeal varieties of pasta are available and these provide extra fibre.

Pasta originated in Italy, China and Japan, but most of the names for pasta are derived from the Italian language. For example, spaghetti means 'little string', lasagne means 'broadleafed', tagliatelli means 'thin strips' and vermicelli means 'worm like'. Pasta also comes in alphabet and animal shapes as well as little shells, spirals and tiny rods which children love to try.

Spaghetti and Meatballs

500 grams hamburger mince
1 egg
1 onion, finely chopped
¼ cup breadcrumbs, dry
1½ tablespoons grated carrot
    or zucchini
¼ teaspoon ground pepper
tomato sauce (see page 161)

Combine all ingredients and mix well. Shape into small balls the size of a golf ball. Fry in non-stick, lightly oiled frying pan until evenly browned. Remove from pan and place in saucepan and pour tomato sauce over and simmer until tender (approximately one hour). Serve with hot spaghetti and salad. Freeze remaining meat and sauce mixture for a quick meal next time.

Spaghetti Marinara

1 tablespoon olive oil
1 onion, sliced
2 cloves garlic, crushed
2 tablespoons tomato paste
    (no added salt)
425 g can tomatoes (no added
    salt)
2 tablespoons chopped fresh
    parsley
½ tablespoon chopped fresh
    mint
¼ teaspoon black pepper
½ cup dry white wine
½ cup water
500 g scallops, cooked
500 g green prawns
½ cup squid rings
500 g wholemeal spaghetti

Heat oil in a heavy-based pan and sauté onion and garlic until tender. Add tomato paste, tomatoes, parsley, mint and pepper. Cook gently until mixture thickens. Add wine and water and simmer for 2 minutes. Add seafood and mix thoroughly over low heat for no longer than 3 minutes. Cook spaghetti in boiling water until tender. Drain and serve topped with marinara sauce, crusty bread and crisp green salad.

Spaghetti Carbonara

500 g spaghetti noodles
2 eggs
½ cup chopped ham
½ cup grated cheese
½ cup white wine
¼ teaspoon ground black
  pepper

Cook spaghetti in a large saucepan of boiling water until tender but still firm. Drain spaghetti and add ham and wine. Beat eggs well and add to spaghetti. Toss mixture over a low heat and add cheese and pepper, making sure spaghetti is well coated with the egg mixture. Add more wine if the mixture is too dry. Serve in small bowls sprinkled with grated cheese and chopped parsley. **Note:** All the alcohol from the wine evaporates during cooking.

Fettucine with Pesto Sauce

3 cups fresh basil leaves
¾ cup olive oil
4 cloves garlic, crushed
¼ cup pine nuts
1 tablespoon parmesan cheese
250 g dry or fresh spinach
  fettucine

Combine basil leaves, oil, garlic, pine nuts and cheese in a blender and blend thoroughly. Cook pasta in boiling water until *al dente*, drain. Toss pasta with pesto sauce. Serve immediately.

Butterfly Pasta with Capsicums

4 small capsicums
2 cups tinned tomatoes (no added salt)
1 onion
2 tablespoons olive oil
2 tablespoons chopped basil, fresh
ground pepper
2 cups butterfly pasta (farfalle)
grated cheese for topping

Cut capsicums into thin strips, and thinly slice the onion. Heat the olive oil in a pan and cook onion until tender. Add capsicum strips and cook until soft. Add tomatoes and half the juice from the cans. Season with basil and pepper to taste. Simmer for 15 minutes until some of the water evaporates and the mixture thickens. Cook pasta in a saucepan of boiling water until tender, drain well and place in a serving dish topped with capsicum mixture and a little grated cheese. Serve with crusty bread and green salad.

Canneloni

In Italian, canneloni means 'pasta shaped in big tubes' and is made from flat sheets of noodles which are rolled up into tubes. Canneloni noodles are available from shops or you can make your own at home from a fine pancake. Cannelloni are spread with a filling, rolled up and topped with sauces. This recipe uses ready made canneloni which are filled with a chicken and cheese mixture.

Filling

2 cups cooked chicken, chopped
250 g chicken livers (optional)
2 rashers lean bacon
½ cup mozzarella cheese, grated
1 tablespoon olive oil

Cook canneloni in a large saucepan of boiling water for approximately 12 minutes until tender. Drain and dry on kitchen paper. To make filling, heat a large pan and sauté chicken livers in olive oil for

Sauce

4 tablespoons plain flour

1 litre milk

½ cup ricotta cheese

¼ teaspoon ground white
pepper

¼ teaspoon ground nutmeg

five minutes. Remove from heat and allow to cool. Remove rind and fat from bacon and chop into small pieces. Combine bacon, chicken livers and chopped chicken in a blender until the mixture becomes smoother.

Add half of the mozzarella cheese. To make sauce, melt one tablespoon of butter in a saucepan and stir in flour. Stir for two minutes. Add milk and stir until the sauce boils and thickens. Reduce heat. Gently simmer sauce for a further five minutes; stir constantly and add ricotta cheese, the other half of the mozzarella cheese, pepper and nutmeg. Add 1 cup of the sauce to the chicken mixture and blend thoroughly. Spoon chicken filling into canneloni and place in a shallow ovenproof dish which has been lined with a little of the sauce. Top canneloni with the remaining sauce and the remainder of the grated mozzarella cheese and bake for 30 minutes at 190°C.
Serve with crisp green salad.

Lasagne

375 g lasagna noodles

Bolognese sauce (page 203)

3 cups ricotta cheese

¾ cup grated cheese

7 tablespoon, chopped parsley

2 eggs, lightly beaten

½ teaspoon ground pepper

Prepare bolognese sauce. Cook lasagne in a large saucepan of boiling water until tender. Drain and spread on kitchen paper. Combine ricotta cheese, parsley, grated cheese, beaten eggs and pepper. Lightly grease an oven proof dish, and line

with lasagne noodles. Spread with half the ricotta cheese filling and half the bolognese sauce. Place another layer of lasagne noodles on top of the bolognese sauce and follow with ricotta cheese and the remaining bolognese sauce. Bake at 180°C for 40 minutes. Cut into squares and serve with bread and salad.

Chicken Lasagne

½ cooked chicken
2 onions, chopped
5 zucchini, sliced
1 cup sliced mushrooms
425 g can tomatoes (no added salt)
½ cup tomato paste (no added salt)
1 clove garlic, crushed
1 teaspoon fresh oregano, chopped
1 teaspoon fresh sweet basil, chopped
1 tablespoon parsley, chopped
1 packet instant lasagne noodles (wholemeal)
½ cup mozzarella cheese, thinly sliced (reduced fat)
500 g ricotta cheese (reduced fat)
½ cup grated tasty mozzarella cheese (reduced fat)

Remove all fat and skin from chicken and chop meat into bite-sized pieces. Place onions, zucchini, mushrooms, tomatoes, tomato paste, garlic and herbs in a large pan and simmer until tender. Add a little water if sauce becomes too thick. Combine sauce with chicken. Place a layer of lasagne noodles in a large baking dish and cover with half the chicken sauce. Cover sauce with another layer of noodles and then a layer of ricotta cheese and mozzarella. Cover cheese with remaining chicken sauce, noodles and top with grated cheese. Bake, uncovered, in a moderate oven (180°C) for 40 minutes. Pierce with a knife and continue cooking for 5–10 minutes.

Potato Gnocchi with Bolognese Sauce

Gnocchi (pronounced nok-ee) is a European dish which combines potato, milk, flour and cheese to form small rods which are served with sauce. Children like gnocchi because it is novel, not too strong in taste and it has an interesting shape and texture.

Gnocchi

3 cups mashed potato (warm)

1 egg

1 cup plain flour

Bolognese Sauce

500 g lean minced steak

2 rashers bacon

1 tablespoon olive oil

1 onion, finely chopped

1 clove garlic, crushed and
  chopped

1 tablespoon parsley, chopped

1 bay leaf

1 × 500 g can whole tomatoes
  (no added salt)

½ cup white wine

½ cup water

2 tablespoons tomato paste
  (no added salt)

¼ teaspoon ground black
  pepper

½ teaspoon basil, chopped

To make gnocchi, add lightly beaten egg to potato and mix thoroughly. Add enough flour to make a firm but soft dough. Divide dough into pieces and roll out with floured hands to thick lengths about 10 mm (about ½ inch) in diameter. Cut into 2.5 cm (1 inch) lengths and pinch the centre of each one between the finger and thumb. Drop one at a time into a large saucepan of rapidly boiling water. As soon as the gnocchi float to the surface, remove, drain and place in a serving dish. Serve with bolognese sauce and a little grated cheese. Gnocchi may be served with other sauces such as tomato sauce or a plain cheese sauce (page 217).

To make Bolognese sauce, trim the rind and fat from bacon and chop into small pieces. Heat oil in a large saucepan and add minced steak, bacon, garlic, onion, parsley and bay leaf. Stir frequently, smoothing out lumps, and cook until browned. Add tomatoes with juice from the can, wine, water, tomato paste and ground black pepper. Cover and simmer for approximately one hour. Add chopped basil and cook for a further five minutes. Serve bolognese sauce with any pasta, a salad and a sprinkling of grated cheese. This recipe freezes very well and makes a quick and easy meal.

Vegetable Side Dishes

Scalloped Potatoes

3 large potatoes
1 egg, lightly beaten
1 cup milk
½ cup grated cheese
1 small onion
¼ teaspoon white pepper
¼ teaspoon ground nutmeg

Simmer milk in saucepan with whole onion. Peel potatoes and slice into thin rounds. Place slices in ovenproof dish and sprinkle with pepper and nutmeg. Cool milk to lukewarm and remove and discard onion. Add egg to milk and pour over potatoes. Sprinkle with cheese, and bake at 180°C for 40–50 minutes, until potatoes are soft.

Minted Potatoes

1 kg baby potatoes
1 cup low fat natural yoghurt
2 tablespoons chopped mint
½ teaspoon black pepper

Boil potatoes in their jackets until tender. Combine yoghurt, mint and pepper and serve with hot potatoes.

Foil Baked Potatoes

Scrub potatoes well and remove eyes. (Avoid potatoes with green spots as these contain a toxin called solonine which can cause gastric upsets.) Wrap potatoes in foil and roast in the oven for 40 minutes. Serve with plain yoghurt mixed with lemon juice or cottage cheese.

Stir Fry Vegetables

4 stalks celery
2 cups cabbage, shredded
4 shallots
2 carrots
1 cup baby corn pieces
2 tablespoons vegetable oil

Chop celery, shallots and cabbage into thin diagonal pieces. Heat oil in wok or pan and toss cabbage and carrots for three minutes. Add celery and shallots and stir until tender but still crisp. Add corn pieces. Can be served with any meat, fish or poultry dish.

Cabbage Lentil Rolls

2 cups cooked lentils
½ cup onion, chopped
1½ cups tomatoes, chopped
1 tablespoon vegetable oil
¼ teaspoon oregano
8 large cabbage leaves

Prepare lentils according to directions on the packet, but do not add salt. Heat oil in large pan and cook onions until tender. Add other ingredients, cover, and simmer for five minutes. Add some water if the mixture is too dry. Cook cabbage leaves in boiling water for five minutes. Spoon bean mixture on one end of cabbage leaf and roll up into little parcels. Bake in covered casserole dish for 20 minutes until cabbage is tender.

Pesto Rosse with Eggplant

2 small eggplants
300 g sun-dried tomatoes,
    drained, reserve oil
1 red capsicum, chopped
2 cloves garlic, crushed
freshly ground black pepper
1 teaspoon chopped fresh
    oregano

Wash and halve eggplants and cover with salt. Leave for 30 minutes to allow salt to absorb bitter taste. Rinse thoroughly and pat dry. Combine remaining ingredients in a blender. Mixture should form a thick paste. Add some oil from the sun-dried tomatoes or some olive oil to make a smoother paste. Place mixture on eggplant and roast in a hot oven (200°C) until tender.

Eggs and other dishes

Spanish Omelette

3 eggs, lightly beaten
1 medium potato, finely
    chopped
1 onion, finely chopped
3 tablespoons olive oil

Heat large pan with 1 tablespoon of oil and cook potatoes and onion until soft. Beat eggs until foamy. Add a little more oil to pan and add ⅓ of mixture at a time, lifting mixture to allow moist egg to run under. Repeat until all the egg has been added. Cook until underside is browned. Invert plate over pan and turn out omelette. Return to pan to cook other side. Serve with green salad.

Chicken and Broccoli Quiche

Wholemeal Pastry

2 cups wholemeal flour
2 tablespoons polyunsaturated
  oil
2 tablespoons sesame seeds
⅓–½ cup cold water

Filling

1½ tablespoons
  polyunsaturated oil
1½ cups broccoli florets
½ cup chopped shallots
1 cup evaporated skim milk
2 eggs
½ cup grated tasty cheese
½ teaspoon black pepper
½ teaspoon ground nutmeg
1 cup chopped cooked chicken
  (no skin or fat)

To make pastry, mix flour, oil and sesame seeds. Gradually add cold water until dough is formed. Roll out dough and line an oiled quiche tin or pie plate. Cover with greaseproof paper and rice, to prevent rising. Bake blind in a hot oven (200°C) for 15 minutes. Remove paper and rice and allow to cool. To make filling, heat oil in a pan and sauté broccoli and shallots until tender. Lightly beat milk, eggs, cheese, pepper and nutmeg. Add chicken, cooked broccoli and shallots. Pour into pastry shell. Bake in a moderate oven (180°C) for 30–40 minutes until quiche is set and lightly browned. Serve hot or cold with vegetables or a salad.

Spiced Basmati Rice

1 cinnamon stick
2 cloves
4 cardamom pods
muslin cloth
3 cups basmati rice
1 teaspoon saffron (optional)

Place cinnamon, cloves and cracked cardamom pods in muslin cloth and tie up with string. Boil rice in a large saucepan of water with spice bag until rice is tender, about 10–15 minutes. (Do not add salt.) Remove spice bag and mix through saffron.

Filo Ricotta Roll

Unlike most other pastries, filo pastry is made mainly from flour and water and is very low in fat. Filo pastry sheets can be filled with mixtures of cheese, meat, vegetables and fruit. If you brush the sheets with skim milk and egg whites, instead of oil, the fat content remains quite low.

1½ cups ricotta cheese
1 egg, beaten
3 tablespoons sultanas (optional)
4 sheets filo pastry (frozen)
1 egg white, beaten
¼ cup skim milk
¼ cup dried breadcrumbs
½ cup finely chopped walnuts

Beat egg white in a bowl and add milk. Brush each sheet of pastry with the egg/milk mixture and sprinkle with breadcrumbs. Stack pastry sheets on top of each other. Combine cheese, walnuts, whole egg and sultanas and spread along short end of the pastry. Roll up. Bake at 200°C for 30 minutes until lightly browned.

Variations:
• Substitute grated vegetables, beans or lentils for sultanas.
• Fill the pastry with cherries or apple instead of cheese.

Pilaf

1 cup long grain rice, uncooked
1 onion, chopped
½ cup raisins
½ cup slivered toasted almonds
4 cups chicken stock
½ tablespoon vegetable oil

Heat oil in pan and cook onion until tender. Add rice and cook for three minutes, stirring. Bring chicken stock to boil in saucepan and add to rice. Cover tightly (or place in ovenproof dish) and cook in oven (200°C) for 30 minutes or until rice is tender. Remove from oven and add raisins and almonds.

Carrot Walnut Loaf

500 g carrots
2 onions
1 cup soft wholemeal
    breadcrumbs
3 eggs
1⅓ cups milk
½ tablespoon butter or
    margarine
¼ teaspoon pepper

Peel and chop the carrots and cook in boiling water for five minutes. Finely chop the onions and cook in the butter until tender. Combine onions and carrot. Add walnuts, breadcrumbs, eggs, milk and pepper to carrot mixture and mix well. Spoon the mixture into a lightly greased loaf tin and decorate with walnuts. Cover with foil and bake at 190°C for one hour. Serve hot or cold with a tomato or cheese sauce.

Vegetarian eating

Research into the health of vegetarians, particularly in wealthier countries, shows they have better general health than non-vegetarians and suffer less from lifestyle diseases such as high blood pressure, being overweight, obesity, heart disease, certain cancers and diabetes. The incidence of intestinal disorders, such as constipation, haemorrhoids and diverticulitis (inflammation of the bowel) are also much lower among vegetarians.

A narrow range of foods may present problems during the critical periods of growth and development during pregnancy, breast-feeding, infancy and childhood. With this in mind, one of the main problems of extreme vegetarian diets, such as vegan diets, for young children is getting enough energy and protein from a diet high in bulk, water and fibre from foods such as vegetables, fruits and cereals. While this may be an advantage for adults (particularly those who are trying to lose weight), it is inadequate for children because they become 'full' very easily before their nutrient needs can be met. These children will be at risk of stunted growth, low weight for height, muscle wastage, anaemia and fatigue.

Vegetarian diets can be classified into two major groups; the nutritional difference between these two diets is of great importance for children.

Lacto-ovo-vegetarians are those who eat no meat, poultry or fish but include dairy products, eggs, cereals, nuts, fruit and vegetables. This type of diet will satisfy the nutrient requirements of young babies, children and adults.

The other group, vegans, are those who exclude meat, fish, poultry, dairy products and eggs, but include cereals, dried peas, beans, lentils, nuts, fruits and vegetables. Research has shown that this type of diet is nutritionally inadequate for young babies and children, but is suitable for most adults if care is taken to ensure an adequate intake of protein, energy, vitamins and minerals.

An optimum vegetarian diet for children should include a variety of foods such as eggs, milk, cheese and dairy products; dried beans and lentils; nuts and seeds; fruits and vegetables and cereals, grains and bread. The following vegetarian recipes can be enjoyed by the whole family, and many can be made beforehand and frozen to provide a cheap, quick and nutritious meal.

Gnocchi with Tomato Sauce

500 g potatoes
1 tablespoon polyunsaturated
 oil
¼ teaspoon white pepper
½ cup wholemeal plain flour
1 egg, lightly beaten
1 cup grated cheese

Tomato Sauce
½ tablespoon olive oil
½ cup chopped onion
2 cloves garlic, chopped
1 cup chopped tomatoes
½ cup water
2 tablespoons tomato paste
 (no added salt)
2 drops tabasco sauce
¼ teaspoon oregano
½ teaspoon chopped fresh
 basil

Peel, chop and boil potatoes until soft. Mash with oil and pepper until smooth. Add flour and egg and mix well. Divide mixture into small balls and roll into strips 2.5 cm thick. Cut 1 cm lengths from strips and press each piece between finger and thumb. Drop each piece of gnocchi into a shallow pan of boiling water, reduce heat and poach for 5 minutes or when gnocchi floats to surface of pot. Remove and drain on absorbent paper. Place gnocchi in ovenproof dish and cover with grated cheese and cook in a hot oven (200°C) for 10–15 minutes until golden brown.

To make sauce, heat oil in pan and cook onion and garlic until soft. Add tomatoes and remaining ingredients, except basil, and simmer until tender and sauce thickens. Add basil and simmer for 3 minutes.

Serve gnocchi hot with tomato sauce.

Walnut Pasta Bake

⅔ cup wholemeal short cut
  macaroni
2 tablespoons wholemeal
  breadcrumbs
2 tablespoons chopped walnuts
2 tablespoons grated cheese

Tomato Sauce
500 g canned tomatoes (no
  added salt)
1 medium onion, finely
  chopped
1 clove garlic, crushed and
  chopped
1 bay leaf
1 tablespoon parsley, chopped
1 teaspoon dried oregano or
  basil
ground black pepper
1 tablespoon oil

Heat the oil in a pan and
sauté onion and garlic until
soft over a low heat. Add
tomatoes, bay leaf, and herbs
and a pinch of pepper. Bring
to the boil and simmer for
30 minutes until mixture
becomes smooth. Remove bay
leaf. Cook macaroni in water
until soft (do not add salt).
Drain and place in slightly
greased ovenproof dish or
casserole dish. Pour over sauce
and bake for 25 minutes in
moderate oven (200°C).
Remove from oven, mix
through breadcrumbs and top
with walnuts and cheese, then
bake for further ten minutes
until golden brown on top.
Serve hot with salad or green
vegetables.

Macaroni Cheese

⅔ cup macaroni, uncooked
2 tablespoons margarine
¼ cup flour
1 cup cheese
1 cup milk
1 cup tomato puree (no added
  salt)
1 onion, chopped
1 capsicum, chopped
1 teaspoon mustard

Cook macaroni in boiling
water for 12–15 minutes, or
until tender. Drain. Melt
margarine in saucepan,
remove from heat and stir in
flour, paprika, mustard and
¼ teaspoon black pepper.
Return to heat and cook one
minute, stirring constantly.
Add milk gradually, stirring

¼ teaspoon paprika

¼ teaspoon ground black
   pepper

until sauce boils and thickens;
remove from heat. Add
cheese, tomato puree and mix
well over low heat. Add more
puree if the mixture is too dry.
Lightly fry capsicum and
onion in a pan until soft and
add to sauce. Add macaroni
to sauce and mix thoroughly.
Place mixture in a casserole
dish and sprinkle with grated
cheese. Bake at 200°C for
25–30 minutes or until top is
golden brown. Serve with
salad or vegetables.

Pasta with Lentil and Tomato Sauce

1 cup pasta (try different
   shapes – spirals, shells,
   penne)

½ cup brown lentils (dry)

1 large tomato, chopped

2 tablespoons tomato puree
   (no added salt)

1 onion, chopped

¼ cup carrot, grated

¼ cup zucchini, grated

1 teaspoon olive oil

1 clove garlic, crushed and
   chopped

¼ teaspoon ground black
   pepper

Soak lentils overnight, drain
and discard water. Heat oil in
pan and cook onion until soft.
Add garlic, tomato, carrot,
zucchini and simmer until
vegetables are tender. Cover
lentils with cold water and
boil gently until tender. Drain.
Add lentils to vegetable
mixture and mix thoroughly.
Add tomato puree and season
with black pepper. Add extra
puree if the sauce is too dry.
Boil pasta of your choice
until tender and serve with
lentil sauce, grated cheese
and salad.

Lentil Lasagne

100 g wholemeal lasagne
   noodles
⅔ cup brown lentils (dry)
tomato sauce (page 161)

Topping
1 tablespoon margarine
1 tablespoon wholemeal plain
   flour
2 cups milk
2 eggs, beaten
¼ teaspoon pepper
¼ teaspoon ground nutmeg

Soak lentils in cold water for at least 30 minutes (overnight if possible). Cook lasagne in boiling water until tender (do not add salt). Drain and spread on kitchen paper or a clean tea towel. Drain lentils and discard water. Cover with cold water and gently boil until tender.

Make tomato sauce, and add lentils, mixing thoroughly. Lightly grease an ovenproof dish and spoon in a layer of sauce mixture. Cover sauce with a layer of lasagne and repeat layers and finish with sauce. To make the topping, melt margarine in saucepan. Remove from heat and stir in the flour. Return to stove and cook for one minute. Gradually stir in milk, bring to the boil and stir continuously for three minutes. Gradually whisk sauce into the bowl of beaten eggs. Season with pepper and nutmeg. Pour the topping over the ovenproof dish and push a knife down through the lasagne layers to allow topping sauce to seep through. Bake at 190°C for 50–60 minutes until topping is brown. Serve with salad or vegetables.

Spinach Lasagne

1 tablespoon margarine
2 onions, chopped
2 cloves garlic, crushed
2 × 400 g cans tomatoes (no
   added salt)
250 g packet lasagne noodles
½ cup grated cheese

Sauté onions and garlic in oil and add tomatoes and juice from cans. Simmer, covered, for 30 minutes. Boil lasagne noodles until soft. Pour one-third of this mixture into ovenproof dish and top with a

Vegetable Layer

250 g packet frozen spinach, thawed and chopped

1 cup zucchini, sliced

½ cup mushrooms, sliced

180 g can tuna

Cheese Sauce

2 tablespoons margarine

¼ cup plain flour

1 cup milk

1 cup cottage cheese

½ cup grated cheese

2 eggs

layer of lasagne noodles. To make cheese sauce, melt margarine, stir in flour and cook for one minute, and gradually stir in milk. Bring to boil, stirring constantly. Remove from heat and allow to cool slightly. Stir in cheeses and eggs and mix thoroughly. Spoon one-third of cheese sauce mixture over lasagne. Mix the spinach, zucchini, mushrooms and drained tuna and spread half this mixture on top of the cheese layer.

Repeat layers adding tomato mixture, then lasagne, cheese sauce and vegetables. Finish with cheese sauce and top with grated cheese. Bake at 200°C for 15 minutes and serve slices with salad or vegetables.

Chinese Rice

3 cups brown rice, cooked

5 shallots, chopped

½ cup celery, chopped

½ cup red capsicum, chopped

1 egg

½ cup peas, cooked until tender, not soft

½ cup corn kernels, drained

2 tablespoons vegetable oil

Heat large non-stick fry pan or wok on medium heat and lightly brush with vegetable oil to prevent sticking. Lightly beat egg in bowl and add to pan. Cook, remove, and chop into small pieces. Add shallots, celery, capsicum and corn to pan with 1 tablespoon of oil and toss until tender. Season with a little ground

black pepper. Add rice and heat through, adding one tablespoon of oil to prevent sticking. Add egg and peas. Serve with chopsticks. For a non-vegetarian rice dish, add chopped ham and a small can of peeled prawns.

Risotto

This is an Italian word which means 'rice and vegetable combination' and is a fun food for children, as well as being a good way to use small amounts of left-over vegetables or fish. Risotto can be served with green salad or as an accompaniment to other dishes; alternatively it can be a nutritious meal on its own.

1 cup rice (dry)
1 red capsicum, thinly sliced
½ cup mushrooms, sliced
1 clove garlic, crushed and
  chopped
½ cup peas (frozen)
½ cup celery, thinly sliced
1 medium onion, chopped
500 mls vegetable or chicken
  stock
½ cup Edam cheese, grated
¼ teaspoon ground black
  pepper
1 tablespoon olive oil
1 tablespoon chopped parsley

Heat oil in large pan and fry onion, garlic, celery. Add rice and mix thoroughly. Add capsicum slices, mushrooms and peas. Pour on stock, add pepper and bring to the boil, stirring occasionally. Lower the heat, cover pan and simmer without stirring for 40 minutes, until rice is tender. Add more stock if the rice dries out too much. Stir in half the cheese. Place risotto on to serving dish and sprinkle with cheese and parsley.

Rice and Vegetable Pie

Rice Base

1 cup brown rice (dry)
1 egg, lightly beaten
1 teaspoon margarine
1 small onion, chopped
sesame seeds
paprika

Filling

1 cup zucchini, sliced
1 large onion, chopped

To make base, cook rice in boiling water until tender (approximately 40 minutes). Drain. Heat margarine in pan and cook onion until soft. Add rice and egg and mix well, then press into 20 cm pie plate and cover base and sides. Make filling by cooking vegetables in oil until tender but not soft. Season with pepper and curry

½ cup baby corn pieces
½ cup mushrooms, sliced
1 carrot, thinly sliced
2 teaspoons vegetable oil
¼ teaspoon pepper
1 teaspoon mild curry powder

Cheese Sauce
⅓ cup plain flour
1 cup milk
2 tablespoons margarine
½ cup grated cheese
2 teaspoons parsley, chopped
¼ teaspoon ground black
    pepper

powder. Fill pie case with vegetable mixture. To make cheese sauce, melt margarine in saucepan, stir in flour and cook for one minute. Remove from heat and add milk, stirring thoroughly. Return to heat and add pepper. Bring mixture to the boil, simmer and allow to thicken. Stir in cheese and parsley and allow cheese to melt thoroughly. Pour sauce over vegetables and sprinkle with a little paprika for colour and sesame seeds. Bake at 190°C for 35–40 minutes. This can be a complete meal but goes well with salad or colourful vegetables.

Carrot Souffle

500 g carrots, sliced
50 g margarine
¼ cup wholemeal plain flour
1 cup skim milk, warm
3 eggs
¼ teaspoon ground black
    pepper
2 tablespoons chopped mint
1 tablespoon grated Edam
    cheese

Boil sliced carrots until tender. Drain and mash well or puree in blender. Separate egg whites and yolks. Melt the margarine in a saucepan, stir in the flour and cook for one minute. Gradually stir in the milk and bring to the boil. Simmer for three minutes, stirring constantly. Remove from heat and allow to cool slightly. Beat one egg yolk and add to carrot mixture with pepper and mint. Beat egg whites until stiff and fold them through the carrot mixture with a metal spoon. Gently spoon the mixture into a souffle dish and bake for 45 minutes at 190°C.

Mexican Quiche

500 g lamb, diced
1 cup pineapple pieces
  (canned, unsweetened)
1 small onion, chopped
½ red capsicum, sliced
2 cups water
¼ teaspoon garlic flakes
¼ teaspoon pepper
¼ teaspoon paprika
2 tablespoons white wine
1 teaspoon cornflour

To make pastry, rub margarine into flour with finger tips until it resembles fine breadcrumbs. Slowly add 1 tablespoon cold water and mix through flour thoroughly. Add enough water to make a firm, moist dough. Roll out on a floured board and line a lightly greased 20 cm (8 inch) flan tin. Simmer shallots and capsicum in a little water until tender. Drain and mix with sweet corn. Arrange vegetables on the pastry base. Beat eggs lightly and combine with cheese, milk, yoghurt and a little pepper. Pour mixture over vegetables and sprinkle with paprika for extra colour. Bake at 200°C for 50 minutes or until the quiche is set and browned on top. Serve hot or cold slices with salad or vegetables.

Egg Fingers

4 hard boiled eggs, finely
  chopped
1 tablespoon brown rice,
  cooked
1 tablespoon fresh
  breadcrumbs
1 tablespoon cheese, grated
3 teaspoons parsley, chopped
1 teaspoon dry breadcrumbs
1 egg white, beaten
1 tablespoon oil

Combine hard boiled eggs, rice, fresh breadcrumbs, cheese and parsley. Stir in the egg yolk and mix well. Form one tablespoon of mixture into fingers. Brush each finger in beaten egg white and roll in dry breadcrumbs. Lightly brush non-stick pan with oil and cook fingers until golden brown. Serve with salad and fruit 'swords' or kebabs (page 259).

Vegeburgers

2 cups soft-cooked soya beans
½ cup cooked brown rice
½ cup grated carrot
½ cup finely chopped onion
½ cup finely chopped celery
2 teaspoons soy sauce (salt reduced)
2 tablespoons fresh parsley, chopped
¼ teaspoon ground cumin
¼ teaspoon pepper
50 g wholemeal breadcrumbs
¼ cup grated cheese
polyunsaturated oil for frying

Drain and mash beans and rice. Combine bean and rice mixture with carrot, onion, celery, soy sauce, parsley, cumin and pepper. Add breadcrumbs and cheese and mix thoroughly. Form into burgers. Coat with a little flour. Cook in a non-stick pan brushed with oil. Turn burgers when golden brown on one side. Serve in wholemeal buns with salad and Spicy Tomato Sauce, recipe following.

Spicy Tomato Sauce

½ tablespoon oil
½ cup chopped onion
1 cup chopped tomatoes
½ cup water
2 tablespoons tomato paste (no added salt)
½ teaspoon curry powder
¼ teaspoon dried oregano
2 drops tabasco sauce
½ teaspoon chopped fresh basil

Heat oil in pan and sauté onion until soft. Add tomatoes and simmer until tender. Add remaining ingredients, except basil, and simmer until liquid has reduced. Add basil and simmer 5 minutes. Serve.

Lentil Burgers

2–3 tablespoons olive oil
1 onion, chopped
3 cups chopped carrots
1 cup chopped celery
1 cup uncooked lentils
2½ cups chicken stock (no added salt)
1 teaspoon ground coriander
½ teaspoon ground black pepper
¼ teaspoon ground cumin
3 cups wholemeal breadcrumbs
2 tablespoons chopped fresh parsley
1 egg, lightly beaten
2 tablespoons wholemeal plain flour

Heat 1 tablespoon oil in a large pan and sauté onion, carrots and celery until soft. Place lentils, chicken stock, coriander, pepper and cumin in a saucepan, bring to boil and simmer until lentils are tender, about 30 minutes. Combine lentils and vegetable mixture and mash well. Add breadcrumbs, parsley and egg to lentil mixture and mix thoroughly. Form mixture into flat patties, coat with wholemeal flour and cook in a non-stick pan with remaining oil, until golden brown. Serve in wholemeal buns with grated carrot, lettuce, tomato and bean sprouts and Spicy Tomato Sauce (page 219).

Soy-bean Patties

2 cups cooked soya beans (canned beans are suitable)
2 tablespoons wholemeal flour
1 egg
1 onion, chopped
1 cup wholemeal breadcrumbs
1 tablespoon parsley, chopped

Puree soya beans. Combine with all other ingredients, except breadcrumbs, and mix well. Form into small patties, flatten and coat with breadcrumbs. Heat non-stick pan and lightly brush with oil. Cook patties until golden brown on each side. Serve 1–2 patties per child with green salad or vegetables. Make Soy Burgers by placing a pattie on a hamburger bun with tomato, shredded lettuce and tomato sauce.

Soya Bean Casserole

1 cup soya beans, dry (or
   2 cups, cooked)
1 tablespoon polyunsaturated
   oil
1 onion, chopped
1 teaspoon dried thyme
2 tablespoons chopped fresh
   parsley
2 cloves garlic, crushed
1 teaspoon chopped fresh dill
½ teaspoon black pepper
1 cup vegetable stock (no
   added salt)
¼ cup grated tasty cheese
3 tomatoes, peeled and sliced
3 zucchini, sliced
extra grated tasty cheese
paprika

Soak soya beans in water overnight. Drain and discard water. Cover with water, bring to boil and simmer for 2 hours or until beans are tender. Drain. Heat oil in a large pan and sauté onion with all the herbs and spices until tender. Add beans and vegetable stock and simmer for 15 minutes until liquid is reduced. Add cheese and mix thoroughly. Spoon half mixture into a lightly oiled casserole dish and cover with a layer of tomato slices and then a layer of zucchini slices. Repeat layers until all beans, tomatoes and zucchini are used up. Top with extra grated cheese and sprinkle with paprika. Cover with a lid or aluminium foil. Bake in a moderate oven (180°C) for 2 hours. Serve with green vegetables or salad.

Ricotta and Bean Spread

3 cups uncooked lima beans
½ cup ricotta cheese
2 tablespoons parsley, chopped
1 tablespoon lemon juice
black pepper
½ teaspoon oregano

Soak lima beans in water overnight. Drain, cover with water and simmer until soft. Drain well and puree in a blender to a thick paste. Mix in all other ingredients and refrigerate. Serve as a sandwich filling with grated carrot or chopped capsicum.

Curried Lentil Triangles

1 tablespoon polyunsaturated oil
1 onion, chopped
1 clove garlic, crushed
3 teaspoons curry powder
1 teaspoon grated ginger
½ teaspoon black pepper
2 cups cooked lentils
1 tomato, chopped
½ cup chopped celery
2 tablespoons tomato paste
  (no added salt)
½ cup grated cheese
375 g packet filo pastry
1 cup shredded tasty cheese,
  extra

Heat oil in a pan and gently sauté onion, garlic, curry powder, ginger and pepper for about 3 minutes. Add lentils, tomato and celery and simmer until tender. Add tomato paste and cheese and mix thoroughly. Cool. Divide filo pastry into individual sheets and brush with skim milk. Fold pastry by thirds into long strips. Coat with grated cheese. Place 1½ tablespoons of mixture on bottom corner of pastry and fold over to make a triangle. Continue folding pastry in this way until you finally have a triangular parcel. Pierce with a fork to prevent bursting during cooking. Bake on an oiled tray in a hot oven (200°C) for 20–30 minutes until browned. Makes about 24.

Variations:
- Cauliflower and cheese – sauté 2 cups cauliflower, chopped shallots and parsley. Add 1 cup skim milk cottage cheese. Season with pepper and cumin.
- Chicken and mushroom – sauté 1 cup sliced mushrooms, 1 cup cooked chicken and 1 chopped onion. Combine with ½ cup ricotta cheese and season with chopped parsley and pepper.

Mexican Chilli Beans

½ cup tomato purée (no added salt)
½ cup cracked wheat
1 tablespoon olive oil
1 onion, chopped
2 cloves garlic, crushed
½ cup chopped carrots
½ teaspoon chopped fresh basil
½ teaspoon ground cumin
½ teaspoon chilli powder
¼ teaspoon ground coriander
¼ teaspoon cayenne
¼ teaspoon pepper
½ cup chopped capsicum
½ cup chopped celery
1 cup chopped tomatoes
3 cups cooked red kidney beans, drained

Simmer tomato purée and cracked wheat in a large saucepan until wheat is tender. Heat oil in a large, heavy-based pan and sauté onion and garlic until tender. Add carrots, basil, spices and seasonings and cook until vegetables are tender. Add capsicum, celery and tomatoes and cook for a further 5 minutes. Add beans and wheat and simmer until all ingredients are cooked. Check seasonings – you may like to add more chilli powder to taste. Serve with hot flat bread and grated cheese. Serves 6.

Crusty Beans

2 cups lima beans (uncooked)
250 g tomato paste (preferably salt free)
1 tablespoon oil or margarine (melted)

Soak lima beans overnight. Discard water. Cover beans with water in a saucepan and gently boil until tender. Drain. Add tomato paste and margarine and mix well. Bake in a shallow baking dish at 175°C until crusty and brown. Serve with vegetables or salad, on toast, bread or rice.

Vegetarian Pie

1 teaspoon polyunsaturated oil
2 cups chopped Chinese
  cabbage
1 cup diced potato
1 cup sweet corn kernels,
  drained
1 cup sliced mushrooms
1 onion, chopped
½ cup diced parsnip
½ cup chopped carrots
1 cup cashews
1 cup vegetable stock (no
  added salt)
2 tablespoons tomato paste
  (no added salt)
1 tablespoon soy sauce (salt
  reduced)
2 teaspoons chilli sauce
1 teaspoon mixed dried herbs
¼ teaspoon pepper

Topping
½ cup wholemeal plain flour
2 tablespoons wheatgerm
2 tablespoons rolled oats
2 tablespoons polyunsaturated
  margarine
½ cup grated tasty cheese
¼ teaspoon cumin
¼ teaspoon coriander
2 teaspoons freshly chopped
  parsley
paprika

Heat oil in a large wok or frying pan and sauté vegetables until tender but not soft. Add cashews, vegetable stock, tomato paste, soy sauce, chilli sauce, herbs and pepper. Simmer until liquid reduces and mixture thickens. To make topping, combine flour, wheatgerm, oats and margarine and blend until mixture resembles breadcrumbs. Add cheese, cumin, coriander and parsley. Place vegetables in a lightly oiled casserole dish and cover with topping. Sprinkle with paprika. Bake in a moderate oven (180°C) for 30–40 minutes until browned. Serves 4.

Vegetable Cakes

¾ cup red lentils
1 onion, finely chopped
1 celery stalk, finely chopped
2 small carrots, grated
½ cup green beans, cooked
   and chopped
1 cup fresh breadcrumbs
3 eggs
½ teaspoon ground black
   pepper
¾ cup dry breadcrumbs
1 tablespoon vegetable oil

Soak lentils overnight and discard the water. Cover with cold water and boil gently until tender. Drain. Combine lentils, onions, celery, carrots, beans, fresh breadcrumbs, 2 eggs and pepper in a bowl. Let mixture stand for 30 minutes to allow flavours to develop. Shape mixture into ten small balls and flatten into cakes. Beat the remaining egg and dip each vegetable cake in egg and then dry breadcrumbs. Lightly brush non-stick pan with oil and cook vegetable cakes for 10 minutes on each side or until golden brown. Serve 2 cakes per child with a salad; as vegeburgers in a hamburger bun; or as a Lebanese roll with hummus and tabbouli (pages 156, 166) rolled up in Lebanese flat bread.

Cauliflower Curry

2 tablespoons polyunsaturated
   oil
½ teaspoon ground ginger
½ teaspoon turmeric
¼ teaspoon cayenne pepper
¼ teaspoon cinnamon
½ teaspoon coriander
½ teaspoon mustard seeds
½ teaspoon cumin seeds
¼ teaspoon ground cloves
1 kg cauliflower, cut into florets
½ cup water
1 cup shelled fresh peas
2 tablespoons chopped Italian
   parsley leaves
2 tomatoes, diced

Heat oil in a wok or large pan and add all spices. Cook over a low heat for 5 minutes. Add cauliflower and water. Mix thoroughly, cover tightly and steam until tender. Add peas and parsley and cook for 5–8 minutes. Add tomatoes last and heat through. Serve this curry with hot chappatis. Serves 4.

Corn Patties

1 egg, separated
½ cup skim milk
1 cup corn kernels, drained
⅔ cup wholemeal self-raising
    flour

Combine egg yolk and milk in a bowl and beat gently. Add corn kernels. Fold through flour and mix thoroughly. Beat egg white until stiff and fold through corn mixture. Drop ½ tablespoon of mixture into a lightly oiled non-stick pan and cook each side until golden brown. Serve with coleslaw, salad or as a vegetarian burger. Makes about 12.

Corn Chowder

1 teaspoon polyunsaturated oil
310 g can corn kernels,
    drained
1 onion, chopped
3 potatoes, peeled and
    chopped
½ cup chopped celery
2 cups chicken stock (no
    added salt), or chicken
    consommé (no added salt)
2 cups evaporated skim milk

Heat oil in a large pan and lightly sauté corn, onion, potato and celery. Add stock, simmer until all ingredients are cooked. Remove from heat and gently add evaporated milk – do not boil. Serve hot with wholemeal bread rolls. Serves 4.

Baby Pumpkin House

3 baby golden pumpkins (as
  small as possible)
½ onion, chopped
1½ cups brown rice (cooked)
1 cup brown lentils (dry)
1 cup frozen mixed vegetables
½ teaspoon dried mixed
  herbs
3 tablespoons tomato paste
  (no added salt)
3 tablespoons ricotta or
  cottage cheese
1 tablespoon vegetable oil
paprika

Cook whole pumpkins in a slow oven for one hour or in a microwave oven for 15 minutes. Soak lentils in water overnight, drain, cover with cold water and boil gently until tender. Drain. Remove pumpkins from oven and allow to cool. Slice the top off each small pumpkin and save this to make a 'roof'. Remove seeds. Carefully scoop out pulp from each pumpkin and reserve. Heat oil in a heavy base pan and cook onions until tender. Add rice, lentils, mixed vegetables, herbs, pumpkin pulp and tomato paste and cook until vegetables are tender. Fill each pumpkin shell with rice mixture and top with cheese and a sprinkle of paprika for colour. Bake at 190°C until hot. Replace 'roof'. Serve with broccoli 'trees' or another green vegetable.

Variation: Instead of pumpkins use 3 red capsicums, blanching the seeded capsicums in boiling water for three minutes.

Potato Surprise

4 large potatoes, scrubbed and
dried
3 teaspoons chopped chives
¼ teaspoon black pepper
60 mls milk
3 eggs

Prick potatoes lightly with a fork, place on oven rack and bake for 1½ hours at 190°C. Remove from oven and allow to cool slightly. Cut top off each potato and scoop out inside with a teaspoon, taking care not to break the skin. Mash the potato flesh with the milk, chives and pepper. Gradually beat in the eggs. Stuff each potato with the filling and place in a baking dish. Bake for 10–12 minutes or until the top is lightly browned. Garnish with a sprig of parsley. Serve one potato per child with other colourful vegetables or as a meal on its own.

Italian Potatoes

500 g potatoes
1 tablespoon olive oil
2 cloves garlic, chopped
425 g can tomatoes (no added
salt)
2 teaspoons chopped fresh
oregano (or ½ teaspoon
dried)
¼ teaspoon ground black
pepper

Wash and cube potatoes. Do not peel. Cook in boiling water until tender, but not soft. Drain. Heat oil in saucepan and cook garlic until golden. Add tomatoes including liquid from can, and oregano. Simmer until thickened. Season with pepper. Arrange potatoes in a warmed serving dish and cover with tomato sauce. Serves 4.

Variations:
- Use 2 teaspoons of chopped fresh basil instead of oregano.
- Add ½ teaspoon chilli powder to sauce mixture for Chilli Potatoes.

Cabbage Rolls with Pine Nuts

fresh cabbage leaves
½ cup brown rice
1 onion, chopped
2 tablespoons tomato purée
   (no added salt)
1 large tomato, chopped
½ cup pine nuts
¼ cup chopped parsley
tomato sauce (page 161)

Blanch the cabbage leaves by cooking in gently boiling water for five minutes. Drain. Cook the rice in boiling water until tender. Drain. Combine rice, onion, parsley, tomato and tomato purée and pine nuts and mix thoroughly. Spoon one tablespoon of rice mixture in the centre of each cabbage leaf and fold into a neat parcel. Place each cabbage roll into an ovenproof dish and pour over enough tomato sauce to cover the base of the dish but do not completely immerse the rolls. Cover with lid or aluminium foil and bake at 150°C for 1½ to 2 hours. Serve 2–3 rolls per child with hot tomato sauce.

Note: Small children aged under five years old will require supervision when eating nuts.

Variations:
- Cabbage Rolls with Sultanas – combine rice, tomato purée, onion, ½ cup grated cheese, 2 tablespoons sultanas and 1 teaspoon mild curry powder.
- Soya Bean Roll – combine ½ cup mashed soya beans, rice, onion, tomato, tomato puree and 1 clove chopped garlic.

Savoury Cheese Roll

Wholemeal Pastry

1 cup wholemeal plain flour
2 tablespoons margarine
3–4 tablespoons cold water

Filling

1 cup grated cheese
2 small onions, chopped
2¼ tablespoons tomato
   paste (salt free)
ground black pepper
1 tablespoon chopped parsley

Make pastry by rubbing margarine through flour until it resembles fine breadcrumbs. Add enough cold water to mix to a firm dough. Roll out on to a floured board into an oblong shape. To make filling, combine cheese, onion, tomato paste, parsley and a little pepper and mix thoroughly. Spread cheese mixture on to pastry, leaving a 1-centimetre clear margin around the edges. Roll up like a swiss roll and place on a lightly greased baking tray in a slightly curved shape. Cut three centimetre slices through the roll, allow some of the inside to be exposed and brush with a little milk. Bake at 200°C for about 20–30 minutes until golden brown. Serve with salad or vegetables.

Variations: This roll is very versatile and can be filled with most things that children like. Try combining ricotta or other cheese, tomato paste and onion with two-thirds cup of:

- Sautéed mushrooms
- Spinach, boiled and chopped
- Soya beans or lima beans, cooked and mashed
- Sweet corn kernels
- Asparagus pieces
- Celery and walnuts, chopped and sautéed.

Cheese Balls

2 cups cottage cheese
2 cups dry breadcrumbs
   (preferably wholemeal)
1 onion, finely chopped
1 egg
1 tablespoon parsley, chopped
¼ teaspoon sage

Combine all ingredients in a bowl and mix thoroughly. Add a little milk if mixture is too dry and mould into small balls. Place on lightly greased oven tray and bake at 200°C for 30 minutes. Serve hot with tomato sauce (page 161) or cold with salad.

Gado Gado

This is an Indonesian dish which is eaten alone or as a salad with small serves of fish or seafood.

1 lettuce
¼ cabbage, finely shredded
3 medium potatoes
1 cup frozen beans
4 hardboiled eggs, diced
3 carrots
2 tomatoes, firm and diced
onion flakes

Peanut Sauce

1 medium onion, finely chopped
½ cup peanut butter (salt free)
2 cups water
1 teaspoon sugar
½ teaspoon chilli powder
¼ teaspoon Chinese Five
   Spice
1 tablespoon white vinegar
1 teaspoon soy sauce

Boil potatoes in their jackets, until tender but not soft. Rinse in cold water and dice. Put beans and cabbage into boiling water and cook until tender. Drain and cool. On a large serving plate arrange vegetables in layers. Firstly, a layer of crisp shredded lettuce, then potatoes, cabbage, beans, carrots, tomatoes and egg. Sprinkle with onion flakes and top with peanut sauce. To make peanut sauce in saucepan, cook onion in one teaspoon of oil until transparent. Add Chinese Five Spice and chilli powder. Add water, peanut butter and bring gently to the boil. Reduce heat and stir until smooth. Season with soy sauce, vinegar and sugar. Eat with chopsticks as a complete meal or serve with grilled fish.

Kibbled Wheat Bread

1 teaspoon sugar
275 mls warm water
15 g dried yeast
15 g polyunsaturated margarine
350 g wholemeal flour
100 g burghul (cracked wheat)

Dissolve sugar in half the water and mix with yeast. Leave in a warm place until frothy. Rub margarine into flour and burghul. Mix to a firm dough with yeast liquid. (The dough should leave the sides of the bowl clean.) Knead on a lightly floured board for 10 minutes until smooth, cover and leave until doubled in size. Knead the dough again for 3–4 minutes and shape into a round. Place on warmed baking tray, cover, stand until doubled in size. Use a knife to wedge the top of the loaf and brush with milk. Sprinkle top with burghul. Bake at 230°C for 35–40 minutes.

Variations:
- For plain bread, replace burghul with 100 g wholemeal flour.
- Divide dough into three long segments and plait.
- Divide dough into pieces the size of a golf ball for bread rolls.
- Sprinkle dough with sesame or poppy seeds.
- To make herb bread add chopped onion, mixed dried herbs, garlic and chopped parsley.

Stuffed Dates

1 tablespoon cream cheese
1 tablespoon chopped nuts
6–8 whole dates

Combine cheese and nuts and mix well. Stone the dates carefully and stuff with cream cheese filling. Serve 3–4 per child with salad and bread.

Variation: Use prunes instead of dates.

Rock Cakes

2 cups wholemeal self-raising
  flour
1 teaspoon cinnamon
3 tablespoons margarine
½ cup sugar
½ cup mixed dried fruit
1 egg
½ cup milk

Sift flour and cinnamon and return bran from the sieve. Rub in margarine until mixture resembles breadcrumbs. Make a well in the centre and add remaining ingredients gradually. Spoon 1 tablespoon of mixture on to a greased oven tray and bake at 180°C for 15 minutes until golden brown.

Sensible snacks and food for entertaining

Snacks

Snacks are a source of energy between meals. Children cannot manage the large meals that adults become accustomed to, so snacks play an important role in the daily energy and nutrient intake for children.

Children's snacks should be nutritious not only because of their contribution to the daily allowances for nutrients, but also because they reduce the incidence of tooth decay and becoming overweight. Each time a child eats food containing sugar, the bacteria on the surface of the teeth use the sugar to form a sticky acidic coating called plaque, which causes tooth decay. Snacks which contribute to tooth decay and being overweight include sweets, sugary cakes and biscuits, cough drops, ice blocks, chewing gum and soft drinks. Sticky foods such as dried fruits, caramel and toffee also promote tooth decay by sticking to the tooth surfaces. Dried fruit is a nutritious snack for children but should be served with fresh fruit, nuts or vegetables to help clean the teeth, and may be followed by water or a sugar-free drink. Weight control can be improved by encouraging some form of daily exercise for children, such as walking to school, cycling or sport. Sitting in front of the television will do little to promote healthy lifestyle habits in children, so lay down some firm rules about the number of viewing hours your children are allowed each day. Some children watch up to seven hours of television daily and this habit is unhealthy from both a physical and a social point of view. Playing with adults, animals or children or spending time on hobbies, sport, school work and small chores are much more healthy pastimes for children than watching television.

Television is also a more direct threat to your child's health. The fast food industry, the entertainment industry and advertisements aim at selling snack food to children. You will notice that television advertisements for snack foods are shown primarily between four and six o'clock each afternoon, during children's prime viewing time. These snack foods and drinks are mostly high in sugar, fat and salt, and provide very little nourishment for children. You can limit your child's consumption of these foods by simply not providing them in the home, by limiting their consumption outside the home and at school to once or twice a week, and by encouraging children to spend their pocket money more wisely on non-food treats.

Providing nutritious snacks for your children means competing with these food advertisements, but it is possible to make home made food attractive, interesting, and just as much fun. These recipes will give you some ideas on suitable healthy snacks which children enjoy and can also be used at birthday parties (there is also a separate section dedicated to children's parties, following). The occasional consumption of sugary or salty foods is something children may be permitted without any detrimental effects on health, nutrition or dental health, but on a daily basis, eating these foods is unsuitable and requires guidance by parents. If they are attractively presented, children will soon learn to enjoy eating more healthy snacks, and this will help to develop long term healthy eating habits.

Tiny Corn Tarts

bread slices (any sort)
1 egg
2 tablespoons milk
440 g creamed corn

Cut circles from sliced bread to fit into patty pans. Beat egg and milk in a bowl. Brush both sides of bread circles with milk mixture and press into lightly greased patty tins. Bake at 190°C until crisp and golden. Fill with hot creamy corn. Serve hot or cold.

Variations:
- Tuna Tarts – fill tarts with tuna heated in a saucepan, topped with grated cheese, warm under griller until cheese melts.
- Baked Bean Tarts – fill tarts with hot baked beans.
- Banana Tarts – heat mashed banana, sultanas and 1 tablespoon of fruit juice in a saucepan and serve in hot tart shells.

Pineapple Dip

1 cup cottage cheese
½ cup crushed pineapple
  (unsweetened)
apple sticks
celery sticks

Combine cheese and drained pineapple in a bowl. Use fruit or vegetable sticks for dipping.

Miss Muffet Spiders

sultana grapes
prunes
toothpicks

Remove the stone from prunes to avoid choking and discard. Slide a toothpick through a grape lengthways and a prune to make the head and body of the spider. Bend eight toothpicks to make eight legs for each spider.

Cinnamon Toast Fingers

sliced raisin bread
butter or margarine
ground cinnamon

Toast slices of bread and lightly spread with butter or margarine. Sprinkle with cinnamon and cut into fingers.

Cheese Toasts

2 slices thickly sliced bread
  (about 4 cm thick)
½ cup mild cheese (grated)

Remove crusts from bread and cut bread into cubes. Toast under griller, turning until evenly browned. Roll in cheese and place on a sheet of aluminium foil. Cover completely in cheese and grill until cheese melts and bubbles. Break into cubes and serve hot with a mug of soup.

Fruit Balls

2 cups dried mixed fruit
½ cup apple juice
½ cup chopped nuts
½ cup dessicated coconut
½ cup skim milk powder

Finely chop dried fruit and soak in apple juice overnight. Combine nuts, coconut, milk powder and fruit mixture and mix thoroughly. Add more milk powder if the mixture is too wet. Form into balls and wrap each ball in plastic or foil and allow to set in refrigerator before serving.

Red Cheese Balls

1 cup mild cheddar cheese, grated
½ cup ricotta cheese
red paprika
milk

Combine the grated cheddar and ricotta cheese in a bowl and mix thoroughly. Add 1–2 teaspoons of milk if the mixture is too dry to form into balls. Shape into small balls and roll in red paprika. Wrap each ball in plastic or foil and chill in refrigerator until firm.

French Toast

sliced bread
1 egg
½ cup milk
¼ teaspoon ground pepper

Lightly beat egg, milk and pepper in large bowl. Cut bread slices in half and dip in egg mixture. Lightly brush non-stick pan with oil and cook bread until golden brown on each side.

Mushroom Munch

6 large mushrooms
1 onion, chopped
1 tomato, chopped
½ cup cheese, grated

Remove stalks from mushrooms. Toss onion and tomato in a saucepan until tender. Fill mushrooms with tomato mixture and place in a baking dish. Cover with foil and bake at 190°C for 15 minutes. Top with grated cheese and place under griller until cheese melts.

Cheese Bread

1 French bread stick
table margarine
½ cup grated cheese
chopped parsley

Cut French bread stick in 3 centimetre slices, without cutting right through the base of the roll. Lightly spread each slice with a scrape of margarine. Sprinkle with cheese and allow cheese to settle between slices. Top with parsley and wrap in aluminium foil. Heat at 200°C for 20 minutes until roll is heated through. Serve individual slices with a cup of soup or hot milk.

Oat Cookies

1½ cups wholemeal flour
1½ cups rolled oats
½ cup dessicated coconut
2 tablespoons raisins, chopped
¼ cup dates, chopped
2 tablespoons lemon juice

Combine the flour, oats, coconut, raisins and dates in a bowl. Add the oil, lemon juice, milk and vanilla and mix thoroughly. Press into a flat tin lightly oiled and bake

½ cup vegetable oil
1 cup milk
1 teaspoon vanilla essence

at 190°C for 40–50 minutes. Cut into 25 squares and serve one or two per child with a hot milk drink.

Wholemeal Scones

1 cup wholemeal self-raising flour
1 cup white self-raising flour
½ teaspoon mixed spice
1 tablespoon butter or margarine
½ cup sultanas (optional)
1 tablespoon brown sugar
1 cup milk

Sift flours and mixed spice into a bowl and add bran left in the sieve. Rub butter into flour with fingertips until it resembles fine breadcrumbs. Add sultanas and sugar. Fold in milk using a knife and mix to a soft dough. Knead on a lightly floured board until smooth. Roll out until 2 cm thick and cut into rounds. Place on a lightly greased tray and brush with milk. Bake at 240°C for 12–15 minutes until golden brown on top. Serve hot or cold with a scrape of butter or margarine.

Pumpkin Scones

1 tablespoon margarine
2 tablespoons brown sugar
1 egg
1 cup cold mashed pumpkin
¾ cup milk
2 cups white self-raising flour
1 cup wholemeal self-raising flour

Cream margarine and sugar then add egg, pumpkin, milk and lastly flour. Roll out on to floured board and cut into round shapes. Place on a lightly greased baking tray and bake at 220°C until risen and 'hollow' when tapped. Serve hot and lightly buttered.

Coconut Log

1 cup dried apricots, chopped
½ cup sultanas
½ cup dates, chopped
½ cup raisins, chopped
2 tablespoons sunflower seeds
½ cup skim milk powder
½ cup desiccated coconut
2 teaspoons lemon juice

Place the dried fruit in a bowl and cover with a cup of boiling water. The mixture will soften after ten minutes. Combine the fruit with sunflower seeds, lemon juice, milk powder and coconut. Mix well. Roll mixture into a 5 cm wide log shape and roll in coconut. Wrap in aluminium foil and allow to set in refrigerator. Cut into slices and serve 1–2 per child with a milk drink.

Cottage Potatoes

1 or 2 potatoes
2 tablespoons cottage cheese
chopped chives
paprika

Wash the potatoes and prick with a fork to prevent the skin bursting. Cook on an oven rack at 200°C for about an hour. When ready, split the top open and fill with 1 tablespoon of cottage cheese. Sprinkle with chives and paprika for extra colour. Serve hot or cold.

Peanut and Apple Loaf

2 cups wholemeal self-raising
   flour
2 tablespoons margarine
1 egg
1 cup milk
2 tablespoons brown sugar

Sift flour into a bowl and add remaining bran from sieve. Rub margarine into flour with fingertips. Add sugar, nuts and apple and mix well. Lightly beat egg and milk and

1 cooking apple, chopped
1 cup unsalted peanuts,
  chopped

thoroughly mix through dry ingredients. Bake in lightly greased loaf tin at 190°C for 30 minutes.

Golden Pineapple Nuggets

5 tablespoons pineapple juice
½ cup white self-raising flour
½ cup wholemeal self-raising
  flour
3 tablespoons margarine
2 tablespoons brown sugar
½ cup crushed pineapple
  (unsweetened)
½ cup sultanas
1 egg
¼ teaspoon mixed spice

Drain pineapple and reserve liquid from can. Rub margarine into flour with finger tips. Add sugar, pineapple and sultanas. Lightly beat the egg and mix with pineapple juice. Combine thoroughly with flour mixture. Spoon ½ tablespoon of mixture on to a lightly greased baking tray and cook at 180°C for 20 minutes.

Banana Walnut Bread

3 ripe bananas, mashed
2 eggs, lightly beaten
1 cup white self-raising flour
2 cups wholemeal self-raising
  flour
½ cup chopped walnuts
⅓ cup brown sugar

Mix mashed bananas and eggs together in a large bowl. Add sugar and flour and mix well. Add walnuts and blend until thoroughly mixed. Add a little yoghurt in the mixture if too dry. Put mixture into a lightly greased loaf tin and bake at 190°C for one hour. Serve sliced and lightly buttered.

Raisin and Zucchini Loaf

2½ cups wholemeal self-raising
  flour
½ teaspoon cinnamon
125 g butter
½ cup sugar
2 eggs
½ cup natural yoghurt
1 cup chopped raisins
1 cup firmly packed grated
  zucchini
¼ cup roughly chopped
  walnuts
¼ cup sunflower seeds
extra sunflower seeds

Sift the flour and cinnamon together, adding the coarser particles left in the sieve. Cream the butter and sugar until light and fluffy. Add eggs, one at a time, beating well between each addition. Fold in the yoghurt, raisins, zucchini, walnuts, sunflower seeds and then flour. Spoon into a greased 23 cm × 12 cm (9" × 5") loaf tin, and sprinkle with the extra sunflower seeds. Bake in a moderate oven for 70 minutes, or until cooked through when tested. Serve hot or cold spread lightly with butter or margarine.

Fruit and Nut Loaf

1½ cups wholemeal
  self-raising flour
½ cup white self-raising flour
⅓ cup sugar
1 tablespoon skim milk powder
2 eggs
½ cup chopped nuts
  (unsalted)
½ cup chopped dried fruit
½ cup vegetable oil
½ cup orange juice
½ cup water
1 teaspoon mixed spice

Combine dry ingredients in a bowl. Beat eggs lightly and add the juice, water, nuts, dried fruit, vegetable oil in a separate bowl. Fold the egg mixture into the dry ingredients and mix lightly. Spoon into a lightly greased loaf tin and bake at 180°C for approximately one hour.

Tuna Mould

1 tablespoon gelatine	Dissolve gelatine in hot water.
1 cup tuna (in brine), drained	Drain tuna. Allow to cool
¼ cup chopped capsicum	slightly and combine with
¾ cup chopped celery	yoghurt and other ingredients.
1 cup lemon juice	Mix thoroughly. Pour into a
1 cup low fat yoghurt	fish shaped mould and chill
¼ cup hot water	until firm. Turn out mould on
¼ teaspoon pepper	to a bed of shredded lettuce
	and radish flowers.

Soybean Spread

1½ cups canned soybeans	Rinse and drain soybeans
¼ teaspoon thyme	and combine with other
1 tablespoon chopped chives	ingredients. Mash or blend
1 teaspoon chopped parsley	until smooth. Chill and serve
1 teaspoon paprika	as a sandwich filling or a dip
	with vegetables.

Entertaining

Choosing nutritious, low fat snacks is the key to a healthy diet. Serving sensible healthy snacks and drinks at parties will be greatly appreciated by your guests who are often trying to control their weight. Children's parties, especially, should provide fun party foods which are also reasonably healthy and won't result in the common nausea and vomiting we often see after our children have been to birthday parties. For more children's party ideas, see the following section.

Remember also that many of your adult guests will be trying to avoid drinking alcohol, so make sure you can offer them an enjoyable non-alcoholic alternative. Here are some delicious non-alcoholic suggestions:

- Ginger ale punch with mint leaves
- Lemonade and fruit juice with fruit pieces and lots of ice

- Low-joule mixers such as diet lemonade, diet tonic and diet Coke
- Non-alcoholic mixers such as lemonade, mineral water or soda. Try a shandy, or wine and soda spritzer, or champagne and orange juice.

Cornmeal Bread

2 cups polenta (yellow cornmeal)
½ cup wheatgerm
2 teaspoons baking powder
2 teaspoons brown sugar
1¼ cups skim milk
1 egg, lightly beaten
1 tablespoon polyunsaturated oil

Combine polenta, wheatgerm, baking powder and sugar in a large bowl. Whisk together milk, egg and oil. Pour over polenta mixture. Fold through until well combined. Spoon mixture into a lightly oiled 20 cm sandwich tin. Bake in a moderate oven (180°C) for 20–25 minutes. Serve hot or cold.

Variation: 1–2 tablespoons chopped fresh herbs (parsley, chives or shallots) may be added to the dry ingredients.

Carrot Cake

2 tablespoons polyunsaturated margarine
3 tablespoons brown sugar
1 egg
1 cup wholemeal self-raising flour, sifted
½ cup white self-raising flour
1 cup grated carrot
½ cup chopped walnuts
1 tablespoon grated orange peel

Cream margarine and sugar together until well combined. Add egg. Beat well. Add flour, carrot, walnuts, peel and cinnamon. Mix well. Gradually blend in orange juice and vanilla. Mix lightly until well combined. Spoon mixture into a lightly oiled 10 × 20 cm loaf tin. Sprinkle with extra chopped walnuts if liked. Bake

½ teaspoon ground cinnamon
⅔ cup orange juice
½ teaspoon vanilla essence
extra chopped walnuts
   (optional)

in a moderate oven (180°C) for 45–50 minutes or until a skewer inserted in the centre of the loaf comes out clean and dry. Cool on a wire rack and store in an airtight container.

Surprise Chicken Parcels

½ tablespoon polyunsaturated
   oil
¼ cup sliced mushrooms
½ cup sliced celery
½ capsicum, chopped
4 shallots, chopped
1 clove garlic, crushed
¼ teaspoon each dried basil
   and tarragon
freshly ground black pepper to
   taste
2 cups cooked chicken, skin
   and fat removed
½ cup chicken stock (no
   added salt)
2 teaspoons soy sauce (salt
   reduced)
6 sheets filo pastry
2 tablespoons skim milk or
   orange juice
sesame seeds

Heat oil in a frying pan. Sauté mushrooms, celery, capsicum, shallots and garlic until tender. Season with herbs and pepper. Add chicken, stock and soy. Simmer until mixture begins to thicken. Cool. Working with one sheet of filo at a time, fold in half widthways to form a square. Brush with a little milk or juice. Spoon one-sixth of the chicken mixture onto the pastry. Roll up to form a parcel, tucking ends in. Brush outside with a little more milk or juice. Sprinkle with sesame seeds. Place on a lightly oiled baking tray. Continue with remaining pastry and filling. Bake in a hot oven (200°C) for 10–15 minutes or until crisp and golden. Serve hot with salad.

Brown Bread Plait

3 × 7 g sachets dried yeast
1¾ cups lukewarm water
1 teaspoon sugar
1 tablespoon gluten flour
  (optional)
4 cups wholemeal plain flour
2 cups white flour
1 teaspoon salt
50 mg ascorbic acid tablet
  (vitamin C, optional)
2 teaspoons polyunsaturated
  margarine
sesame seeds

Dissolve yeast in warm water with sugar. Place flour, salt, crushed ascorbic acid tablet and margarine in a bowl. Rub margarine into flour with fingertips. Make a well in the centre and gradually add yeast mixture, mixing with a knife. Mix thoroughly. If too dry, add a little more water. Turn dough onto a lightly floured board and knead until dough is smooth. Dough will spring back when pressed with finger if kneaded well enough. Rest dough for 5 minutes. Divide dough into three sections and roll out into lengths. Plait the three lengths and seal each end by folding dough under. Brush with water and sprinkle with sesame or poppy seeds. Place plaited dough on lightly oiled baking tray and cover with cloth. Set aside in a warm spot (preferably on top of stove) and allow to rise until doubled in size, about 30 minutes. Bake in a very hot oven (220°C) for 25–30 minutes until golden brown and sounds hollow when tapped.

Variations:
- White bread – use 6 cups of white flour. This is a very tender loaf.
- 100% wholemeal bread – use 6 cups of wholemeal flour. This is a much heavier loaf than the brown bread.
- Shape dough into 20 small rolls or two loaves.
- Top with a variety of seeds or cracked wheat.

Fruit Ice Blocks

Blend soft fruit such as banana, canned pear, apple or apricots, rockmelon, watermelon, mango, etc., with a little fruit juice. Pour mixture into ice-cube trays or small moulds. Insert a toothpick or ice-cream stick. Freeze to make healthy ice-blocks. For every ½ cup of fruit purée use ¼ cup of fruit juice (e.g. orange juice).

Apple Spice Cake

3 cooking apples, peeled, cored and sliced
4 tablespoons water
4 whole cloves
2 tablespoons polyunsaturated margarine
¼ cup brown sugar
1½ cups wholemeal self-raising flour
1 teaspoon mixed spice
½ teaspoon ground cinnamon
½ cup chopped walnuts
½ cup chopped raisins or dates
3 tablespoons skim milk

Place apples in a saucepan with water and cloves. Cover. Simmer until apples are pulpy. Remove cloves. Drain well. Cool. Cream margarine and sugar until light and fluffy. Sift flour with mixed spice and cinnamon, returning any husks. Mix into creamed mixture with walnuts, raisins and milk. Spoon mixture into a lightly oiled 10 × 20 cm loaf tin or 20 cm sandwich tin. Bake in a moderate oven (180°C) for 1–1¼ hours or until a skewer inserted in the centre of the cake comes out clean and dry.

Cool on a wire rack. Serve warm or cold with a scraping of low fat spread or ricotta cheese. Store in an airtight container.

Cheese Pinwheels

1 cup wholemeal self-raising
flour
1 cup white self-raising flour
1 tablespoon polyunsaturated
margarine
1 cup skim milk
1 cup shredded tasty cheese
1 onion, finely chopped
½ cup chopped celery
¼ teaspoon each dried basil
and oregano
¼ cup shredded tasty cheese,
extra

Sift flours into a large bowl, returning any husks. Rub in margarine using fingertips until well blended. Make a well in the centre of the flour. Add milk all at once, mixing with a knife to form a sticky dough. Turn dough onto a lightly floured surface. Knead lightly. Roll out to form a rectangle about 1 cm thick. Sprinkle cheese, onion, celery and herbs evenly over dough. Roll up into a log from the long side and slice at 2 cm intervals. Place circles on a lightly greased baking sheet, close together, cut-side up. Sprinkle with a little extra cheese. Bake in a hot oven (200°C) for 15–20 minutes. Cool on a wire rack. Serve warm or cold. Makes about 16.

Variation: Fruit Pinwheels – omit savoury filling. Instead, spread dough with honey and top with dried fruit.

Cheese and Yoghurt Scones

2 cups wholemeal self-raising
flour
1 teaspoon mustard powder
pinch cayenne pepper
2 tablespoons polyunsaturated
margarine
⅔ cup shredded tasty cheese
200 g tub natural yoghurt (low
fat)

Sift flour, mustard and cayenne together into bowl, returning any husks. Add margarine. Rub in using fingertips until well combined. Blend in cheese and yoghurt until mixture forms a dough. Turn dough onto a lightly floured surface. Knead for

skim milk
sesame seeds

several minutes. Roll out to form a round about 2 cm thick. Cut into rounds using a scone cutter or the top of a round glass jar. Place on a lightly oiled baking tray. Brush with a little skim milk. Sprinkle with sesame seeds. Bake in a very hot oven (220°C) for 12–15 minutes or until scones sound hollow when tapped. Transfer to a wire rack to cool. Serve hot or cold spread with a little low fat spread. Makes about 16.

Prawns with Curry Sauce

1 onion, finely chopped
1 clove garlic, crushed
½–1 tablespoon curry powder
1 cinnamon stick
1 tablespoon polyunsaturated
   margarine
1½ cups plain skim milk
   yoghurt
¼ teaspoon ground black
   pepper
500 g cooked king prawns

Gently sauté onion and garlic, curry powder and cinnamon in margarine until soft. Remove from heat, place in serving bowl and cool. When curry mixture is cool, blend in yoghurt and pepper. Refrigerate overnight. Shell and devein prawns. Arrange on serving platter on a bed of crisp lettuce with a bowl of curry sauce for dipping.

Ratatouille Cups

Filling
1 tablespoon olive oil
2 onions, finely chopped
2 cloves garlic, crushed
200 g button mushrooms,
  sliced
1 eggplant, chopped
6 zucchini, sliced
3 tomatoes, peeled and
  chopped
2 capsicum, finely sliced
1 teaspoon tomato paste (no
  added salt)
1 teaspoon dried basil
¼ teaspoon ground pepper
½ cup grated cheddar
  cheese
2 tablespoons natural skim
  milk yoghurt

Cups
½ loaf sliced wholemeal
  bread

To make a ratatouille, heat oil in large saucepan and sauté onion and garlic until soft. Add mushrooms, eggplant and zucchini, and cook until tender. Add all other ingredients and mix thoroughly. Simmer until liquid reduces. You can make this mixture one day ahead and let it stand overnight in refrigerator. Make bread cups by removing crusts from bread slices and pressing bread into patty tins. Bake in a slow oven (150°C) for 15–20 minutes until crunchy. Fill bread cups with hot ratatouille mixture and serve hot or cold as an appetiser or light lunch. Makes 10.

Mexican Nachos

4 wholemeal pita bread
1½ cups grated tasty cheese
  (try fat reduced)
310 g can red kidney beans,
  drained and mashed

Chilli Sauce
1 tablespoon olive oil
1 onion, chopped

To make chilli sauce, heat oil in saucepan and sauté onion and curry powder until tender. Add all other ingredients and simmer for 10–15 minutes until liquid reduces. Cut pita bread into triangles. Split each slice in half to make 'chips'. Bake in a very slow oven

½ teaspoon curry powder
425 g can tomatoes (no added salt)
1 teaspoon sugar
½ teaspoon ground chilli
¼ teaspoon ground oregano

(120°C) for 15 minutes or until crunchy. Arrange pita chips in a baking tray. Sprinkle with half the cheese and spread with kidney beans. Pour over a layer of chilli sauce and finally top with remaining cheese. Heat in a slow oven (150°C) until cheese is melted and nachos are piping hot. Serves 4.

Chicken Liver Pâté

3 slices bread (one day old)
250 g chicken livers
2 tablespoons chopped onion
½ cup dry white wine
½ cup chicken stock
2 tablespoons chopped parsley
2 teaspoons soy sauce (salt reduced)
1 teaspoon grated root ginger
2 tablespoons polyunsaturated margarine
½ tablespoon dry sherry
¼ teaspoon nutmeg
½ teaspoon ground black pepper

Crumb the bread and combine with livers, onion, wine, stock, parsley, soy sauce and ginger in a saucepan. Simmer until livers are cooked. Cool. Strain liquid off liver mixture and place in blender with margarine, sherry, nutmeg and pepper. Blend until smooth or beat by hand. Press mixture into individual pots and refrigerate overnight. Serve on wholemeal toast fingers or pita triangles with vegetable crudités. Serves 4.

Wholemeal Dippers

Remove crusts from bread slices and cut into triangles or cut Lebanese or pita bread into small triangles. Bake in an ovenproof dish at 150°C until bread is crunchy. Serve with dips instead of high fat chips or salted biscuits.

Wholemeal Cheese Damper

2 cups wholemeal self-raising flour
2 cups white self-raising flour
1 cup grated tasty cheese
1 teaspoon sugar
1½ cups skim milk

Combine flour, cheese and sugar in a bowl. Add milk and mix to a soft dough. Add more milk if the mixture is too stiff. Turn onto a floured board and shape into a round damper. Cut a cross on top of loaf. Bake on a lightly greased tray in a moderately hot oven (190°C) for 45–50 minutes until cooked through and golden brown. Serve hot with a scrape of margarine.

Dolmades

2 teaspoons olive oil
6 shallots, chopped
2 tablespoons pine nuts
1½ cups rice, cooked
2 tablespoons chopped parsley
1 tablespoon chopped dill
2 tablespoons chopped mint
juice of 1 lemon
28 packaged vine leaves
extra lemon juice

Heat the oil in a saucepan, add shallots and pine nuts, sauté for 3 minutes. Add rice, parsley, dill, mint and lemon juice. Mix thoroughly. Rinse vine leaves with cold water and pat dry with absorbent kitchen paper. Place rice mixture into 24 vine leaves and roll up tightly. Line saucepan with remaining vine leaves, place rolled-up vine leaves into pan. Sprinkle with extra lemon juice and cover with 1 cup water. Top with a plate. Cover saucepan with a lid and simmer gently for 1 hour.

Crunchy Onion Fingers

1 cup self-raising flour
1 cup white self-raising flour
1 tablespoon polyunsaturated
  margarine
1 cup skim milk
2 teaspoons olive oil
1 onion, chopped
2 tablespoons ricotta cheese
  (reduced fat)
1 clove garlic, crushed
1 tablespoon chopped parsley
cayenne and black pepper to
  taste
¼ cup shredded cheddar
  cheese
paprika

Sift flour into a bowl. Add margarine. Rub in using fingertips until well combined. Form a well in the centre of the flour. Add milk all at once, mixing with a knife to form a sticky dough. Turn dough onto a lightly floured surface. Knead lightly. Roll out into a rectangle to line a 23 × 30 cm lamington tin. Heat oil in a small frying pan. Sauté onion, ricotta, garlic, parsley, cayenne and pepper until onion is tender. Spread over dough. Sprinkle with cheese and paprika. Bake in a hot oven (200°C) for 20–25 minutes or until crisp. Serve with soup or as an appetiser, cut into fingers. Makes about 60.

Homemade Popcorn

2 tablespoons polyunsaturated
  oil
½ cup popping corn

Heat oil in a large saucepan and add corn. Shake to cover with oil. Cover pan with lid firmly until corn stops popping. Season with pepper if desired. Serve hot or cold. Makes about 3 cups.

Salmon Ricotta Dip

1 cup ricotta cheese (reduced fat)
½ cup salmon (no added salt)
2 tablespoons chopped parsley
1 tablespoon finely chopped shallots
¼ teaspoon ground pepper
2 drops tabasco sauce

Mix all ingredients in a bowl. Allow to stand in refrigerator for 1–2 hours or overnight. Serve dip with a platter of fresh vegetable crudités such as cucumber, zucchini, celery, carrot, capsicum, cauliflower and baby mushrooms. Makes about 1½ cups.

Pineapple Dip

2 cups skim milk cottage cheese
1 cup crushed pineapple (unsweetened, well drained)

Combine cheese and pineapple. Serve with a platter of fruit pieces tossed in lemon juice to prevent browning. Try apple sticks, firm pear sticks, orange wedges and fresh pineapple wedges to use as 'dipping' sticks. Makes about 3 cups.

Savoury Cheese Spread

500 g ricotta cheese (fat reduced)
½ cup chopped celery
½ cup chopped capsicum
1 tablespoon French mustard
1 tablespoon currants
1½ teaspoons caraway seeds
1 teaspoon black pepper
½ teaspoon paprika

Mix all ingredients except paprika and form into a ball. Sprinkle with paprika. Chill for 1–2 hours or overnight to allow flavours to blend. Serve on a platter with vegetable crudités or sticks and dark ryebread fingers. Makes 1 ball.

Children's Parties

Special occasions such as children's parties should include attractive, colourful and tasty foods – but there is no reason why this food should not also be nutritious. Foods high in sugar, fat and salt may occasionally be included in children's diets, but it is often at parties when these foods make children feel nauseous and then spoil the occasion.

Providing healthy foods and drinks for children's parties can be an easy and healthy way to celebrate. You can try serving any of the lunch or snack and entertaining suggestions in the previous sections, as well as these special ideas.

Cherry Tomato Stars

1 cup cottage cheese
2 tablespoons green capsicum
20 cherry tomatoes
paprika

Finely chop green capsicum and combine with cottage cheese. Cut each cherry tomato into quarters from the top, almost to the base. Do not cut completely through the tomato. Spread tomato out into a star shape and fill with cheese mixture. Top with paprika.

Cheese Crackers

4 crispbread or cracker biscuits
   (unsalted)
½ cup ricotta or cottage cheese
2 tablespoons grated apple
lemon juice
cinnamon

Mix the apple with ½ teaspoon of lemon juice. Spread biscuits with ricotta cheese topped with grated apple and a sprinkle of cinnamon. Serve cold or warmed under griller.

Fruit 'n' Nuts

2 cups sultanas
2 cups dried apricots
2 cups sunflower seeds
1 cup nuts (unsalted)

Combine all ingredients in a bowl. Fill small plastic bags or white paper bags or patty papers with the mixture and seal with an elastic band. These are suitable for 'play lunch' and are an easy snack when travelling.

Celery Boats

sticks of celery
ricotta cheese
sliced processed cheese

Slice celery into four centimetre chunks and fill with ricotta cheese. Cut cheese slices into four triangles and pierce with a toothpick to make a 'sail'. Stand the sail upright in the cheese boat.

Spiny Ant Eater

1 granny smith apple
1 processed cheese wedge
1 carrot
2 currants
lemon juice

Place cheese wedge on a flat slice of apple. Dip apple in lemon juice to prevent browning. To make 'spines' cut carrot into thin strips and stick each strip into cheese. Completely cover cheese wedge with carrot spines. Place the currants on toothpicks to make two eyes.

Quick Dip

1 cup ricotta cheese
3 tablespoons salmon (no
    added salt)
1 tablespoon parsley, chopped
¼ teaspoon ground pepper
vegetable sticks

Mix all ingredients in a bowl. Prepare a platter of vegetable sticks such as cucumber, zucchini, carrot, capsicum, celery, cauliflower pieces and baby mushrooms for dipping.

Lettuce Rolls

1 cup cottage cheese
½ cup chopped walnuts
2 tablespoons chopped
    cucumber
6 lettuce leaves

Combine cucumber, cheese and walnuts. Spoon into lettuce leaves, roll up and secure with a toothpick.

Sandwich Castles

2 slices wholemeal bread
2 slices white bread
2 sandwich cheese slices
1 tomato
1 slice ham
shredded lettuce

Lightly spread bread with butter, margarine or mayonnaise. Place ham and lettuce on one slice of white bread. Top with 1 slice of wholemeal bread, tomato slices, white bread, cheese and tomato slices, and wholemeal bread. Press down firmly on sandwich. Trim crusts. Spear with nine toothpicks, each 2 cm apart. Carefully slice into nine cubes. Serve each castle with a toothpick.

Pinwheels

sliced bread
peanut butter
ricotta cheese
currants

Remove crusts from bread and spread thinly with peanut butter. Spread a row of ricotta cheese and currants across one end of the bread, approximately ½ cm in width. Roll up firmly. Wrap each roll firmly in plastic wrap and chill. Cut each roll into five pinwheels. Pinwheels can be made with other colourful spreads such as Date and Walnut spread (page 155), fish or meat paste.

Fruit Dip

½ cup ricotta cheese
3 tablespoons low fat flavoured
   yoghurt
fruit pieces

Slice firm fruit such as apple, pears, orange segments and fresh pineapple into five centimetre sticks. Dip apple in lemon juice to prevent browning. Dip the fruit sticks into a bowl of mixed ricotta cheese and yoghurt.

Double Decker

4 cracker biscuits (no added
   salt)
grated carrot
shredded lettuce
peanut butter

Place alternate layers of carrot, lettuce and peanut butter between cracker biscuits.

Peanut Pyramids

processed cheese slices
crunchy peanut butter

Thinly spread cheese slices with peanut butter. Top with cheese and repeat cheese layers three times. Cut cheese into four triangles and secure with a toothpick.

Fruit Swords

pineapple pieces (fresh or
   unsweetened)
strawberries
banana
red apple

Cut pineapple, apple and banana into cubes. Dip in lemon juice to prevent browning. Thread fruit pieces and whole strawberries on to skewers.

Miss Mouse

2 eggs, hard boiled
4 slices wholemeal bread
lettuce (finely shredded)
1 glacé cherry
celery
8 currants
4 bean sprouts

Cut each egg in half lengthwise for the 'mouse'. Cover the bread slices with lettuce to make 'grass' for the mouse. Place the egg half on the lettuce cut face down. Use a piece of cherry for the 'nose', thin strips of celery as 'whiskers' and bean sprout as the 'tail'. To make 'eyes' pierce each currant with a small piece of toothpick and insert into egg.

Go-Carts

2 individual cheese portions
carrot rings
sultanas
grapes

Pierce carrot rings with a toothpick (for the wheels) and secure a sultana on the end of each wheel. Attach carrot to cheese 'go-cart' with toothpicks. The 'driver' consists of a large grape attached to the cheese with a toothpick. 'Wheels' can also be made from cucumber, zucchini or radish rings. 'Drivers' can also be raisins, prunes or almonds.

Sneaky Snakes

1 green cucumber or zucchini
1 carrot
½ cup ricotta cheese
1 tablespoon mayonnaise
2 currants

Run a fork down the sides of the cucumber to make 'stripes' for the snake. Combine ricotta cheese and mayonnaise, then slice cucumber and carrots into thin rings and press rings together alternately with cheese and mayonnaise mixture. Secure with a long skewer and with two currants make the eyes. Serve on a bed of shredded lettuce.

Tasty Tidbits

bread slices
corn niblets
cheese, grated
1 egg
capsicum, chopped
meat, chopped

Place bread on oven tray. Combine all other ingredients and spread on bread. Bake at 180°C for 15–20 minutes until golden brown. Cut into bite size pieces.

Tomato Cocktail

1 cup tomato juice (no added salt)
½ cucumber (peeled and chopped)
¼ teaspoon sweet basil
2 drops tabasco sauce
4 ice cubes

Blend all ingredients except ice and pour into tall glasses. Add ice and serve with a straw.

Party Punch

1 large bottle sparkling mineral water
500 mls orange juice
1 cup tinned fruit salad (unsweetened)
crushed ice

Combine all ingredients in a punch bowl and allow children to serve themselves in paper cups.

Tropical Punch

1 litre soda water or sparkling mineral water
7 litres orange juice
500 mls pineapple juice (unsweetened)
ice

Combine orange juice, pineapple juice and ice in a punch bowl or large jug. Add soda water just before serving.

Apple Cider

2 litres apple cider
2 cups orange juice
1 cup lemon juice
5 cups pineapple juice (unsweetened)
1 cinnamon stick
5 whole cloves

Combine juices in a large saucepan. Add spices and simmer for 60 minutes. Strain to remove cloves and cinnamon. Serve in punch bowl with diced orange and whole apples floating in the bowl.

Ice Cream Cake

1 can evaporated skim milk
½ cup skim milk powder
2 tablespoons castor sugar
4 egg whites
4 kiwi fruit, chopped
1 cup strawberries, sliced
2 teaspoons vanilla

Chill evaporated milk in freezer until icy cold. Chill mixing bowl. Beat milk, milk powder, and vanilla with electric beaters of food processor on high speed until thick. Chill in freezer for 30–40 minutes, but do not allow to freeze. Remove from freezer and continue beating for five minutes. Mix in chopped kiwi fruit and strawberries. Beat egg white until stiff and fold through milk mixture carefully. Do not beat as this allows air to escape. Line round cake tin with aluminium foil and pour mixture into tin. Freeze overnight. To serve, lift foil and ice cream out of tin and peel off the foil. Decorate with colourful fruits, flowers, nuts and candles.

Melon Basket

1 whole watermelon
4 red apples
3 cups grapes
2 bananas
1 rockmelon
3 kiwi fruit

Draw a 10 cm belt over the top half of watermelon with a knife. Cut away all of the top half of the melon, except the 10 cm 'handle'. Make melon balls from the inside flesh of the watermelon and rock-melon. Chop apple into cubes and slice kiwi fruit. Fill the watermelon 'basket' with melon balls, grapes and apple pieces. Slice banana and kiwi fruit on top. Decorate handle of the basket with colourful ribbons and flowers. Children may use toothpicks, to obtain fruit pieces.

Desserts

Try some of the following healthy dessert ideas:

- Melon balls with yoghurt
- Ricecream with strawberries
- Grapes, cheese and crackers
- Breakfast cereal and milk
- Bananas on a Paddlepop stick, rolled in desiccated coconut
- Jelly made with canned fruit pieces
- Fruit salad and ice cream (try low fat brands)
- Cubes, or moulds, of frozen fruit juice
- Frozen grapes
- Ice cream (low fat brands) with Milo sprinkled on top.

Also, try these ideas which are listed in other sections of this book:

- Fruit ice blocks (page 137)
- Cinamon Apples (page 140)
- Strawberry Ricotta Pancakes (page 148)
- Fresh Fruit Salad (page 149)
- Citrus Cup (page 149)
- Cinnamon Rice (page 150)
- Spiced Apple Yoghurt (page 153)
- Strawberry Frozen Yoghurt (page 153)
- Fruit Swords (page 259)

Index

A practical guide to feeding children from birth to the preschool years

Eat right, don't fight

Jan O'Connell, Rosey Cummings and Gina Ralston

Sleep Right, Sleep Tight

A practical, proven guide to solving your baby's sleep problems

ROSEY CUMMINGS, KAREN HOUGHTON & LE ANN WILLIAMS

How to Motivate Your Child

for School and Beyond

Andrew Martin

BACK OFF BULLY

A crash course in stopping bullies

MARK DOBSON

What to do when
your children turn into

TEENAGERS

Dr David Bennett & Dr Leanne Rowe